"Sports fans have long argued amongst themselves about the 'right' way to be a fan, their duties to 'their' teams, and the comparative value of everything from their favorite players to women's versus men's athletics. *The Ethics of Sports Fandom* aims to settle some of these classic disputes and raise new ones, with a philosopher's eye to questioning even the most dearly held beliefs of die-hard sports fans, while it defends fans from their unkinder critics."

—**Erin Tarver**, *Emory University, USA*

"Adam Kadlac's *The Ethics of Sports Fandom* is an engaging and compellingly argued book. Kadlac argues that fans need to view their teams from an appropriate distance: we did not win at the weekend, the team did. One might think that this pushes the fans away from the team and makes fandom less important, yet Kadlac does an admirable job of arguing why fandom is a valuable part of our lives, rather than mere escapism. Along the way, he addresses a variety of ethical issues, like the ways fans objectify players, the harms players suffer, how fans so rarely are fans of women's teams, and the divisive nationalism international sports can arouse. In doing this, he shows both how fandom can be valuable, but also the ways in which we need to change in order to avoid some of the ethical problems fandom can bring."

—**Jake Wojtowicz**, *Rochester, NY, USA*

THE ETHICS OF SPORTS FANDOM

Fans largely regard sports as an escapist pursuit—something that provides distraction from the cares and concerns of "real life." This book pushes back against a fully escapist account of sports fandom and argues that we should understand the value of fandom in terms of the ability of sports to prompt fans to reflect meaningfully on the notion of a good life. Even if we are not engaged in high-level athletics, it is possible to learn a great deal from those who are: what sacrifices are required to achieve our goals; how to persevere through failure and disappointment; and about teamwork and the rewards of accomplishing things together. Moreover, partisan fandom, which has been criticized from various quarters, can teach us valuable lessons about love and what it means to be invested in things over which we have no control. If our reflection on the efforts of individual athletes helps us reflect on our own pursuit of the good life, our attachments to teams can help us to cultivate a certain kind of humility and openness to all that life has to offer.

The Ethics of Sports Fandom is an accessible resource for researchers and students interested in the ethics and philosophy of sport that offers an analysis of several different aspects of contemporary fandom: fantasy sports, the ways that fans interact with athletes on social media, violent sports, women's sports, and the support for our countries' national teams. In all these areas, reflecting on what it means to respect athletes as individual human beings engaged in their own pursuit of the good life requires that fans consider their sports-related behavior in a new light.

Adam Kadlac is Teaching Professor of Philosophy at Wake Forest University, USA. His published work has appeared in a number of venues, including *American Philosophical Quarterly*, *Journal of Applied Philosophy*, and *Philosophical Studies*.

THE ETHICS OF SPORTS FANDOM

Adam Kadlac

NEW YORK AND LONDON

First published 2022
by Routledge
605 Third Avenue, New York, NY 10158

and by Routledge
2 Park Square, Milton Park, Abingdon, Oxon, OX14 4RN

Routledge is an imprint of the Taylor & Francis Group, an informa business

© 2022 Adam Kadlac

The right of Adam Kadlac to be identified as author of this work has been asserted in accordance with sections 77 and 78 of the Copyright, Designs and Patents Act 1988.

All rights reserved. No part of this book may be reprinted or reproduced or utilised in any form or by any electronic, mechanical, or other means, now known or hereafter invented, including photocopying and recording, or in any information storage or retrieval system, without permission in writing from the publishers.

Trademark notice: Product or corporate names may be trademarks or registered trademarks, and are used only for identification and explanation without intent to infringe.

Library of Congress Cataloging-in-Publication Data
Names: Kadlac, Adam, author.
Title: The ethics of sports fandom/Adam Kadlac.
Description: New York, NY: Routledge, 2022. | Includes bibliographical references and
    index.
Identifiers: LCCN 2021032707 (print) | LCCN 2021032708 (ebook) |
    ISBN 9781032120195 (hardback) | ISBN 9781032122311 (paperback) |
    ISBN 9781003223696 (ebook)
Subjects: LCSH: Sports spectators—Psychology. | Sports spectators—Attitudes. | Sports—
    Moral and ethical aspects.
Classification: LCC GV715 .K34 2022 (print) | LCC GV715 (ebook) |
    DDC 796.01/9—dc23
LC record available at https://lccn.loc.gov/2021032707
LC ebook record available at https://lccn.loc.gov/2021032708

ISBN: 978-1-032-12019-5 (hbk)
ISBN: 978-1-032-12231-1 (pbk)
ISBN: 978-1-003-22369-6 (ebk)

DOI: 10.4324/9781003223696

Typeset in Bembo
by Apex CoVantage, LLC

CONTENTS

Acknowledgments	viii
Introduction: Probing the Ethics of Fandom in a Post-Pandemic Age	1
1 On "We"	14
2 Why Sports Are Like Shakespeare	30
3 Love 'em Like a Brother: In Defense of Partisan Fandom	46
4 Avoiding the Pitfalls of Objectification	61
5 A Cautious Defense of Football	77
6 Egalitarian Fandom	95
7 Cosmopolitan Fandom	114
Conclusion: A Few Guidelines for Being a Good Fan	129
Works Cited	135
Index	142

ACKNOWLEDGMENTS

I owe a great debt of gratitude, as always, to my own home team: my wife, Tisha, and my children, Gideon and Sadie. They don't always care very much about sports, but they care quite a bit about me, and I am consistently humbled by their love and support. I can't imagine my life without them.

My foray into the philosophy of sport had its start at the Beautiful Game Conference in Basel, Switzerland, back in 2016. I count myself incredibly fortunate to have developed some rich friendships with a number of the people I met there (and with whom I have subsequently reconvened on several occasions). Many thanks to Victoria Allen, Ridvan Askin, Aline Bieri, Jan Chovanec, Catherine Diederich, Dan Haxall, David Kilpatrick, Eva Lavric, George Kioussis, Michael O'Hara, Cyprian Piskurek, Ian Plenderleith, Philip Schauss, Emily Ryall, Kristof Vanhoutte, and Connell Vaughan for all the conversations that have inspired some of the thoughts that made their way into this book.

Cyprian was, I believe, the first person to give me feedback on the entire manuscript. My erstwhile Wake Forest colleague Julian Young and my father, Jeff Kadlac, later joined that list. Their suggestions were encouraging as I was working out the core arguments of the book and trying to decide how to fit them together. Two reviewers for Routledge, Jake Wojtowicz and Erin Tarver, provided exceedingly thoughtful and thorough comments to which I have attempted to respond while preparing the text's final version. It should go without saying that any defects in the book are entirely my responsibility.

I originally conceived of this project as focused entirely on the ethical issues surrounding American football and was able to present early drafts of the material that became Chapters 4 and 5 to audiences at Davidson College, the Center for Bioethics, Health and Society at Wake Forest, and the Rethinking Community Conference, also at Wake Forest. The feedback I got from these encounters convinced me to shift/widen my focus to sports fandom in general. It also helped to sharpen my thoughts about objectification and reconfigure my argument about the ethics of playing football. A summer grant from the Center for Bioethics, Health and Society also enabled me to complete some foundational research (and explore some intellectual "dead ends") in the summer of 2017.

Among its many other attractions, the philosophy department in which I work has a vibrant works-in-progress group that was kind enough to read more refined versions of several chapters before the pandemic shut down the world in March 2020. Many thanks to Emily, Austin, Adrian

Bardon, Jonathan Barker, Nick Colgrove, Francisco Gallegos, Stavroula Glezakos, Ana Iltis, Justin Jennings, Ralph Kennedy, Win Lee, and Christian Miller for their probing questions and comments as well as their collegial support. I probably could have written the book while working in a different environment, but the process certainly wouldn't have been as enjoyable. In his capacity as department chair, Win was also able to secure me a reduced teaching load in the spring of 2019 during which I was able to draft much of the text that became Chapters 1, 2, and 3.

Working at Wake Forest affords me the opportunity to work with some fantastic and engaged students on a regular basis. I periodically teach a class on sports and society to first-year undergrads and have consistently benefitted from hearing their perspectives on the world of sports. They have often been unwitting guinea pigs for my half-baked thoughts and ideas, and their regular patience with me as a teacher is much appreciated.

Finally, thanks to Andrew Weckenmann, Allie Simmons, and the rest of the staff at Routledge for their help in bringing this project to fruition and to Meridith Murray for her excellent work compiling the index.

INTRODUCTION

Probing the Ethics of Fandom in a Post-Pandemic Age

On March 11, 2020, Utah Jazz center Rudy Gobert tested positive for the novel coronavirus that was already wreaking havoc around the world. The first official death from COVID-19 in the United States was reported on February 29, and many sports organizations had begun to alter their operations in light of public health concerns.[1] Nevertheless, Gobert's test proved to be something of an inflection point for major spectator sports. The NBA abruptly postponed all of its games until further notice.[2]

Gobert's test was confirmed on Wednesday, and by the weekend, the NCAA had canceled its postseason basketball tournaments—events that generate around $1 billion dollars a year.[3] There would be no March Madness in 2020. The NHL promptly cleared its schedule, and all the major European soccer leagues announced the suspension of their matches. The PGA Tour cancelled one of its marquee events—The Players Championship—and shortly thereafter every tournament for the foreseeable future. The Masters would not be played for the first time since 1945.[4] Major League Baseball closed down all spring training activities and postponed the start of its regular season. A couple of weeks later, on March 24, the International Olympic Committee decided to reschedule the 2020 Summer Games in Tokyo for the following year. Sports were going into an extended hibernation, and it was not at all clear when they would wake up.

For those of us who regard ourselves as sports fans, not having access to the games we love immediately threw us into various stages of grief. I had friends on Facebook who forcefully expressed their anger, though it wasn't always clear if they were angry at those who canceled the events (because they thought such decisions were overreactions) or whether their ire was directed at the universe for taking away something they love. In retrospect, it might not have been anger so much as panic—addicts who were suddenly worried about where they were going to get their next fix.

Other fans were somewhat more tempered and reflective. Tim Layden registered something of a lament on *NBCSports.com*, noting that the loss of sports was the loss of an important "oasis" in a culture that is otherwise deeply divided. "In the age of social media," he wrote, sports "are where we gather, even when we are not gathered. They are what we share, when we can't agree on anything else, here in our fractured 2020."[5] In the *New York Times*, Will Leitch suggested that when sports eventually returned, we would find that our bond with them had weakened. He thus suggested that "the illusion that we couldn't live without them, that they were both eternal and

DOI: 10.4324/9781003223696-1

2 Introduction

vital, will be shattered. That would probably be healthy in the long term. But as with any loss, it would also be sad."[6] And on Twitter, Jim Weber was more sweepingly existential in his assessment: "Imagine if man had never created sports and this is what life was like all the time . . . Brutal."[7]

My own emotional response to the loss of sports was difficult to parse. Given the tragedies playing out around the world, I was initially uncomfortable devoting any mental space to sports, much less complaining about their absence. It felt unseemly to express frustration at not being able to watch a game when people were dying and suffering immense economic hardship—kind of like a kid whining that the movie theater is closed in the middle of a hurricane. We all had more important things to worry about.

When my mind did turn to sports, my strongest feelings didn't have anything to do with games that people would have watched on television. Instead, they first hit me as I was talking to my wife about the U12 girls soccer team I coach and how I had missed seeing them play the first game of their spring season (which, like every other sporting event in the world, had been indefinitely postponed). This reaction was, in part, an expression of sadness for what I would be missing. They are a terrific group of kids, most of whom were having their first experience with soccer, and while their skills are (to put it tactfully) unpolished, they enthusiastically support each other and are always eager to learn. These qualities make them really fun to coach, and I was going to miss that fun.

More than my loss, however, I realized that my greater fear was what they might be missing should we be unable to play our season, namely, all of the learning and team-building and competition that make sports worth playing in the first place. None of these girls have professional careers in their future, and billion-dollar industries are not organized around their talents. They play simply because soccer is a game worth playing, and missing competition and practices meant missing all that the sport has to offer: the rewards of improving at something difficult; the joys of becoming part of a team; the satisfied exhaustion after a closely contested game. My strongest emotion wasn't for my loss; it was for the girls.

Those same thoughts made me sad for other athletes in my life. My son's club soccer season was likewise thrown into limbo, and questions loomed for his high school team in the fall. The window of his life as a competitive athlete was closing as he neared graduation, and a lost season for him felt more significant, since fewer and fewer games lay in his future. I love watching him play more than any other sports-related activity in my life, but what I began to mourn was what he was losing: time on the field, playing a game he loves with his friends. A look at the family calendar on a Saturday in early April reminded me that he was supposed to have a game that day (which turned out to be gorgeous spring day here in North Carolina). I'm not ashamed to admit that tears welled up at the thought of what he was missing.

I also thought about the college athletes I have in my classes who were by then scattered around the world, riding out the end of the semester at home. Some of them aspire to play professionally, and the pursuit of those longer-term ambitions was suddenly put on hold. But I also teach a large number of athletes—the overwhelming majority, in fact—for whom playing in college is the pinnacle of their athletic career. It is an opportunity they have worked years to obtain, and the loss of a season for them struck me as some kind of cruel joke. All the hours of practice and games (and parents driving them around to practices and games) only to have the dream of competing at the collegiate level taken away by a stupid virus. For them, I felt a palpable sense of injustice.

Lying in the background of these reactions was the fact that I had, by that point, been working on a book about sports fandom for the better part of two years—a project whose significance seemed questionable in a cultural landscape devoid of sports. To begin with, I was deprived of the very experience that had propelled my reflection on the topic. The fuel for the intellectual work had always been my own devotion to the teams I support, and without that regular engagement with sports, the writing felt largely unmotivated.

Moreover, I had real questions about what the world would look like when the book finally made its way to readers. Would sports have returned to normal, or would games still be on hold? The latter case was hard to imagine, given the time it takes for a book manuscript to get published, but there was enough uncertainty about damn near everything at that time that I certainly couldn't rule out the possibility. And even if sports had returned, maybe Leitch was right in suggesting that our relationship to them would be changed. Maybe the sort of fandom that most interested me— the sort where people are willing to forego other plans in order to watch a game and where their emotional state is affected by the exploits of their favorite teams—would no longer be recognizable for most fans. If that turned out to be the case, then the book might end up as an interesting piece of anthropology: a snapshot in the history of that peculiar animal *homo fanaticus*. But it wouldn't find much traction as a work in ethics, because it would be about how best to navigate a sporting landscape that no longer existed.

Despite these misgivings, two considerations led me to stick with the project as originally conceived (albeit with this revised introduction). First, I ended up being convinced that the world of sports would eventually return to something resembling its pre-pandemic state. Games had been placed on hiatus before (in the midst of world wars, for example), and they had found a way to come back. As long as there are people, I suspect that they will want to compete in athletic contests, and as long as there are athletic contests, I suspect that people will want to watch. The return of spectator sports to cultural prominence might happen quickly, or it could take years, but I believed that it would happen. And given that exploring the particular hold that sports have on us is one of the motivating concerns of the book, I thought I might have something to say about the enduring nature of this attachment.

More fundamentally, however, I thought that my own reaction to the sporting world's Grand Pause proved to be a roundabout illustration of the central line of the book's argument. For my central contention in the pages that follow is that while there is unquestionably value in being a sports fan, and that our lives can be enriched through the various practices and rituals of fandom, that value is best obtained when fans largely forget themselves and direct their attention more fully to the athletes who play the games. After all, fans are observers of, rather than participants in, the games they watch. When sports are canceled, fans lose the opportunity to observe the remarkable exploits of others, but the athletes miss out on playing the games, whether they are 11-year-old soccer players running around a field in front of their parents or multimillionaires whose names are known by a billion people around the world.

Perhaps a global pandemic, and the distance from sports it imposed on us, would enable us to have fresh eyes when we could finally start watching and attending games again. And perhaps the time away would help us to better appreciate what happens on the field: who really wins and who really loses and how we, as fans, can benefit from the athletic exploits of others. If so, then maybe the sadness I felt for the athletes in my life provided a glimpse of the sort of fandom I wanted to cultivate. At the very least, that line of reflection provided the fuel I needed to put the finishing touches on the initial manuscript.

The Allure of Escapism

There are, of course, plenty of fans who have no desire to ever think too much about their relationship to sports, much less do so in the wake of a once in a century pandemic. Such people are more than happy to think quite a lot about sports: they analyze coaching strategy, criticize player performance, opine about how to improve their favorite teams, and argue with other fans about

4 Introduction

everything under the sporting sun, from who will win the weekend's upcoming games to how to rank the best players of all time. However, those same people may balk at the suggestion that their existence as fans is something that deserves much attention. For them, fandom should be uncomplicated—an escape from the messiness of everyday life. While canceling sports thus meant depriving them of that escape, when sports returned, the last thing they wanted to do is place their fandom under a microscope. They just wanted to enjoy the games again. Why muddy these clear waters by submitting them to philosophical scrutiny, much less raising specifically *ethical* questions in the realm of sports? Aren't we better off just letting people have fun and confining our ethical reflections, if we engage in them at all, to the real life concerns we are trying to block out?

Even in the best of times, it is not hard to see why there might be a reluctance to subject our fandom to too much scrutiny. We love sports, and we fear that if we look too closely at the relationships we have to the games, athletes, and teams we love, we may be unsettled by what we see. We are like beer lovers who don't even want to ask whether their relationship to alcohol is altogether healthy or, I hazard to say, investment bankers who would rather not think about the moral features of their industry. Why risk changing our lives too much or, heaven forbid, giving up the things we love? Better to simply avoid thinking about them and continue on as we always have.

I confess that during the many days at home trying to wait out the coronavirus, I found this view more attractive than I had at any other point working on this project. I had never wanted to deny the value of shielding ourselves from "real life" every now and then. We can't spend every waking moment thinking about the world's problems (or even just the problems in our own lives), and if sports provide a way for some people to occasionally zone out, then far be it from me to deny them such a pleasure. Despite what some people in my life probably think, "Philosopher as Killjoy" is not a role I'm at all eager to play.

Indeed, throughout the spring and summer of 2020, I felt the pull of a thoroughly escapist approach to sports rather acutely. News from around the world was brutal and periodically forgetting about "real life" became something of a necessity. I found it incredibly difficult to concentrate for any sustained length of time, so getting absorbed in books proved to be difficult even with more than enough time to devote to reading. And while movies and television shows often did the trick, none of them offered the particular kind of emotional engagement that I often get from sports. Plus, I started to miss the rituals that are familiar to all fans, in some form or other: the gameday sweatshirt, the post-game analysis on Twitter (usually terrible), the Premier League matches early on Sunday mornings before anyone else in the house is awake, the anticipation of my favorite team's next big matchup. My own fandom has historically provided a structure to my life that itself would have been a nice distraction in difficult times. So, despite everything I have to say in the pages that follow, let me here register a new appreciation for the escapist benefits of fandom.

That said, I don't think it is ultimately desirable to entirely exempt our fandom from reflective scrutiny. To begin with, as I think the comparisons to alcohol use and investment banking suggest, the mere fact that we like something does not mean that, all things considered, that thing occupies a good place in our lives. We may very well like things that are not good for us (or, at the very least, like them in a way that is not good for us). I really like beer, but it doesn't follow that it is good for me to drink as much as I want whenever I might happen to want it. I also like money (and periodically wish I had considerably more of it than I do), but it doesn't follow that a life heavily organized around the goal of making as much money as possible is a life well-lived. In the same way, a simple appeal to our deep love of sports does very little to vindicate all the time we devote to sports as fans. The love of something—no matter how deeply embedded in our lives—does not exempt that love from examination.

Similarly, the mere assertion that one wants to escape from everyday concerns is not, by itself, a justification that such an escape is worth pursuing; nor does it show that we cannot better maintain our psychological health via other means. It may very well be true that we all need a break from thinking about the state of our marriages, how well our kids are doing, the incompetence of our political leaders, and whether anything like world peace will ever be possible. But maybe sitting in front of the television or going to the stadium are not the best ways to achieve those ends. Maybe it would be better to go for a hike in the mountains or immerse oneself in more obviously constructive hobbies like woodworking or portrait painting. Indeed, engaging in these sorts of activities would seem to provide some of the escapist benefits of watching sports without taking us on the kind of emotional roller coaster we often ride when we watch a sporting event. And hikes and artistic pursuits have more obviously positive outcomes as well: a hike burns calories and an afternoon toiling in the workshop might yield a nice coffee table. What does the sports fan have to show for an afternoon spent on the couch or screaming in the stadium?

Those who insist on a wholly escapist approach to fandom also fail to acknowledge all the ways in which the world of sports stubbornly resists being isolated from "real life." Nearly every day there is a sports-related story on the news that concerns something of significance beyond the realm of sports. High-profile athletes get in trouble with the law or speak out on controversial political issues. Owners threaten to move their teams to different cities, and local governments decide how (or whether) to respond. Doping scandals mar the purity we want to attribute to athletic competition. Native Americans protest the use of Indian-themed nicknames and mascots. Yet another football player commits suicide, and medical researchers tell us that playing the game probably ruined his brain.

To be sure, many sports fans complain about these intrusions; they are decidedly inconvenient for people who are trying to forget about life for a while. Unfortunately, the regularity with which these stories are covered by the sports media should, I think, lead us to question the assumptions that motivate the complaint. After all, sports and real life are not separate for the individuals who play them. Why should we expect to keep them separate as fans? The athletes who perform on the field are also fathers, sons, mothers, daughters, brothers, sisters, and friends whose athletic pursuits are but one part of their own efforts to live good human lives. When non-sports-related news emerges concerning prominent athletes, it may very well destroy the illusion that athletes are mere bodies whose sole purpose is to help our favorite teams win. But that is an illusion that is better destroyed anyway.

Finally, an escapist view of fandom is challenged by all of the ridiculous and damaging things that fans do under the guise of "supporting their teams." They attack—both physically and verbally—the supporters of opposing teams and even athletes on the field. They riot and damage physical property, both when their teams win and when they lose. They tie their emotional well-being to events over which they have no control. They miss important events in the lives of their loved ones because of conflicts with games they want to watch, and they forego the opportunity to enrich personal relationships because their fan-related commitments take precedence over things like going to dinner with friends. If "real life" has a way of stubbornly inserting itself into the realm of sports, fans also have a way of allowing what happens on the field to affect the way they conduct themselves when they are not engaged with sports.

These sorts of examples are only some of the myriad ways in which sports and "real life" can become intertwined. However, I think they are more than sufficient to motivate the idea that being a sports fan is exactly the kind of pursuit that calls out for some philosophical—and, indeed, ethical—justification. Are we really making our lives better by spending a significant amount of time watching sports or living and dying with the fortunes of our favorite teams? And if that sort of devotion can be justified, what sorts of commitments might be required for fans who want to be the best fans they can be? To insist that it is important to examine the ethics of fandom is,

6 Introduction

therefore, to insist that these are important and abiding questions—questions I aim to explore in the pages that follow.

My Life as a Fan

I come to this inquiry from a deep well of personal experience. As I write, I'm 44 years old, and my first sports memory dates from when I was 6: Ohio Stadium in the fall of 1982 when the University of Wisconsin Badgers football team beat Ohio State 6–0. I was born in Madison, Wisconsin, and my father is a University of Wisconsin-Madison (UW) alum, so even though we had moved to central Ohio in the summer of 1980, we were thrilled with the result. It rained the entire game—a coldish October rain, as I recall—but the contingent of Badger fans in the crowd certainly didn't care. Beating Ohio State was (as it continues to be) its own reward.

As it happens, my second sports-related memory concerns events later that same month when the Milwaukee Brewers lost Game 7 of the World Series to the St. Louis Cardinals. I actually don't remember anything about the game, which my parents had let me stay up well past my bedtime to watch. What I do recall is being emotionally devastated and running upstairs to my room to cry. Already, at the age of 6, I had experienced the full range of emotions that sports fandom has to offer: the glorious highs of victory often destroyed soon thereafter by the excruciating agonies of defeat.

My sporting loyalties were thus cemented early, and most of them run through the state of Wisconsin: the Milwaukee Brewers, the Green Bay Packers, and the Wisconsin Badgers. Indeed, such was the pull of these teams throughout my youth that when it came time for me to think about colleges—a decision that really should involve a number of factors other than what sports teams one happens to like—I was more or less blind to all other possibilities and applied to only one school: the University of Wisconsin-Madison. The academics, campus, and my family connections in the state definitely played a role in that decision, but if I'm honest, it was the Badger football, basketball, and hockey teams that ultimately drew me there. The chance to see games in person and root for the Badgers as a student was simply too much for other schools to overcome. Plus, I found the prospect of rooting for any other college teams unthinkable. Being a student at a different school while following the Badgers from afar was too much of a strain on my loyalties to contemplate.

I mean this quite literally. As a high school student, I visited the University of Notre Dame, undeniably a top-flight academic institution with a beautiful campus and its own tradition of athletic excellence. Had I applied, I think I would have had a chance to be admitted, and at some level, I probably should have given the school serious consideration. However, the idea of sitting in Notre Dame Stadium and watching the Irish while the Badgers were 250 miles away playing in Camp Randall seemed ridiculous to me. I suppose I could have skipped Notre Dame games to watch Wisconsin play on television, but what sense would that make when I could just go to UW, where I really wanted to be anyway? So I did.

Looking back on my 18-year-old self, it might not have been the most laudable way to go about making a college decision, but it's not a decision I've ever regretted.[8] I ended up living in Madison for seven years, during which the Badger football team won back-to-back Rose Bowls, the Badger men's basketball team went to the Final Four, and the Packers won a Super Bowl. I had season tickets for the Badger men's hockey team for three seasons and made more than a few road trips to Milwaukee for Brewers games. I loved my time in Madison and getting to watch all my favorite teams up close was a central part of the overall experience.

While I have been devoted to the Badgers, Packers, and Brewers for as long as I can remember, I have also developed some new attachments in recent years. And somewhat surprisingly, given my background, they have been to soccer teams.

I did not grow up playing the (so-called) Beautiful Game. Save for one season at the local YMCA when I was (I believe) in first grade, I had basically no connection to the world's most popular sport in my youth. I played baseball and basketball through elementary school and into middle school, and then took up golf and played competitively through high school. I had friends who played soccer, but I think most everyone I knew still regarded it as something of a fringe sport in the 1980s and 1990s. There was no American professional soccer to speak of (the North American Soccer League having folded in 1984), and I don't recall anyone at my high school wearing a jersey of one of the big European clubs. When the World Cup came to the United States in 1994 (the summer before my senior year), it was clearly a significant cultural event, but it didn't convert anyone I knew into a passionate soccer fan. Indeed, I didn't really think much more about the game for the next ten years or so (except to occasionally needle the handful of devoted soccerheads in my circle of friends for their hipster devotion to a decidedly non-American pastime).

Despite my lack of familiarity with the game, when it came time to select a sport for my son to play, my wife and I picked soccer without much thought. Our reasoning was simple. Soccer involves a lot of running, and we wanted Gideon to be involved in a team sport that is physically demanding. Baseball is a wonderful game, but even when it is played at the highest levels, it involves an incredible amount of time just standing around; when kids are first learning how to hit, throw, and catch, it can be downright tedious. I worried how my son's temperament might fare in that environment, whereas at least in soccer, the kids are in constant motion. They might hardly ever touch the ball, but they will still be running around trying to get their kicks in. So Gideon started playing soccer at age 4, and has done so ever since.

Somewhere along the way—probably around the time that games started to resemble something like real soccer, as opposed to mass chaos only vaguely connected to the ball and goals—I fell in love with the sport. Its nuances started to make sense to me, and I felt that I was progressively able to understand what I was watching beyond the rudimentary events of scoring and conceding goals. Even at the youth level, sports are more enjoyable when you are able to appreciate the details: a subtle bit of skill that opens up space; a completed pass that looks simple but requires impressive vision on the part of the players involved; a defender patiently delaying the attack until help can arrive from his teammates. I eventually got roped into coaching my son's team, and have continued to coach at the youth level even as my son has moved on to more competent instructors.

The irony of being a soccer coach who never really played soccer is not lost on me, but that irony is probably better explored in a different book.[9] And anyway, this is a work on sports *fandom*, and in that connection what is important is that my developing love of soccer has coincided with an explosion of the sport on television in the United States. As I've noted, high-profile European games were almost never on TV when I was growing up. Now, American soccer fans can watch pretty much anything they want: English Premier League, La Liga games from Spain, the German Bundesliga, France's League 1. All of the UEFA Champions League games are aired live, and if you want to pay for an extra cable channel or online streaming service, you can even get the English Championship, Dutch Eredivisie, or Portugal's Primeira Liga, not to mention all the games from North and South America: MLS in the United States, Mexico's Liga MX, and top league and cup games from Brazil, Argentina, and Uruguay. As my wife regularly points out: "There. Is. Always. A. Soccer. Game. On. Television."

Unlike other sports, I'm happy to watch soccer games in which I have no rooting interest. I can't remember the last baseball game I watched on television that didn't involve the Brewers, and

8 Introduction

I watch markedly less American football than I did ten years ago. I barely paid attention to the last few Super Bowls or college national championship games because they didn't involve the Packers or Badgers. But a Liga MX clash between Tigres and Cruz Azul, involving (at most) two players I recognize and narrated in Spanish (which I do not speak)? Sure. I'll watch.

I've also developed some genuine attachments to soccer teams, a fact that proves that sporting loyalties don't have to date from childhood in order to exercise a significant hold on us. Though I haven't lived in Ohio since 1995, I support the Columbus Crew in MLS, and for European soccer, it's Tottenham Hotspur. Not one of the mega powers of the Premier League, they are a competitive club with an interesting history and a handful of connections to American players. My adoption of Spurs was probably arbitrary, but at this point, it feels like it happened organically. And then there is the US Men's National Team. I had paid some attention to every World Cup since 1994, with a clear eye on the progress of the United States. But following the national team is now a year-round process as I try to keep tabs on various roster developments and mark out time for friendlies, World Cup qualifying matches, and secondary tournaments like the Gold Cup.

I offer this bit of self-indulgent autobiography, not because my experience as a sports fan is at all remarkable, but rather because I suspect it is exceedingly common. Many fans can probably trace their strongest feelings about sports to their childhood, while some have also likely developed new passions and loyalties along the way, whether through the discovery of a new sport or by developing a relationship with a new team. Moreover, most fans can probably relate to the experience of having made a non-sports-related decision on the basis of how it would affect one's sporting interests—if not a choice as weighty as where to attend college, then surely something along the lines of whether it would be better to go to a movie with friends on Friday night or Saturday night. ("Sorry. The Badgers play on Saturday. Can we do Friday instead?")

A Map of the Terrain Ahead

My aim, then, is to try to make sense of this sort of devotion to sports: to ask what sort of value, if any, being a fan might add to one's life and what sorts of norms should govern those of us who want to be the best fans we can be. I think it is relatively easy to see the potential value of *playing* sports, even if you aren't interested in playing them yourself. For example, when I mourned my son's inability to play soccer during the coronavirus pandemic, I was sad for all the benefits of the game that he would be missing: the physical activity, the development of certain technical skills, the mental engagement required to know one's positional assignments, the unique camaraderie that teammates can develop over the course of a season, the thrill of testing oneself in competition. But I wasn't missing out on any of those things because I wasn't the one who would have been playing the games. I would have just been standing on the sideline.

Thus, even if playing soccer can be part of a flourishing life, it doesn't follow that those who watch other people play soccer are improving their lives by doing so. After all, sex can, fairly clearly, be part of a good human life, and some might even argue that it is an essential part of such a life. But it doesn't at all follow that watching other people have sex makes our lives better, or that people who devote significant amounts of time and energy to observing the sexual activity of others are spending that time and energy wisely.[10] In the same way, confidence in the value of participating in sports does not automatically support the value of watching sports, much less devoting significant portions of one's life to following the exploits of various teams.

At some level, fans certainly know that they are not participants in the games they are watching. They know that they do not make baskets, score goals, or throw touchdowns as they cheer from the stands or the comfort of their living rooms. They know that fan-related behavior is not inherently taxing on the human body and that the chance they will tear their ACL or get a concussion is, therefore, markedly lower than the athletes they are watching. And they know that, as fans, they can *at most* indirectly affect the results of the games they care about. They can cheer and yell and financially support their teams by purchasing tickets and sweatshirts. But precisely because they cannot score goals or throw touchdown passes, they know that these efforts are merely supportive.

However, even though fans know all this, I think that we far too often lose track of the distinction between ourselves and the athletes we support. We think that their victories are our victories—that their losses are our losses—and that we are therefore justified in exercising a kind of ownership over their lives. We think, to put it bluntly, that they *owe* us something: that their primary goal should be to satisfy *our* desire for victory and that the most important thing about their failures is that they constitute a frustration of *our* deepest longings. With our emotional well-being tied closely to the outcome of various games, we thus allow our passion and self-absorption to crowd out genuine respect for the humanity of the athletes we watch on the field of play.[11] Though I certainly wouldn't argue that every problem with sports fandom can be traced to this kind of attitude, I do think that any plausible ethic of fandom must start with its rejection. In other words, any account of the role that being a fan can play in a good human life needs to be organized around a commitment to the fact that athletes are independent and autonomous persons engaged in their own pursuit of the good life.

In the next chapter, I begin to address these broader questions by examining a practice that tends to obscure this fact, namely, the peculiar way in which fans employ first-person plural pronouns when discussing the performance of the teams they support. "We won" or "We didn't play well today" are common phrases in the mouths of fans, even though such fans do not play in the games they watch. My contention is that this practice has the tendency to elide the distinction between observers and participants and that greater sensitivity to the language we use when talking about our favorite teams is an important way of paying respect to athletes and the effort they put into their performance. Thus, while it may not always be wrong to use "we," being more critical in how we choose to do so can be a useful habit for fans who want to develop a healthy relationship with what happens on the field.

Having motivated the importance of the participant/observer distinction for our understanding of fandom, Chapters 2 and 3 consider what value there might be in engaging with sports as an observer. In Chapter 2, I look at criticisms of sports fans that paint them as fundamentally brutish. According to this view, sports might be worthwhile to play, but when we engage with them as fans, they tap into some of our basest instincts. If we want to live the best lives possible, we are, therefore, far better off devoting our time to other pursuits. My response to this line of thought is to argue that observing sports as fans can enrich our lives in much the same way that cultural products like literature and drama can do so—products whose value is rarely questioned as vociferously as sports and that seem to be plausible constituents of flourishing human lives. Thus, those who think that consuming (rather than producing) the works of Shakespeare can be part of a flourishing human life should come to similar conclusions about being a sports fan.

Establishing this point does not, however, establish that there is any value in being a partisan fan—that is, a fan who is invested in the performance of particular teams. Chapter 3 thus takes up this issue and argues, against some critics of partisanship, that the benefits of partisan fandom are analogous to the benefits of personal relationships. While some defenses of partisanship have invoked a similar analogy and compared a love of sports teams to romantic relationships, I contend that familial love of the sort we can share with our parents, siblings, and children better captures the unique nature of fans' attachment to their favorite teams. Taking this approach, we can see how it is possible to regard the devotion of the fan as an attachment that satisfies a basic human need to love, rather than viewing it as a matter of loyalty that they are somehow obligated to maintain. Put

10 Introduction

differently, I argue that human beings need to love things, and that sports teams are worthy objects of that love.

The remainder of the book is an exploration of a number of challenges that fans confront on the contemporary sporting landscape. Chapters 4 and 5 are explicitly occasioned by the current state of American football.[12] As we learn about the physical and psychological toll that the game takes on those who play it, it becomes increasingly difficult to resist concluding that whatever enjoyment fans get from watching football comes at a remarkable cost to players. As a result, anyone who wishes to continue as a football fan should grapple with what we owe to those who are willing to put their health at risk in these ways.

With these facts in mind, in Chapter 4, I draw on the feminist literature on objectification and argue that it is wrong to regard athletes solely in terms of the performances they are able to generate with their bodies. This position may strike some readers as obvious, but I suggest that the pitfalls of objectification are not as easy to avoid as we might think, because they extend from the way we respond to athletes who speak out on political issues to the seemingly innocuous world of fantasy sports. Taking the humanity of athletes seriously thus requires greater vigilance on the part of fans than is commonly acknowledged.

In Chapter 5, I delve more fully into the ethics of playing football and, by extension, other violent sports. For though this is a book on sports fandom, it does not seem possible to vindicate the practice of watching football without showing that it is ethically permissible to play a game that poses the sorts of risks faced by football players. While we can assume that there are no ethical problems with individuals playing most sports, and thus consider the ethical dynamics of watching basketball and soccer with that assumption in the background, we cannot take the ethical permissibility of football for granted in the same way.

I thus offer a tentative defense of football that appeals to the idea that it is legitimate for athletes to risk serious injury (including the possibility of future brain damage) when they are pursuing goods that (a) cannot be obtained without that risk and (b) they regard as valuable enough to their own pursuit of the good life to be worthwhile. After attempting to articulate how individuals might arrive at the conclusion that such trade-offs are worth making, I consider whether children should be allowed to make similar decisions. On that point, my suggestion is that while we should not permit very young children to risk their future mental health, the desires of older adolescents should be given increasing weight. Provided they think through the stakes of their decisions, I think it can be permissible for 16- and 17-year-olds to play football.

In Chapters 6 and 7, I consider the ethics of rooting for two different kinds of teams: women's teams and national teams. Unlike American football, and other big-time spectator sports, the challenge with women's sports is that they draw such little attention when compared to their male counterparts. For those of us who claim to be committed to gender equality, this fact should be unsettling. After all, women should have as much opportunity to pursue the good life through the use of their athletic talents as men have, and young girls should have as much opportunity to draw on the experiences of other female athletes as men have to draw on the experience of their athletic heroes. As a result, I argue that sports fans of all genders should support women's sports teams as fans: by buying tickets to the games, purchasing team merchandise, and watching games on television. This proposal may seem fairly pedestrian, but when developed in sufficient detail, I suggest that such actions have the possibility of subverting any number of troubling norms surrounding gender and sexuality, both within the world of sports and in our culture more broadly.

Support of national teams raises yet another set of issues as competition on the international stage is often fraught with nationalistic impulses and political overtones that are absent from many domestic contests. I explore this dynamic by looking at controversies surrounding the makeup of various national teams, particularly the inclusion of dual nationals.

Nevertheless, while political circumstances can heighten the dramatic tension of certain athletic contests, we should be slow to map geopolitical conflicts onto sports. When the United States played the Soviet Union in the 1980 Winter Olympics hockey tournament, it was just a hockey game played by men on both sides attempting to win the gold medal, not a referendum on the superiority of capitalism over communism. Striving to keep this fact in view should, therefore, guide the manner in which we express our nationalistic commitments in the realm of sports. It should also temper the enthusiasm with which we view sports as a vehicle for the advancement of our favorite social and political causes.

I then conclude by offering four guidelines that I think encapsulate some of the broader themes of the book and provide a rough-hewn framework for thinking about the stream of controversies that regularly intersect with the realm of sports. While I am (for various reasons) resistant to moral sloganeering, I think it can nevertheless be appropriate to have some rules of thumb to fall back on as we attempt to navigate a complex world. I thus offer a few "takeaways" for readers who may find them useful.

Why This Set of Topics?

Examining this limited array of issues quite clearly does not constitute a comprehensive account of all the ethical issues surrounding fandom, nor do I intend it as such. I have, for the most part, avoided discussing phenomena that strike me as obviously immoral or whose connection to sports is only incidental to an understanding of their ethical significance. For example, racist fan chants— a practice that is still disturbingly rampant in world soccer (and more common in American sports than is probably recognized)—can be straightforwardly criticized on the grounds of their racist content. The fact that they occur in the context of sports does not fundamentally change the way in which we understand the norms surrounding racist speech. Racist speech is wrong whether it is fans yelling at players, players yelling at other players, or people hurling racist epithets at each other while they are walking down the street. Similarly, it is wrong for fans to threaten violence toward players and other fans for the same reasons that it is wrong to threaten violence toward other people generally. The fact that the individuals involved are players and/or fans doesn't shed any additional moral light on the situation.

While there are, no doubt, interesting psychological and sociological questions about why individuals engage in those sorts of behaviors, I don't think there is much of philosophical interest surrounding the *ethics* of those behaviors.[13] It is not, I think, a vexing ethical question whether racist fan chants are repugnant, and I don't recall ever seriously entertaining the thought that more fan violence might be a good thing. As I see it, the moral stakes in these behaviors can be fairly well understood without thinking much, if at all, about sports: racism is bad, and so is expressing racist thoughts; violence is bad, and so perpetrating violence without any necessity is bad as well. The fact that it is fan violence is more or less irrelevant to understanding why it is bad.

I have, therefore, attempted to focus on issues that are uniquely faced by fans or whose particular normative contours are somehow put in a new light by their presence in the world of sports. We all have to confront the use of racist language and violence, whether or not we are sports fans, but only fans are really occupied with the question of whether they should support their country's national soccer team or whether there is anything problematic about deriving pleasure from a sport that inflicts harm on many of the people who play it. One can, quite clearly, live a full and wonderful life without caring about sports at all, and none of the arguments that follow are intended

12 Introduction

to suggest otherwise. But if one is going to be a sports fan, figuring out how to do so in the best manner possible will, I hope, lead one to address these kinds of questions.

By the same token, one might have ethical commitments that one is not sure how to consistently apply in the realm of sports. For example, the phenomenon of objectification seems to be morally significant, and feminists have therefore been concerned about objectifying portrayals of women in pornography and the media more generally. But those who are concerned to avoid objectifying others might also be concerned about the subtle ways in which an objectifying attitude can corrupt the ways that fans relate to athletes. As such, we can consider objectification to be a general moral issue but one that takes on a specific character in the context of sports. My discussion in Chapter 5 is therefore offered in this spirit: to figure out how a general moral commitment might put pressure on fans to think about their relationship to athletes in ways that go unrecognized. In the same way, the ethics of nationalism might be of a general interest that takes a particular form when it comes to rooting for national sports teams—the sort of issue I consider in Chapter 8.

One final caveat. Despite the moral significance of all the topics I discuss, I don't intend my conclusions as rigid moral rules that are disobeyed only by bad or evil people. Though I certainly present arguments in the pages that follow, I offer them in a largely personal and inquisitive spirit: as an attempt to understand the role that being a fan might play in my own life and, just as importantly, how I might become a better one. If readers perceive a lot of finger wagging in the pages that follow, I will have failed to convey the mindset that has led to the views I offer. At the end of the day, I will be happy if I have urged readers to think critically about their own fandom and challenged them to consider how they, too, might be better fans. It is ultimately up to them to decide if I have been successful.[14]

Notes

1. "CDC, Washington State Report First COVID-19 Death," *CDC Online Newsroom*, February 29, 2020, www.cdc.gov/media/releases/2020/s0229-COVID-19-first-death.html.
2. Ben Golliver, "NBA Suspends Season after Jazz's Rudy Gobert Tests Positive for Coronavirus," *The Washington Post*, March 12, 2020, www.washingtonpost.com/sports/2020/03/11/nba-suspends-play-player-test-coronavirus.
3. Andrew Lisa, "The Money Behind the March Madness NCAA Basketball Tournament," *Yahoo.com*, March 9, 2020, https://finance.yahoo.com/news/money-behind-march-madness-ncaa-194402803.html.
4. The 2020 Masters would eventually be played in November with no fans in attendance.
5. Tim Layden, "Coronavirus KO'd Spring Sports; Now We're Living without Them," *NBC Sports. com*, March 13, 2020, https://sports.nbcsports.com/2020/03/13/sports-crystallized-coronavirus-for-america-now-we-adjust-to-life-without-them.
6. Will Leitch, "How Will Sports Recover from This Hiatus?" *The New York Times*, March 15, 2020, www.nytimes.com/2020/03/15/opinion/sports-coronavirus.html.
7. Jim Weber (@JimMWeber), "Imagine If Man Had Never Created Sports," *Twitter*, April 10, 2020, https://twitter.com/Jimmweber/Status/1238952465099296768 (At last check, the tweet had been deleted.)
8. Warren St. John made a different decision, as he details in *Rammer, Jammer, Yellow Hammer* (New York: Three Rivers Press, 2005). An Alabama native and lifelong fan of the Crimson Tide, St. John nevertheless decided to attend Columbia University—a fact that imposed certain obstacles in his quest to follow Alabama's football team during his college years. When I first read the book several years ago, I confess that my reaction to St. John's decision was puzzlement. Why not just go to the University of Alabama and avoid these problems? Sure. Columbia is, by most any measure, a better school than Alabama. But he could have gone to every Alabama home game for four years, not only as a fan, but as a student and future alum. Surely that possibility should have carried more weight with St. John than it did. With the benefit of a few more years' maturity, I now concede that the overall benefits of going to Columbia might outweigh the costs St. John endured as a sports fan. Nevertheless, it's a decision I don't think I could have made. Perhaps a full scholarship to Cornell or Brown could have lured me away from Madison, but even then, it would have been a close call.

Introduction **13**

9. Unfortunately for me, though certainly not for readers, I think it's probably a book that Jim Haner has already produced with his excellent *Soccerhead: An Accidental Journey into the Heart of the American Game* (New York: North Point Press, 2006).
10. This analogy between sex and sports is also employed by Randolph Feezell in Chapter 4 of *Sports, Philosophy, and Good Lives* (Lincoln: University of Nebraska Press, 2013).
11. I recognize that not all sports are played on fields. Nevertheless, for stylistic reasons, I will often use the phrase "field of play" when referring to the arena of athletic competition even if the "field" is a court, track, course, pool, or rink. Also for stylistic reasons, when the field in question is one on which soccer is played, I will sometimes refer to it as a "pitch."
12. From this point on, I try to be consistent in referring to Association Football (played by Tottenham Hotspur and the Columbus Crew) as soccer and the American version of football (played by the Green Bay Packers) as simply football.
13. In saying this, I don't at all mean to deny that there are fascinating sociological and anthropological questions about fan behavior. For journalistic examinations along these lines, see Bill Buford, *Among the Thugs* (New York: Vintage, 1993) and Justine Gubar, *Fanaticus: Mischief in the Modern Sports Fan* (Lanham: Rowman & Littlefield, 2015). For a more academic approach, see Lisa A. Lewis, ed., *The Adoring Audience: Fan Culture and Popular Media* (New York: Routledge, 1992); Andrei Markovits and Emily Albertson, *Sportista: Female Fandom in the United States* (Philadelphia: Temple University Press, 2012); and Andrei Markovits and Lars Rensman, *Gaming the World* (Princeton: Princeton University Press, 2010).
14. Consider this my effort to deflect any charge of moral grandstanding of the sort outlined by Justin Tosi and Brandon Warmke, "Moral Grandstanding," *Philosophy & Public Affairs* 44, no. 3 (June 2016): 197–217.

1

ON "WE"

Among the many peculiar habits of sports fans is their tendency to use pronouns of the first-person plural variety when describing the exploits of their favorite teams. "We didn't play well today." "Our defense has to improve if we are going to have any shot at the title." "I really hope we beat the Buckeyes this weekend." "If only we had a decent striker, our fortunes might finally start to change." None of these phrases would raise an eyebrow if uttered among fans bantering about the prospects of the teams they support, even though such individuals have only been witness to—rather than participants in—the events in which they are so invested.

In a 2011 column for the now-defunct *Grantland* website, Chris Jones takes aim at this practice, arguing that "[i]f you don't play for, or you are not an employee of, the team in question, "we" is not the pronoun you're looking for. 'They' is the word you want." Jones's case for this conclusion is largely ontological as he points out that a team without fans still exists and that first-person plural pronouns invoked in other entertainment contexts sound ridiculous. He thus writes: "If someone read a book and said to me, 'We really killed that opening chapter,' I'd wonder if I were talking to Gollum."[1] Bill Simmons issues similar, if somewhat more lenient, advice in a 2002 essay for *ESPN. com* when he suggests that readers be "very careful when using the word 'we' with your favorite team. Use it judiciously. Just remember, you don't wear a uniform, you don't play any minutes, and you're not on the team."[2]

In this chapter, I want to explore this practice in somewhat greater depth and ask what potential costs might attend unreflective uses of "we" on the part of sports fans.[3] My central contention is that such uses are corrosive insofar as they distort the proper relationship between fans and the teams and players they support. After all, to be a fan is, fundamentally, to be one who takes pleasure in the achievements of others (and likely experiences displeasure at their failures), and those who employ first-person pronouns when talking about their favorite teams thus run the risk of representing the successes of others as their *own* successes (and the failures of others as their *own* failures). To insist that fans maintain a distinction between themselves and their favorite teams when they talk about sports is, therefore, a way to keep the proceedings on the field in perspective: it promotes an appropriate level of respect for the accomplishments of athletes (and the work they put into achieving them) while also highlighting that fans are essentially helpless to affect the events in which they are so heavily invested.

DOI: 10.4324/9781003223696-2

My case for this conclusion is, following Jones's lead, largely ontological. When fans say things like "We won the game" or "We can play so much better than we did today," they are linguistically attributing qualities to themselves that they do not, in fact, possess and thus eliding the fundamental distinction between participants and observers that I think is central to any plausible ethic of fandom. However, before examining some of the specific ways in which use of the first-person plural can lead fans to lose track of this distinction, it is perhaps worth remarking briefly on a concern that readers might have with the way in which I have framed the present argument.

If we take it as a given that all but the most wildly deluded fans know that they do not literally play the games they observe—that they do not score touchdown or goals, commit penalties or game-deciding turnovers, or suffer career-ending injuries—then it might seem excessively nit-picky to focus on a linguistic practice that is as widespread as this one. Why paint fans, who love the teams they support with a passion that is often unequaled elsewhere in their lives, as doing something *wrong* when they express that love using language that is widely accepted by other fans? Isn't this much ado about nothing?

There is certainly something to this response, and in keeping with my aims in this book, I don't intend the point I am making to be overly moralistic: I do not think that fans who use "we" are bad people in virtue of that use or that every deployment of the first-person plural should be met with harsh moral rebuke. Nevertheless, I think this topic serves as an important window into some of the issues I will be exploring in later chapters. At a time when many fans seem to think that their status as supporters gives them a right to engage in all kinds of questionable behavior—from verbally abusing players from the stands and attacking them (often quite viciously) on social media, to demanding that athletes stay silent about controversial political issues and instead just "shut up and play"—it seems appropriate to give some sustained attention to the various contours of the relationship between players and fans. And because I think these behaviors are likely fueled by a sense that fans have a close identification with athletes that gives them a right to engage in these kinds of activities, perhaps the use of "we" is not as innocuous as it might first appear.

Moreover, even if our everyday language does not always express nuanced philosophical theories, the words we use are nevertheless capable of reflecting—and sometimes shaping—broader patterns of thought that should concern us. Think here of debates concerning the use of gendered pronouns or the labels that people deploy for characteristics like ethnicity or sexual orientation. Or consider the ways in which words like "retarded" are gradually expunged from polite discourse because they reflect ways of thinking we believe should be revised. Calling someone retarded may show that the speaker has objectionable views about individuals with disabilities and may, therefore, be grounds for morally criticizing that speaker. But whether or not one has such views is not as important as the way in which the word reflects a broader attitude toward the disabled. Individual speakers may not share such views, or even necessarily be aware of the connection between what they are saying and that broader attitude. Nevertheless, those concerned to bolster respect for those with physical or cognitive impairments should probably work to expunge "retarded" from their vocabulary.

Here's another example that is, perhaps, less morally loaded.[4] Midwives tend to describe their participation in the childbirth process somewhat differently from OB-GYNs. Whereas OBs usually talk about "delivering" babies, midwives may refer to "catching" babies, the idea being that it is pregnant women who deliver their children, not whoever happens to be assisting them in the process. The terminological differences are subtle—it is, after all, just one word—but they reflect broader differences in the approach that many midwives and OBs adopt toward their work. Midwives try to emphasize their role as facilitators and sources of emotional support, whereas the language employed by OBs is part and parcel of a medicalized approach to childbirth.

16 On "We"

My point here isn't necessarily to argue that either of these choices is correct in this particular context. It is instead to show that there are many examples along these lines where we decide to alter the way we talk because doing so is a useful way to alter how we think or to reflect changes in our worldviews that have already taken place. Thus, if it is important to respect the accomplishments of athletes by making sure that we maintain a clear distinction between fans and the teams they support, then we also have good reason to think that the language fans use to talk about their favorite teams can play an important role in either bolstering or undermining that distinction. Understood in this way, a commitment to avoid using "we" can be a useful reminder of the boundaries of our achievement—a way to demarcate what we have truly accomplished (or failed to accomplish) as fans and where the glory more properly belongs to others.

Of all the topics I address in this book, I have been most surprised thus far by responses to the argument that follows in this chapter. In part, I think I simply underestimated the genuine complexity of the philosophical issues associated with "we" when I began this project, and so the pushback has been an invaluable part of my own philosophical development. I know I have still left some loose ends, but I have tried to address the most prominent objections and alternative views without expanding the chapter well beyond the limits of readability.

However, I also think that the views that people have on "we" are as strong as they are because they serve as a kind of proxy for their broader commitments as sports fans. As such, the topic serves as an incredibly useful point of entry into a much wider variety of issues. Thus, readers who don't find themselves initially convinced by what I have to say might consider revisiting the topic once they have made their way through the arguments of subsequent chapters. If the remainder of the book does not make the argument here more compelling (as it very well may not!), I hope that it will at least address some lingering questions and provide a clearer sense of how I see the broader ethical terrain and why I take the stand in this chapter that I will now attempt to defend.

Athletes Pay Different Costs

When I drive into campus during the fall semester, my route takes me past the Wake Forest football team's practice field. Most days, I arrive around 8:30 in the morning, and at that point, the countdown clock that looms over the facility usually shows that there are seven or eight minutes remaining in the session. The team has been at it since 6:30, and while my workday is just about to begin, they have been running, blocking, and tackling for two hours. By the time I see some of the football players in my 9:30 a.m. class, they will have (thankfully) showered, devoured a quick breakfast, and be ready to (at least try to) talk philosophy.

If I find myself at a football game on a Saturday afternoon, among the many things that will distinguish the players from the cheering throngs in the stands is the amount of time and effort that has gone into preparing for the day's events. I will watch the game from the relative comfort of my seat while the players endure a significant amount of physical punishment over three and a half hours on the field. Moreover, having witnessed a small part of their daily routine in the week leading up to the game, I know that their performance on that day will be only a fraction of the overall commitment they have made to excellence in their chosen sport. Hours and hours of practice over many years have preceded whatever performance fans happen to see in the stadium.

Consider, then, fans who talk to their friends about "how well we played today" while leaving the stadium after a win. Such fan are, at least grammatically, attributing to themselves some of the actions that led to the victory. As Jones points out, this is an ontological absurdity. While they were sitting, eating, drinking, and talking with their friends, the players were running, throwing, catching, blocking, tackling, and being tackled. Indeed, none of the discrete events that constitute a team victory require that one so much as take account of fans' existence.

Of course, fans do invest time and emotional energy in the proceedings, and they may very well leave the game exhausted. But game day is only a small piece of the puzzle, and panning back from a narrow focus on the competition reveals significant differences in the investments made by players and fans. While the players were practicing at 6:30 on Wednesday morning, most fans were fast asleep in bed, and the long film sessions needed to analyze the next opponent's offensive scheme differ rather markedly from the fan's latest binge-watching session of Netflix. Even on game day, the differences are stark. While the players will go home with aches, pains, cuts, and bruises, fans will go home with indigestion brought on by greasy food and too much beer. If they have been particularly vocal in their support of the team, they might have to nurse a mildly sore throat.

While I think that the discrepancy in the costs borne by athletes and the costs borne by the fans who support them is particularly salient in the case of punishing contact sports like American football, the phenomenon is present in all spectator sports. I might regularly see the football players practicing because of where my office happens to be located and the route I take into work. But I know that on the other side of campus, the women's soccer team is finishing their own training session and that at various times throughout the rest of the day, most of the athletes at my university will be practicing or in some other way preparing for their next competition. When fans come to see the soccer team on game days, they see extraordinary physical exertion over the course of a 90-minute game—exertion that almost none of the people in the stands could even hope to approximate. When I watch them play, I also think of the summers I have seen them doing interval training in heat and humidity that is, even in the early morning hours, enough to make me sweat profusely simply by walking to the car.

These sorts of discrepancies between the costs borne by athletes and fans should, therefore, be enough to undermine any justification of "we" that appeals to the joint agency of fans and athletes or the idea that fans are, contrary to all appearances, part of the teams they support. They should also be enough to make fans wary of owning the accomplishments of athletes via the language they use. Saying "We won the game" when you do not play in the game can thus obscure the different investments that athletes and fans have made in the proceedings, and a failure to appreciate that difference can, therefore, be disrespectful.

As I've noted, this is not to say that fans have made no investment in the proceedings or that those investments are not legitimate. Fans clearly do invest in the outcome of sporting events, and it is the burden of this book to show that those investments can be worthwhile. Nevertheless, I think that having a clear-eyed assessment of the costs that others incur in the pursuit of their goals is an important part of relating well to that person—of acknowledging their distinctness and value as an individual engaged in their own pursuit of the good life. To the degree that we can encourage this kind of clear-eyed approach to sports through the language we use, it seems to me that we should probably do so. Put differently, if avoiding the use of "we" when we talk about our favorite teams helps us to better appreciate and respect the athletes who play the games we love, then avoiding the use of "we" strikes me as a worthy policy to adopt.[5]

Teams, Fans, and Clubs

For all I have said thus far, it must be granted that there are complexities concerning exactly how we should understand the composition of the teams we support—complexities that might lend ontological credence to defenders of "we." If we are unsure exactly how to draw the boundaries concerning who is part of the team and who is not, then perhaps we should be much more lenient when considering who is licensed to claim victory in the first person. For example, consider questions about what makes any given team the same team over time. Given that their composition changes so regularly, any team I currently support may be made up of completely different players, coaches, and administrators in five years. In what sense, then, will I be supporting *the same team* that I support now?

Indeed, there are cases that push this kind of identity question in even more vexing directions. In 1996, Art Modell moved the Cleveland Browns to Baltimore where they have been playing as the Baltimore Ravens ever since. In 1999, a new team began to play in Cleveland as the Cleveland Browns, even adopting the team's traditional orange and brown uniforms. Which team, then, is identical to the team that played as the Browns in 1985? The "new" Cleveland Browns? The Baltimore Ravens? Neither?

As a solution to these sorts of puzzles, Stephen Mumford suggests that we view sports teams as complex social substances whose identity is determined "not just on the metaphysical facts—the (weakly) mind-independent facts of where they are based," but also by "facts about the behavior of people, including facts about the allegiances of their supporters."[6] Thus, in trying to determine what team in 2018 is identical to the 1985 Cleveland Browns, we should not just examine various objective features of the teams in question—facts about the cities and stadiums in which they have played or the players, coaches, and administrators who have worked in each organization. We must also query the views of Browns fans and ask whether they regard the "new" Browns as identical to the team they supported in 1985. If so, then Mumford thinks such views may be sufficient to make it the case that Browns fans in 2018 are rooting for the same team that Browns fans supported in 1985. According to Mumford:

> [I]t is, therefore, agreement among a community of onlookers, that identity has been preserved through a range of discontinuities, that is in part constitutive of that identity through change. To at least some degree, I argue, facts about allegiance are constitutive of the identity of the club.[7]

What is important in the present context is that if Mumford is right about the role that fan attitudes play in determining the identity of teams over time, that account would buttress the idea that fans are justified in feeling as though they are a part of the teams they support. Indeed, Mumford gestures at this implication when he notes that

> [b]ecause the club is a complex social substance, it is in part constituted by that body of support, *so part of the object of allegiance is a group having a shared allegiance to each other, qua component of the club.*[8]

In other words, because fan support over time helps constitute teams as the teams they are, fans become part of the team. And if fans are, in this way, part of the team, then perhaps they have a right to invoke the first-person plural when talking about the teams they partially constitute.

Jake Wojtowicz has recently advanced a similar line of argument in contending that supporters contribute to the ethical identity of a club where an ethical identity is to be understood as a club's distinctive character: its character as the particular club that it is. In this way, fans can "exercise a powerful influence over core parts of a club's ethical identity" by shaping "its playing style as well as its relationship with other clubs."[9] Sometimes, this influence can be for the better, as when a club is defined in terms of its commitment to social justice. It can also be for the worse, as when fans who consistently hurl racist epithets at opposing players may, over time, render the club itself racist. Wojtowicz thus thinks it appropriate to punish clubs "for bad behaviour in a way that affects the club's sporting success: we are justified in imposing points deductions and competition disqualifications on the basis of fan behaviour."[10]

Importantly, this kind of sanction only makes sense if fans constitute the club in some fundamental way. Without that constitutive relationship, such a punishment would be unfair: it would target one group of people (the players on the field) for the actions of others (the supporters in the stands). However, Wojtowicz argues that clubs are larger entities that are constituted, in part, by fans and the teams they support. If we then acknowledge that fans "shape the ethical identity of the club that succeeds" on the field, we have a justification for punishing the *club as a whole* for its actions. As Wojtowicz concludes:

> We can rightly punish sporting success on the basis of fan behavior because sporting success . . . involves more than just the success of a team: it involves the success of a club, a club whose identity is partly constituted by the fans.[11]

Fans of a club that has been punished by receiving competitive sanctions on the basis of fan behavior thus have every right to say something along the lines of "We've lost points in the standings because of our racist behavior."

I'm largely convinced by the notion that teams are complex social substances whose identity is largely constituted by the views of the fans who support them.[12] However, even if it is true that fan support is part of what determines the identity of teams over time, it doesn't follow that fans become part of those teams in virtue of such support. Suppose we ask whether a particular restaurant is the same restaurant in 2018 as it was in 1985. Perhaps it has moved locations and undergone significant changes to its menu and staff. In my view, it is reasonable to think that at least part of the answer to this question depends on whether patrons of the restaurant regard it as the same restaurant. For even if a restaurant is not exactly a complex social substance, neither is it a "middle-sized dry good" whose identity over time may be thought to depend wholly on its mind-independent qualities. Whether people think of it as the same restaurant is an important part of whether or not it is the same restaurant even though no one would be inclined to say that its patrons are part of the restaurant itself. Their views may, in an important way, determine the identity of the restaurant over time, but they do not thereby become part of the entity whose identity is being determined.

In the same way, it is plausible to say that the views of supporters matter for determining the identity of sports teams over time even if it doesn't follow that supporters become part of the teams they support. Perhaps there is an argument to be made that this latter implication is a key part of Mumford's overall view, but it does not seem to be necessary for his central contention to hold. And without that additional commitment, support for use of the first-person plural among fans seems to be lost. Even if Mumford is right, his argument still doesn't give metaphysical cover to fans who insist on using "we" when talking about the teams they support.

Nor does Wojtowicz's contention that supporters help constitute the ethical identity of a club entail that the *club* is what succeeds on the field rather than the *team*. Thus, even if we grant Wojtowicz's basic argument and leave aside questions of whether the framework he invokes applies in North American contexts where the distinction between a club and team may be more difficult to maintain, I still think the scenario he describes is one in which part of the club (the team) is sometimes punished for the poor behavior of another part of the club (its supporters).[13] Indeed, Wojtowicz grants that the "team has a complaint against any success-directed punishment due to fan behavior," and players on the team might, therefore, be justifiably angry because their prospects for a league championship have been undermined by racist chanting in which they have not engaged (and may very well abhor and condemn).[14] It would be perfectly sensible for players in such a scenario to say, "*We* didn't do anything, and now *we* are having to pay the price for *their* offensive actions." The distinction between the team and its fans doesn't disappear just because both groups are constituent parts of the club.[15] And as long as the team is the entity that plays games, it seems that fans should be wary of owning their accomplishments and, indeed, engaging in behavior for which the team on the field will be disproportionately punished.

All of this is consistent, I think, with the idea that it can sometimes be appropriate to punish the whole for the behavior of some of its parts. In coaching contexts, I have sometimes made an entire team perform "punishment" exercises such as extra running because a few players were not paying attention during practice. But in so doing, I have had no illusions that the whole team was goofing off. The idea was rather to encourage all the players to discipline each other—to have the well-behaved kids keep those who were poorly behaved in line, and to have the poorly behaved embrace accountability to their teammates more fully. However, as I suspect most coaches and grade school teachers know, this strategy only works sporadically. All the kids know who is mis-behaving, and those who are doing what they are supposed to do resent being punished for the misbehavior of others. Similarly, kids who aren't committed to paying attention in practice are generally resistant to shaming by their teammates, and so the punishment often fails to have its intended effect.

It is not hard to see a similar dynamic at play when clubs are punished on the basis of fan behavior. Such punishments are only effective to the degree that fans care about them. If they care more about engaging in morally problematic behavior than the success of the team on the field, then they are likely to breed resentment between the players and their fans. For example, ultra-supporters of the Israeli soccer team Beitar Jerusalem—a group known as La Familia—have long engaged in anti-Muslim activities, and the team has been penalized numerous times with point deductions and other sanctions. But such actions have failed to have much of an effect on La Familia, and the club has turned to more targeted methods in an attempt to discipline this subset of fans.[16] The assumption behind this sort of punishment is that all fans strongly identify with on-field results and will, therefore, experience the punishment of the team in the first-person plural—as "our" punishment. That isn't always the case. Even in cases where fans see themselves as part of the club, it is nearly impossible to eliminate a distinction between what fans do and what teams do as different parts of a broader entity.[17]

Who Is on the Team?

Granting a basic distinction between participants in, and observers of, sporting events still leaves us with tricky questions about who properly counts as a member of the team. Some cases seem fairly straightforward. A fan watching a game on the couch in their living room is clearly a specta-tor, and the basketball player they are watching shoot a three-pointer on the television screen is clearly a participant. But other cases are more complicated. Some players are on the team roster but never see competitive action in games. Is it appropriate for the bench warmer to talk about how "we" won the championship even though they didn't log a single playing minute the entire season? Except in very rare occasions, coaches are not players on the teams they coach even though they are obviously more involved in how games unfold than are spectators watching at home. Moreover, coaches frequently use the first-person plural in discussing the exploits of their teams, talking about how well or poorly "we" played and those areas in which "we" need to improve. Indeed, I talk this way all the time about the youth teams I have coached, even though I stand on the sidelines during games while the kids run around and work up a sweat. Am I inappropriately injecting myself into the proceedings or taking undue credit for their victories when I talk about how well "we" played in a recent victory?

Athletic trainers don't play in games either, but they often sit on the bench with players and are involved in the action by assessing and attending to injuries. Are trainers part of the team?

In his discussion of "we," Jones says that one can use the first-person plural if one works for the team in question. But I'm not sure this is always the appropriate line to draw. Is it really appropriate for those who answer the phones in the ticket office or clean the stadium restrooms to speak as though they are part of the team? And who counts as an employee of the team in scholastic contexts? I teach philosophy at a university that has multiple athletic teams. Might it then be the case that I work for my college's sports teams in the same way that a ticket salesperson works for a professional organization, or is this designation reserved for employees of the athletic department?

A few points by way of response to these sorts of questions. First, I think we can grant the existence of difficult cases without denying that the participant/observer distinction is important and useful. Consider a parallel (well-known to students of philosophy as the sorites paradox). We might not be sure about when, precisely, a number of grains of sand can properly be called a heap of sand or how many hairs a man must have on his head in order for him to avoid being bald. Nevertheless, we can be confident that six grains of sand do not really constitute a heap and that I am not bald (even though my hairline has receded somewhat as of late). Similarly, the fact that I might not be sure whether an athletic trainer is a member of the team need not weaken my conviction that people sitting on their couches watching a game on television are not participants in the contest. Put differently, even if athletic trainers and bench warmers can say "we," it does not follow that fans are similarly licensed to do so.

Indeed, the importance of maintaining the participant/observer distinction is highlighted by the existence of legitimate debates about who may provide ethical assistance to athletes in the course of competition. In this way, S.P. Morris grants that even though it is difficult to draw precise lines in the sorts of cases I have mentioned, such vagueness is "no cause to deny a clear category difference between full-fledged participants (i.e. those on the playing surface) and spectators."[18] He then proceeds to argue that "attempts by non-participants (e.g., spectators) to affect the outcome of a contest, whether intended or merely foreseeable, are unsporting and ought to be discouraged because they undermine fairness." For example, fans should not "cheer to their wits' end" in an effort "not only to urge on the favoured side but to thwart the other." Nor should they talk trash or heckle opposing players in order to obtain an advantage for the team they want to win. Precisely because spectators are not participants, Morris thinks these sorts of activities violate the *raison d'être* of athletic contests that is "to test the relevant abilities of the participants."[19]

One need not accept Morris's ethical prescriptions to see that some restrictions along these lines are necessary to maintain the integrity—and, indeed, the point—of athletic competition. If, in the course of a basketball game, anyone in the stands can simply come onto the court and play, how are the proceedings to be so much as understood as a game? If we are not trying to decide which of the participants will win, then why conduct the contest *as a contest* at all? We might debate where, exactly, to draw the line between participant and spectator, and we might debate what kind of behavior is ethically permissible for each group. But without some such distinction in place, it is hard to see how sports can exist as a comprehensible human activity.

Second, I think the communal nature of team sports makes it easier to obscure the participant/observer distinction than it is in the case of individual sports. For example, I don't ever remember hearing fans of particular golfers, tennis players, or track and field athletes talking about how "we" won a tournament or race. Roger Federer has a devoted fan base all over the world. Yet, when he recently secured his sixth Australian Open title, I doubt that any of his fans celebrated "their" victory. Even coaches of individual athletes, who sometimes have a great deal of influence on their competitive prospects, are rarely heard employing the first-person plural when discussing the fortunes of their protégés. The participant/observer distinction seems to be taken for granted in these contexts, and even those who help athletes a great deal in their endeavors often speak as though they function as observers. It is not at all obvious why the dynamic should be fundamentally different when the object of devotion is a team rather than an individual.

One might reply that the passion exhibited by fans of teams is of a different sort than that displayed by even the most devoted supporters of athletes in individual sports and that, as a result, we should expect the language that fans use in these contexts to differ. While people certainly like some individual athletes more than others, these attachments do not seem to have the identity-constituting power that our connection to teams often has. It is in this vein that Erin Tarver has recently suggested:

> [T]he sports fan comes to understand herself as a particular sort of person by virtue of her participation in [the practices of fandom], which enable their subjects to imbue their lives and self-concepts with new layers of meaning. Examination of the most typical practices of sports fans, including knowledge acquisition, outward demonstrations or performances of sports fandom, and participation in fan discourse, shows that these details of everyday fandom are not extraneous additions but central to its function. Sports fandom matters to fans, then, not merely because the moment of victory is pleasurable. More than this, sports fandom, in its everyday details, is one of the primary ways in which fans tell themselves who they are—and, just as importantly, who they are not.[20]

An individual might, therefore, be a huge fan of Tiger Woods and want him to win every tournament in which he plays. Such a person might even organize his schedule so that he can devote as many hours as possible to watching Woods compete and feel great disappointment on those occasions when he doesn't win. But his devotion to Woods is unlikely to be an important means by which he tells himself who he is and who he is not. Put differently, "Tiger Woods fan" is unlikely to be on a list of biographical information on many people's social media pages.[21]

Contrast this with the role that devotion to one's favorite teams can play in shaping a fan's identity. I do, in fact, have certain team allegiances on my Facebook and Twitter pages, and there is little doubt that my sporting loyalties play some role in helping me locate myself in the world. And for some fans, I have little doubt that the investments of time and emotional energy they make in support of their teams lead them to identify more strongly with that team's successes and failures than they do with individual athletes they support. When your identity is bound up with the fortunes of another—and when that other is already a group rather than an individual—it may seem entirely natural to feel that their accomplishments and failures are, in some way, your own.

However, even if these sorts of considerations help to explain why fans employ the first-person plural as often as they do, I do not think they succeed in overcoming the objections to the practice that I have raised thus far. To begin with, the grammar of statements such as "we won" or "we played really well today" still indicates that the speaker has figured prominently in securing the result. "We won the game" comes across very differently than something like "We fans are so happy that our favorite team won the game." The former expresses a sense of agency—that something has been accomplished rather than witnessed—that is absent from the latter.

Moreover, the "we" at the center of Tarver's account is quite clearly the community of fans, not the team itself. This does not imply that the community in question is at all deficient or that it cannot play the role in people's lives that Tarver thinks it can play. I am merely pointing out that the community of sports fans is different from the community created among players on the team. To appeal again to the analogy between sports and music that Jones puts forward, it would be silly to deny that Deadheads form a vibrant community that plays an important role in constituting the identity of many individuals. Deadheads devote significant amounts of time and energy to following the Grateful Dead, and this devotion is clearly an important way for them to locate themselves in the world—to identify who they are and who they are not. Nevertheless, the community of Deadheads is made up of those who love the music of the Grateful Dead and attend their concerts around the world. Deadheads are not the band itself. In the same way, those devoted to the Green Bay Packers may form a vibrant community that helps to constitute the identity of its members. But no matter the level of devotion, the community of fans is not the same as the team to which those fans are devoted.

Other Uses of "We"

Some defenders of "we" might try to get around the ontological case I have been making by putting forward a more straightforwardly linguistic case for the practice. Such individuals might point to non-sporting contexts in which use of the first-person plural seems to reflect some metaphysical ambiguity even as it does not necessarily exhibit a lack of respect for the accomplishments of others. Indeed, one might argue that there are times when rejecting the use of "we" too strongly is problematic. In this way, one might argue that the language employed by sports fans is more similar to that used in other contexts than I have allowed and that we needn't employ the standards of strict metaphysical precision when evaluating the language of fans.

Thus, consider an American citizen who talks about how "we invaded Iraq in 2003" or laments the fact that "we elected Trump president" even though she has never served in the military and voted for Hilary Clinton in the 2016 election. In certain contexts, these kinds of statements would be unlikely to draw much attention, and, in fact, to deny them would probably raise more than a few eyebrows. For example, speaking with a group of non-Americans overseas, it would be perfectly natural for such a person to talk about how "we invaded Iraq and elected Trump," and an American who wanted to deny these claims would, at the very least, have to be exceedingly clear about what she meant.

Despite the natural tone of such statements, there are clear senses in which they might be false. The speaker hasn't so much as set foot in Iraq (in 2003 or any other time) and has certainly never fired a weapon at any Iraqi soldiers or civilians. And if one supported the losing candidate in 2016, it is not clear exactly how they could be held responsible for putting Trump in the White House. One can, therefore, imagine the very same person on a different occasion *protesting* the claim that "we elected Trump" by saying, "Well, *I* didn't vote for him, so *I* certainly didn't elect him." Here, an appropriate use of "we" is thus consistent with an acute awareness of the actions that one has (and has not) performed, and sports fans may argue that their use of "we" is similarly conscious of such distinctions. They know they aren't really playing the games and are not really part of the team, and so their statements should not be interpreted as evidence of beliefs to the contrary.

However, I don't think these kinds of examples give as much cover to sports fans who want to defend their use of "we" as it might first appear, because I think there are metaphysically strict interpretations of statements like "We invaded Iraq" and "We elected Trump" that can render them true even when uttered by Clinton voters who have never served in the military. Thus, when such people say that "we invaded Iraq," they would seem to be referring to the United States as a political entity—one that is distinct from Iran and Jamaica. Interpreted in this way, to say "We invaded Iraq" is to say that the United States, as opposed to either Iran or Jamaica, invaded Iraq. Similarly, the "we" at issue in "We elected Trump" seems to be the American electorate that, as a whole, did elect Trump president.

Importantly, in both cases, I think it is plausible to regard the speaker as part of the "we" in question. It may not be entirely obvious what it means for a complex entity like the United States to do something like invade Iraq. (Indeed, I don't think it is obvious at all.) Nevertheless, however we are to parse that sort of action, it seems to be true that the United States invaded Iraq in a way that Iran and Jamaica did not. Thus, if by "we" one intends "the United States," it is true that "we invaded Iraq." Similarly for the American electorate. To say that "we" elected Trump might just be to say that the American election went for Trump and that the speaker is identifying herself as a member of the American electorate even if they voted for the other candidate.

In other contexts, of course, "we" can have a different referent. "We invaded Iraq" might mean something different when uttered by a member of the US military than it means when uttered by a civilian, just as "We elected Trump" might mean something different coming from a committed Trump supporter than it does in the mouth of someone who voted for Clinton. Thus, a woman who truthfully says "We invaded Iraq and elected Trump" when she is among non-Americans overseas might vigorously deny that statement if she finds herself among Trump supporters who served in the army.

But if the arguments I offer earlier in this chapter are convincing, it isn't clear that sports fans can appeal to these kinds of shifting referents in an effort to vindicate the truth of their statements. If the referent of "we" is taken to be the fans, then it is false that fans have won or lost games, and if the referent is the team, then it is false that the fan is a part of the team in a way that would license use of the first-person plural. It may very well be true that not all uses of "we" are created equal and that shifting contexts can sometimes affect the truth value of statements that employ the first-person plural. However, it is simply not clear what context is available to sports fans that might render "we" statements true when talking about the exploits of their favorite teams. Try as we might, it doesn't seem that we can get around the fundamental distinction between sporting participants and observers.

Helping the Team Doesn't Make You Part of It

One final response to my skepticism about "we" might be for fans to insist that while they are not strictly part of the team they support, they nevertheless deserve some legitimate credit for the team's accomplishments. For example, when I talk to my students about this very topic, many of them seem to be in favor of using the first-person plural. And when I press them to give reasons why this practice is justified, they point to phenomena like crowd noise at games that can give teams a home field advantage or even the indirect financial support they offer the players via the purchase of tickets and team paraphernalia. The thought here seems to be that their purchases give teams financial resources that fund their on-field exploits; fewer purchases would mean less money to pay for the facilities and player salaries that are essential to team success. By pointing to these sorts of practices, the use of the first-person plural is defended by explicitly trying to take credit for some of the results on the field.

Leaving aside whether this claim makes any sense in ostensibly amateur contexts like collegiate sports in the United States, there is some empirical evidence to support this line of thought. The idea that winning correlates strongly with team payroll is fairly well established.[22] To the degree that expenditures on tickets and team paraphernalia help to boost a team's financial position—and, by implication, its ability to spend more money on player salaries—fans of successful teams may have some legitimate claim to have aided in the endeavor. Moreover, the phenomenon of "home field advantage" seems to be real even if the precise role played by any given feature of playing at home is unclear. Thus, while it isn't obvious whether the familiarity of the environment, the lack of travel, or crowd noise are most responsible for giving the home team an edge, the thesis that crowd size correlates positively with a home team's winning percentage also has some empirical support.[23]

However, even if we grant that behavior along these lines does have a positive impact on a team's performance, it is highly questionable that such an effect is sufficient to justify claims like "we won" or "we played really well today." Helping someone to accomplish a task is not the same as accomplishing that task oneself, no matter how essential or valuable the help might be. I helped my wife through two pregnancies and the delivery of our two children. I tried to be encouraging and supportive through what ended up being (in different ways) two very challenging and medically complicated experiences. However, if someone complimented me on what a great job I did being pregnant or giving birth, the only appropriate response would be to point out that I did not, in fact, give birth—that my wife did a wonderful job in that department—and that I was happy to provide whatever support I could. For me to claim that "we did a really good job delivering the baby" would be to suggest that our roles in the process were on the same footing—a suggestion that should, I think, lead any woman who has had a baby to dismissively roll her eyes. (As might be surmised from these comments, the reasons for my opposition to the phrase "We're pregnant" thus parallel my opposition to the first-person plural among sports fans.)

Similarly, I have never published anything in my academic career that was not improved significantly by feedback from colleagues and reviewers. Indeed, I regard the criticism of others as such an important part of the writing process that I now require my upper division students to comment on each other's papers and revise their work in light of the feedback they receive. Nevertheless, though I always give very thankful acknowledgment for comments on my work, I have yet to give a colleague or reviewer a co-author credit on any publication. Their help has been indispensable. But for better and/or worse, I am the one who wrote the papers.[24] If I ever happened to have a conversation with a colleague in which she made a self-congratulatory remark about a recent publication that "we" just had, I imagine my reaction would not be entirely positive. The fact that this scenario is exceedingly unlikely to happen in the world of academia should, I think, give us pause when we think about the pervasiveness of "we" in fan discourse.

Turning back to the realm of sports, then, it may very well be the case that fan support helps athletes perform better—that home field advantage is a real phenomenon and that the financial support fans offer through their purchase of team paraphernalia does, in fact, help teams become more competitive. Nevertheless, supporting individuals who are engaged in a task is not the same as engaging in that task oneself, and fans who invoke the first-person plural mistakenly place themselves in the latter camp rather than the former.

Nick Hornby pushes the significance of fan support in a slightly different direction in *Fever Pitch*—a book in which he consistently uses "we" when referring to the exploits of his beloved Arsenal Football Club. Reflecting on Arsenal's victory over Liverpool in the 1987 League Cup final, Hornby writes:

> This Wembley win belonged to me every bit as much as it belonged to Charlie Nicholas or George Graham (does Nicholas, who was dropped by Graham right at the start of the following season, and then sold, remember this afternoon as fondly?), and I worked every bit as hard for it as they did. The only difference between me and them is that I have put in more hours, more years, more decades than them, and so had a better understanding of the afternoon, a sweeter appreciation of why the sun still shines when I remember it.[25]

For Hornby, his perceived ownership of Arsenal's triumph was based on the years of devotion he had shown to the club: all the time and emotional energy he spent attending games and having his happiness tied to their results. Indeed, because that devotion had predated nearly every player and manager associated with Arsenal at the time—and would extend well beyond their departures—he suggests that the win likely meant more to him than it meant to those who had secured victory on the field.

Hornby strikes me as exactly right that many fans are more emotionally invested in the fortunes of their favorite teams than are the players on the field, at least when those fortunes are described in certain ways. For example, the players may very much want to win the game, but they might not be overly concerned to do so as a member of Arsenal. If they could win championships playing for Manchester United or Chelsea, they may be perfectly happy to do so. Fans, on the other hand, tend to be devoted to their favorite teams even as those teams go through significant changes in personnel. In this way, a League Cup victory *for Arsenal* is likely more important to the fans than the fact that a victory for Arsenal has been obtained by any particular group of players, and a victory by an Arsenal team with a completely different roster would be celebrated by the fans with just as much fervor. This discrepancy between the loyalty shown by fans and players to various teams is, no doubt, the cause of a great deal of frustration that fans experience when their favorite players voluntarily move on to other teams. Fans want the players to love their teams as much as they do, but as Hornby notes, "the plain truth is that the club means more to us than it does to them. Where were they twenty years ago? Where will they be in twenty years' time, a couple of them?"[26]

And yet, in terms of its connection to the central argument I am making here, I want to insist that being emotionally invested in an event is crucially distinct from bringing about that event, and that despite Hornby's insight, he is wrong to claim that the win belonged to him every bit as much as it belonged to Arsenal's players and coaches. It is, after all, a common feature of our experience that we are often invested in events over which we have no control. I had zero role in building the car that I drive, but it would be strange to argue that the individuals working on the assembly line are more invested in how that process was carried out than I am. Of course, most of them no doubt take pride in doing a good job and don't want anything bad to happen as a result of their efforts, but I am the one who will suffer the consequences if something goes wrong. Similarly, I have no doubt that the overwhelming majority of surgeons care about the quality of their work in the operating room. That commitment, taken together with a basic human concern for the well-being of others, will lead most of them to be emotionally invested in the outcome of their surgeries. That said, if my wife or one of my kids is lying on the operating table, I am surely more emotionally invested in the outcome of the procedure than the person who is performing it.

Despite this high level of concern, in neither of these cases would it be appropriate to say that I had a hand in the way things turned out. I did not build the car (and don't have anything like the required skills to do so), and it would be even less plausible to claim that I could ever be involved in performing any sort of surgery. In the same way, it is not clear why a fan's level of emotional investment in the performance of a team should make any difference regarding whether the fan can take linguistic ownership of that team's performance. Vulnerability, in many forms, is a central feature of the human predicament, and we often care deeply about things over which we have no control. Sports fans may distract themselves from this fact by their use of the first-personal plural, but the pervasiveness of this practice only blinds supporters to their essential helplessness to affect the fortunes of the teams they love.[27]

Putting the Emotional Costs in Context

I want to conclude by considering one final point with respect to fans' use of "we." For all I have said, one might point out that fans do not only invoke the first-person plural when their favorite teams win; some fans also employ that convention when their teams lose. In this way, individuals demonstrating grammatical consistency along these lines avoid some of the criticism I have offered previously. Indeed, one might press the point even further and suggest that when fans say things like "They lost" or "They played terribly today," they adopt an overly critical posture toward the athletes they support. Saying "We lost" or "We played terribly today" at least demonstrates a measure of empathy as fans identify with the plight of their favorite teams. By contrast, fans who criticize a team as "they" in the wake of a loss might sound a note of contempt as they dismiss the performance of "those others" who did not play well enough to win.

As with previous objections, I think there is some truth here. Fans who are contemptuous of athletes who do not secure the results they want are at least as problematic as fans who attempt to take credit for their accomplishments. If employing phrases such as "We lost" and "We didn't play very well today" helps to mitigate some of that contempt, such a result would seem to be a mark in favor of the practice. This point especially seems to hold in the case of fans who are happy to take some credit when their teams win but are dismissive when they lose. If one is willing to say "We won," then they should be equally willing to say "We lost" when things don't go their way.

However, even if use of the first-person plural can go some way to fostering sympathy toward athletes on the field, such use is clearly not required for fans to develop such an attitude. I might be deeply moved by a news story on television about the plight of individuals on the other side of the world. Sympathizing deeply with their suffering, I might decide to donate money to a charitable cause or make changes in my life that allow me to better serve the needs of others. But no matter the level of my sympathy, I would not be inclined to discuss the suffering of others as "our" suffering. Identifying in a strong way with the plight of others does not require that I see their plight as my own. Indeed, in some cases, claiming the struggles of others can indicate a failure to respect those struggles in much the same way that claiming the successes of others can be disrespectful. A man who talks about how much pain "we" were in during labor isn't showing sympathy toward the woman who has just given birth; he is potentially minimizing that pain by suggesting that his experience of the event was at all similar to hers. He might do his best to sympathize, but at the end of the day, she is the one who must deal with the pain.

Thus, if there is a problem with fans claiming the accomplishments of athletes, then there may be a similar problem with claiming their failures. Fans may be expressing sympathy with athletes when they talk about how "we lost" or "how poorly we played." But they may also be obscuring the nature of the frustrations and failures endured by players. To return to the contrast with which I began this chapter, athletes who lose games will have failed to achieve a goal for which they have prepared and practiced. They will have tested themselves in the competitive arena and come up short. They will have found that their skills and performance, at least on that particular day, have not measured up to the skills and performance of their opponents. Fans, on the other hand, may have invested a lot in the day's proceedings and prepared in all sorts of ways. But donning face paint and a team hoodie—even screaming and yelling in the cold and rain—is a different sort of preparation, and a different sort of investment than two-a-day practices in the oppressive August heat.

This is not to deny that a fan's disappointment after their favorite team loses is genuine disappointment. It surely is. An event in which they were emotionally invested did not go the way they wanted it to go, and that experience yields a certain kind of pain. Nevertheless, it is not the same kind of pain that is experienced by the individuals who have competed—who have put in hours of practice and preparation and who have set themselves the goal of winning. The fan's pain is the pain of one who has no control over how things unfold, while the athlete's pain reflects the failure to achieve a goal that one has worked very hard to achieve. They are both pain, but it would be a mistake to say they are the same *kind* of pain.[28]

Recognizing this fact may be an important way to pay appropriate respect to the plight of athletes, but it could potentially have a side benefit for fans as well. Hornby describes the experience of watching Arsenal lose in terms that explicitly focus on wins and losses as something that happen to *fans*. He thus writes about the aforementioned League Cup victory as follows:

> The joy we feel on occasions like this is not a celebration of others' good fortune, but a celebration of our own; and when there is a disastrous defeat, the sorrow that engulfs us is,

28 On "We"

in effect, self-pity, and anyone who wishes to understand how football is consumed must realize this above all things.[29]

I have no doubt that many fans of team sports—not just soccer—experience the thrill of victory and agony of defeat in precisely the ways that Hornby articulates. As an empirical matter, his claims strike me as overwhelmingly plausible.

However, keeping in mind that the losses of one's favorite team are not one's own failures might help to mitigate the despair that some fans experience when their favorite teams are not successful. As I've noted, there can be an acknowledgment of genuine disappointment on the part of fans: something they wanted to happen did not in fact happen, and that can yield genuine disappointment. Nevertheless, if the view I have defended here is compelling, then there are other ways for fans to relate to the teams they love. Such an approach may indeed require them to experience victory precisely as pleasure at the good fortune of others—a change that may ease some of the intense emotions associated with winning. But it may also ease some of the pain of losing. In this way, fans who strive to focus their emotional energy on generating sympathy for the athletes who have put in effort on the field may find themselves keeping matters in proper perspective and avoiding the deepest pits of emotional distress that sports fandom can sometimes offer.

Notes

1. Chris Jones, "What Do You Mean, 'We?'" *Grantland*, October 25, 2001, http://grantland.com/features/what-do-mean-we. For those unfamiliar with this reference, Gollum is a character in J.R.R. Tolkein's *Lord of the Rings* who refers to himself using first-person plural pronouns.
2. Bill Simmons, "Rules for Being a True Fan," *ESPN.com*, 2002, www.espn.com/espn/page2/story?page=simmons/020227.
3. Though I think the context of my discussion should make this point clear, in what follows, when I refer to uses of the first-person plural, I have in mind uses of "we" and "our" that refer to the actions or exploits of one's favorite team.
4. Thanks to my colleague Ana Iltis for suggesting this example.
5. Anecdotal evidence from conversations with athletes in my classes suggests that a non-trivial number of them do not like it when fans employ "we" when discussing the fortunes of the team. To be sure, not all of the athletes I have talked to feel this way, and plenty of them have reported to me that they are fine with the practice and even use it themselves when talking about their favorite teams. Nevertheless, the fact that some athletes feel disrespected when fans use "we" indicates that the sort of response that concerns me here is not merely a theoretical possibility but rather something that is part of the lived experience of real human beings.
6. Stephen Mumford, "Allegiance and Identity," *Journal of the Philosophy of Sport* 31, no. 2 (2004): 191.
7. Mumford, "Allegiance and Identity," 191.
8. Mumford, "Allegiance and Identity," 192 (emphasis mine).
9. Jake Wojtowicz, "Fans, Identity, and Punishment," *Sport, Ethics, and Philosophy* 15, no. 1 (2021): 64.
10. Wojtowicz, "Fans, Identity, and Punishment," 59.
11. Wojtowicz, "Fans, Identity, and Punishment," 67.
12. To be clear, neither Mumford nor Wojtozicz explicitly discusses the appropriate use of pronouns, so I am extrapolating somewhat from their official positions.
13. Wojtowicz acknowledges the potential differences between European soccer clubs and North American sports teams but does not explore those differences in any detail. See Wojtowicz, "Fans, Identity, and Punishment," 65.
14. Wojtowicz, "Fans, Identity, and Punishment," 66.
15. It is also worth noting on this point that Wojtowicz does not attempt to identify the bounds of the club, noting only that it "is a larger, and more amorphous, entity which I do not hope to define" ("Fans, Identity, and Punishment," 66). Thus, problems might arise when considering who is part of the club, and whose behavior might be justifiably punished as the behavior of the club.
16. Ori Lewis, "Fans of Jerusalem Club Fed Up with Racism Form New Outfit," *Reuters*, February 22, 2018. www.reuters.com/article/uk-soccer-israel-nordia-idUKKCN1G61RJ.

17. This conclusion is also consistent with Wojtowicz's claim that the ethical identity of the club is more important than the sporting success of the team. All I am trying to argue is that fans should not own the sporting success of the team even if they are both constituent parts of another entity: the club.

18. S. P. Morris, "The Limit of Spectator Interaction," *Sport, Ethics and Philosophy* 6, no. 1 (February 2012): 48.

19. Morris, "Limit of Spectator Interaction," 49–50.

20. Erin Tarver, *The I in Team: Sports Fandom and the Reproduction of Identity* (Chicago: The University of Chicago Press, 2017), 27.

21. My point here is not to deny that adoration for individual athletes can be deep and passionate. Such feelings can obviously be quite intense. Many athletes are adored by millions, and their successes and failures can serve as an occasion for tears of joy or despair for the fans who love them. I simply mean to suggest that the role played by this attachment in the lives of fans is generally different in the case of individual athletes and teams.

22. R. Simmons and D. Forrest, "Buying Success: Team Performance and Wage Bills in U.S. and European Sports Leagues," in *International Sports Economics Comparisons*, ed. R. Fort and J. Fizel (Westport, CT: Praeger Publishers, 2004).

23. A. M. Nevill, S. M. Newell, and S. Gale, "Factors Associated with the Home Advantage in English and Scottish Soccer Matches," *Journal of Sports Sciences* 14, no. 2 (April 1996): 181–186. For a metadata analysis of the home field advantage, see J. Jamieson, "The Home Field Advantage in Athletics: A Meta-Analysis," *Journal of Applied Social Psychology* 40, no. 7 (July 2010): 1819–1848. The significance of crowd noise in producing such an effect is questioned in R. Pollard and G. Pollard, "Long-term Trends in Home Advantage in Professional Team Sports in North American and England (1976–2003)," *Journal of Sports Sciences* 23, no. 4 (April 2005): 337–350.

24. It is, I think, entirely consistent with my insistence on this point that we have a tendency to overestimate the individual nature of accomplishment. For all I say here, perhaps we should give more credit to others for aiding in our accomplishments than we, in fact, give. And perhaps, in some cases, it is appropriate to care more about the quality of the product than who, exactly, produced it. On this point, see Rob Goodman, "Cognitive Enhancement, Cheating, and Accomplishment," *Kennedy Institute of Ethics Journal* 20, no. 2 (June 2010): 145–160. Nevertheless, I confess deep skepticism that we can entirely eliminate the distinction between those who accomplish things and those who aid in the accomplishments of others.

25. Nick Hornby, *Fever Pitch* (New York: Riverhead Books, 1992), 187.

26. Hornby, *Fever Pitch*, 62.

27. To be fair, Hornby seems to be keenly aware of this fact and elsewhere writes of the value of "investing time and emotion in things I cannot control," that the many "bizarre liturgies" of fans are "designed to give us the illusion that we are powerful after all," and that it is important not to blur the boundaries between players and fans (*Fever Pitch*, 62, 111, 62). I will return to this theme in Chapter 3.

28. The point here is thus about the quality of one's pain rather than its quantity. An athlete may feel varying degrees of distress after losing a game in which they have played, and similarly for a fan who has watched their favorite team lose a closely fought contest. In each case, some may be exceedingly disappointed, others less so. The point is that the disappointment of the fan is the disappointment of one who has watched the game, whereas the disappointment of the athlete belongs to one who has played in it.

29. Hornby, *Fever Pitch*, 187.

2

WHY SPORTS ARE LIKE SHAKESPEARE

Back in 2009, University of Washington psychologist David Barash wrote what can only be described as a scathing (and often mocking) criticism of sports fans in *The Chronicle Review*. After declaring that "the opiate of the masses isn't religion, but spectator sports"—a comparison, it should be noted, made by Aldous Huxley in *Brave New World*—Barash goes on to explicitly compare fans to slop-enthralled animals. "Not that I would try to stop anyone from root, root, rooting to his or her heart's content," he writes.

> It's just that such things are normally done by pigs, in the mud, or by seedlings, lacking a firm grip on reality—fine for them, but I am not at all sure this is something that human beings should do.[1]

Barash's charge is not subtle: sports fans are engaged in a pursuit that, at best, satisfies the lowest parts of our nature and, at worst, is a colossal and debasing waste of time.

Barash's view is a good starting point for my discussion in this chapter, not because it is particularly enlightening or plausible as a general account of fandom, but rather because I think it evokes a depiction of sports fans that has traction in circles where people tend to make distinctions between "high" and "low" culture. As the sociologist David Rowe puts it, for those "subscribing to a hierarchical model of culture, sports may be regarded as its antithesis: a bodily practice, of little cultural consequence, gazed on by passive spectators for the enrichment of the leisure and media industries."[2] In a similar vein, Simon Kuper notes that until recently, Europeans embraced "a rigid divide" that "had long separated 'high' from 'low' culture. Opera was high culture and sport was low—and therefore not worth serious contemplation by writers."[3] And Robert McCabe, writing at the turn of the millennium, worried that the rise in popularity of American sport had "begun to overshadow traditional American cultural expressions and intellectual activities such as reading."[4]

The implication of such views is not exactly that sports fans are unintelligent, though I suspect (admittedly without any evidence) that such an assessment lies in the background. The idea is rather that fans are wasting their time on an activity that deadens their more refined sensibilities. Sports fans are, of course, seeking pleasure in spending their time the way they do. The problem is that it is the pleasure of a pig or a fool satisfied.[5] Those interested in developing the human capacities that distinguish us most sharply from non-human animals should, therefore, devote

DOI: 10.4324/9781003223696-3

their time to more lofty pursuits: reading great literature, perhaps, or taking in a performance of Shakespeare's *Henry V*.

The core of Barash's argument for his conclusion is that fans are indulging two primitive impulses when they invest time and emotional energy in sporting events. On the one hand, they are identifying in a robust way with the objects of their devotion and thereby attempting to see "[them]selves in the exploits of another." According to this line of thought, fans who take pleasure in the achievements of athletes largely derive such pleasure by projecting themselves into the action on the field. Even though they are sitting in the stands or on their couches at home, they nevertheless regard the successes and failures of their favorite teams as their own. For this reason, Barash quips that it may be

> time to rework Andy Warhol's observation that in the future, everyone will be famous for 15 minutes: Thanks to spectator sports, each of us can know fame for most of our lives, so long as we are satisfied with the ever-shifting, warmed-over shadow of someone else's.

On the other hand, Barash thinks that sports fans are looking to satisfy a "yearning to be part of a group" that has its roots deep in our evolutionary history. As individuals congregated together, both to confront the dangers of the natural world and more efficiently divide labor, they also began to confront other groups of similarly organized individuals. Thus, while "considerations of efficiency might have meant that our social units sometimes became oversized, it is easy to imagine how the presence of large, threatening bands of our own species pressured us to seek numbers to find safety."

As Barash explicitly acknowledges, not all membership in groups is to be resisted, and drawing on the work of Arthur Koestler,[6] he therefore suggests that there is "an important difference between primitive identification (fish in a school, birds in a flock) that results in a homogenous, selfless grouping, and the higher level of integration that produces a heterogeneous assemblage whose members retain their individuality." But whereas the latter category—exemplified by "the reader or the theatergoer"—allows an "escape from the self that is always conditional, transient, and within control," the former sorts of groups should be deeply troubling to us. After all, Barash notes:

> [T]he acts of greatest human violence and destructiveness have arisen not from personal aggressiveness or nastiness, but from self-transcendence in the form of seductive, mindless identification with a group. Think of Rwanda's Hutus and Tutsis, Bosnian Serbs and Muslims, Nazis and Jews, Irish Catholics and Protestants, Armenians and Azerbaijanis, Israelis and Palestinians.

And, of course, sports fans. As Barash puts it:

> Spectator sports offer quick and easy entree into an instant community. Never mind that it is ersatz. It is there for the joining; no need to "make the team." Instead, just buy a ticket, a T-shirt, or turn on the television or radio.

Once fans have thus identified with other fans, distinguishing one's own group from others becomes nearly an end in itself. One's identity as a supporter of Manchester United thus licenses antipathy toward Liverpool fans simply because the superiority (if not the survival) of Manchester United fans is at stake. While this outlook might not produce outcomes as tragic as the Rwandan genocide, Barash thinks the similarities between the cases are sufficient to undermine any value sports fandom might be thought to have.

32 Why Sports Are Like Shakespeare

Despite my fundamental disagreement with Barash's negative assessment of sports fandom, I think features of his analysis are plausible, provided their scope is clearly defined and their implications are kept in their proper perspective. Do many sports fans project themselves into the proceedings on the field and thereby attempt to bask in the reflected glory of the athletes they watch? Of course. And does the human search for community take a wide variety of forms, ranging from the innocuous to the terrifying in ways that certainly include sports fans who unite around their favorite teams? Again, the answer is clearly yes. Losing yourself in a crowd can enable all sorts of troubling behavior, and one can certainly understand how comparing film footage of the Nuremburg rallies to crowd shots at large spectator sporting events might give one serious pause.

That said, the fact that some fans desire to identify with the accomplishments of athletes does not entail that every fan is similarly motivated. If it is possible to be a fan without regarding the success of athletes as one's own, there is no obvious reason why we should dismiss *all* fans on the grounds that they are engaged in this kind of self-deluded enterprise. By the same token, it would be foolish to deny that groups of all sorts, including fans, can sometimes do destructive things. Nevertheless, if the group dynamics of fandom can deliver positive benefits without indulging this tendency, then we needn't conclude that being a fan is a hopelessly corrosive pursuit. In properly criticizing some of the worst tendencies of some fans, Barash mistakenly thinks he has successfully dismissed the entire pastime of watching sports.

As I argued in Chapter 1, I think that a central part of being a good fan is to take seriously the distinction between those who participate in athletic contests and those who observe those same contests. Employing the first-person plural when talking about their favorite teams is a prevalent way in which fans fail to acknowledge this distinction, but the sort of projection that troubles both me and Barash is likely present any time fans find themselves basking in the reflected glory of athletes. In this way, fans engaged in "BIRGing" tend to "value not only the collective emotion they feel but, more importantly, the opportunity to feel an enhanced sense of self-worth by identifying with the victory of their teams."[7] When fans experience their teams' victories and losses as their own, they are eliding the participant/observer distinction in potentially corrosive ways.

My aim in this chapter is thus to show that it is possible to appreciate sports without projecting oneself into the proceedings on the field. Drawing on the work of Norbert Elias and Eric Dunning, I begin by arguing that sports can satisfy a deep-seated human need for excitement and drama in much the same way as works of film, theater, music, and literature. Insofar as this sort of excitement enhances the quality of our lives, spectator sports can thus be one source of a valuable social good.

Moreover, just as these sorts of cultural products can also spur various forms of moral reflection, sports have the ability to drive spectators' thinking about their own pursuit of the good life. We can become engrossed in the plot of *Hamlet* during the course of its performance—drawn into the dramatic tension it provides—but the work can also drive us to probe various existential questions for ourselves. I thus contend that sports have the ability to engage a similarly wide array of human capacities: if we accept that it is worthwhile to consume various other cultural products, we should similarly accept the potential value of watching sports. Indeed, because the results of sporting events are not scripted in advance, they often provide greater levels of dramatic engagement than other forms of entertainment, and because athletes are real people pursuing their own vision of the good life, they may engage our capacities for moral reflection in ways that fictional characters and works of art cannot.

What, then, of group identification or the ways in which a desire for community can problematically intersect with the world of sports? On this point, I set the stage for my discussion of partisan fandom in Chapter 3 by arguing that the experience of getting lost in the crowd in sporting contexts is often simply the experience of sharing our awe with others. We marvel at feats of athletic excellence and are astonished at the turns of fate that play out over the course of a game, and the benefit we are able to draw from these exploits is only enhanced by taking them in with people who are similarly captivated and moved by what they are witnessing. If this line of thought is plausible, then watching sports as part of a group is not the essentially dehumanizing endeavor that Barash contends it is. Rather, it has the potential to be one of the more life-enhancing things that humans can do.

Our Human Need for Excitement

Buried not so deeply in Barash's criticism of sports fans is an appeal to the supposed triviality of sports and the idea that pursuits are more worthwhile to the degree that they engage humans' higher cognitive capacities. I think such a view is implicit in the contrast he draws between the sports fan and "the reader or the theatergoer"—the former sorts of crowds being suspect because of the tendency of their members to surrender "personal identity and responsibility," whereas in the latter "the escape from the self is always conditional, transient, and within control." It is also explicit in his admonition that sports fans should spend their time on other activities. "You might try reading a book," he writes, "talking with your family, going for a walk, wrestling with the dog, listening to some music, smelling a flower, making love." Here, the problem is not really with community but rather with the supposed insignificance and passivity of watching sports. Better to do things oneself rather than watch others do them, and better yet to do things that engage our distinctively human faculties.

As an initial response to this form of objection, let me first note that the options Barash presents are not, as he seems to suggest, mutually exclusive. I watch a lot of sports, but I regularly do nearly all of the other activities he proposes as well, many of them daily (though I confess that I much prefer to walk my dog rather than wrestle with her and I am not one to regularly smell flowers), and pretty much every other sports fan I know has a similarly diverse array of interests. We watch sports, but we *do* all sort of other things as well. As Ian Plenderleith points out, the tortured fan who thinks only about sports and cannot ever bear to miss a game is undoubtedly a caricature. Most fans are—as they should be—much less maniacal than that in practice. He writes:

> The fans who are relieved when the season ends, or when their team is playing away so that their Saturday is free, or when they simply decide on a Tuesday night (that would typically be a very wet and windy one in Rochdale, in January) that they can't be arsed—these fans really do exist. This is perfectly normal behavior. We don't believe it's the end of the world if we miss a game, or even several. We go happily to our brother's wedding instead, or take the dog for a long walk. Of course fans are deeply attached to football and largely profess to love their team. And most of us love our mothers too, but we wouldn't want to spend every day of our lives with them.[8]

One can quite clearly be a committed fan and also engage in any number of other worthwhile activities. If the contention is that a life committed to following one's sports teams to the exclusion of all else is not a life well-lived, the point is well-taken. It is also a criticism directed at what I suspect is a vanishingly small group of people.

More to the present point, however, it seems possible for fans to engage with sports in ways that are surprisingly similar to the ways in which people engage with other cultural products, even those where the participant/observer distinction is as relevant as it is in the realm of sports. Thus, consider drama, whether we witness it performed live in the theater or recorded and edited in a

34 Why Sports Are Like Shakespeare

film or television show. In either case, whatever value there is in watching such a performance should be spelled out differently than the value that lies in the act of performing. There may, of course, be some overlap in how we assess these activities. But being an actor is different than being a committed theatergoer, and so the value of watching stage productions, if such there be, will be different than the value of acting in them.

When one begins to examine the value of watching dramatic productions, similarities to watching sports begin to emerge quite rapidly. Indeed, such comparisons have been examined in some detail by the sociologists Norbert Elias and Eric Dunning. According to Elias and Dunning, the requirements of civilization have led people to find sources of excitement in their lives that have progressively marginalized genuine danger and violence. As they point out, it is no longer regarded as normal to "see grown-up men and women shaken by tears and abandoning themselves to their bitter sorrow in public, or panic in wild fear, or beat each other savagely under the impact of their violent excitement."[9] Rather, "the public and even the private level of emotional control has become high by comparison with that of less highly differentiated societies."[10] In other words, getting along in civilized communities not only requires that we refrain from displays of violence toward others and activities that seriously threaten the safety of participants; this task also requires that we manage our emotions in fairly restrictive ways. Overt and dramatic displays of feeling are no longer acceptable in polite society.

However, it is not as though civilization has entirely eliminated the human need for excitement. Those of us living in the twenty-first century are no more content with dullness than were our ancestors; we simply have a narrower range of acceptable sources from which to draw our thrills and fewer venues for the expression of joy and anguish. As a result, Elias and Dunning contend that we seek dramatic tension in various mimetic activities—activities that imitate the "never-ending risks and perils of fragile human life."[11] Far from seeking leisure that provides an escape from tension, they suggest that people continue to seek out "a specific type of tension, a form of excitement often connected, as Augustine clearly saw, with fear, sadness and other emotions which we would try to avoid in ordinary life."[12] Indeed, guaranteeing that we have reliable sources of this kind of tension is a crucial part of maintaining a healthy social fabric, and Elias therefore suggests:

> [A] society which does not provide its members, and particularly its younger members, with sufficient opportunities for the enjoyable excitement of a struggle which may, but need not, involve bodily strength and skill, may be in danger of dulling the life of its members unduly; it may not provide sufficient complementary correctives for the unexciting tensions produced by the recurrent routines of social life.

Thus, without safe sources of excitement, individuals will either succumb to boredom or, more problematically, find unhealthy and destructive ways to add some dramatic tension to their lives.[13]

If mimetic excitement was what they were looking for, theater audiences in the late sixteenth and early seventeenth centuries (whose members were drawn from nearly every segment of society) would seem to have found it in spades. There is violence everywhere, and the great tragedies and histories of the day feature power struggles and quests for dominance that still make them compelling to viewers hundreds of years later. Though at no risk of injury or death themselves, theatergoers would have been able to follow a good dramatic story while also finding a safe outlet to explore the more aggressive aspects of their nature.

Moreover, for all that an appreciation of Shakespeare is now confined to university English departments (and those hoping to flaunt their cultural bona fides), it is worth noting that the theater in Shakespeare's day was a decidedly egalitarian form of entertainment. To be sure, the queen and other aristocrats were often in attendance at performances. But so were scores of working-class people, a fact that motivated a number of criticisms of the theater and inspired efforts to limit its operation. As Stephen Greenblatt notes, because plays "were performed in the afternoon," they often "drew people, especially the young, away from their work." Authorities therefore viewed them as "schools of idleness, luring apprentices from their trades, law students from their studies, housewives from their kitchens, and potentially pious souls from the sober meditations to which they might otherwise devote themselves." And this is to say nothing of the plays' aforementioned content, which often required viewers to expose "themselves to sexual provocation and outright political sedition."[14]

Though they are not often compared explicitly to Shakespearean drama, it seems clear that a great deal of attraction of spectator sports can be characterized in very similar ways. After all, sports provide viewers with drama that is generally free from the threat of death or serious injury. Moreover, such events provide an acceptable forum for the expression of emotions that are regarded as off-limits at our places of work or the everyday routines of family life. In this vein, Elias suggests:

> [S]pectators of a football match may savour the mimetic excitement of the battle swaying to and fro on the playing field, knowing that no harm will come to the players or to themselves. As in real life they may be torn between hopes of success and fear of defeat; and in that case too strong feelings aroused in an imaginary setting and their open manifestation in the company of many others may be all the more enjoyable and perhaps liberating because in society at large people are more isolated and have few opportunities for collective manifestations of strong feelings.[15]

Go to a soccer game, and not only can you expect a contest that has the potential to unfold in a dramatic and thrilling manner but you can also be pretty sure that no one will die and that no matter what happens, it will be okay to sing, dance, scream, yell, cheer, and boo. In short, you know that you will probably be entertained and that you'll be able to behave in ways that will not be acceptable when you return to the office in the morning. For all that Barash worries about the violence created by sports fans, it may be the case that sports provide a venue for people to express violent impulses in largely non-violent ways and therefore serve to make society less violent than it would otherwise be.

Indeed, because the outcome of sporting events is not scripted ahead of time, and because the athletes involved are real people, as opposed to fictional characters, one might think that the mimetic possibilities offered by sports are even more varied, and potentially more emotionally satisfying, than what drama may be able to provide. Viewers might not always know how a play ends, but the author does. By contrast, no one knows for sure how sporting events will turn out, and this means that when we are watching athletes perform, we are, in real time, watching them compose the narrative of which they are a part. J.S. Russell thus writes that fans can be enlarged by watching sports in much the same way that they can be enlarged by reading a novel, "except that it is better than fiction in that the story is real, often vastly more complex than fiction, and you cannot skip to the end to find out what happens."[16] And Andrei Markovits and Lars Rensmann argue that the "uncertainty of results is arguably the greatest difference between sports and related human activities that are very similar to sports, namely entertainment."[17] Thus, the unscripted nature of sports, combined with the fact that they are played by real people who must live with the outcome of athletic contests, only adds to the mimetic excitement that Elias and Dunning identify.

Engaging Our Reflective Capacities

I think that whatever truth there is in an escapist justification of sports fandom is probably best articulated along the lines that Elias and Dunning put forward. Sports are able to serve as an escape

36 Why Sports Are Like Shakespeare

from everyday life precisely because they provide a dramatic tension in which viewers can become absorbed. And in the same way that we might justifiably attempt to forget the stresses of a workday by getting lost in a good mystery novel, we might sometimes achieve the same ends by watching a competitive athletic contest. Perhaps the need for mimetic excitement is just escapism with a fancy name.

This contention is fine, as far as it goes, and as I've noted, I don't want to begrudge anyone their escapist indulgences. For all I argue in this book, I don't see any problem with all fans engaging with sports merely for the mimetic excitement they provide at least some of the time, and I'm open to the possibility that it might be okay for some fans to engage with their sports in an escapist fashion most of the time. Provided we are clear that Shakespeare and Mozart provided a similar kind of escapism in their day, such that we are not inclined to tout their cultural superiority over sports, I don't see any reason to object too strenuously.

This caveat in place, as I note in the introduction, I think such an account is incomplete as an exhaustive explication of the potential value of watching sports. Consider an analogy. One function of eating is simply to obtain the nourishment required to sustain life, and there is no question that some of us eat with that end solely in mind at least some of the time. Anyone who has been on a long camping trip has likely faced scenarios where they have to eat a fairly unappetizing meal at some point simply because they need to ingest the requisite calories for the next day's activity, and some people probably make decisions about what to eat for most of their meals on such basis. Considerations of taste, variety, or culinary sophistication are—for at least some people in some contexts—at most secondary, if they register at all.

But confining oneself to the purely nutritional function of eating would give a highly impoverished view of the role that food can play in a flourishing human life, even if we grant that we all sometimes eat merely to survive. People have devoted their lives to exploring the capacities of the human palate, the various relationships that obtain between taste and nutrition, and the role that meals can play in the development of human relationships and communities. I suspect that most people have enjoyed the experience of discovering a new food, even though it does not provide any nutritional value beyond what they have eaten before. And the entire restaurant and hospitality industries are a testament to the fact that food and drink can do more for us than provide nutrition and hydration, even if such qualities never entirely recede from view.

In the same way, I want to suggest that sports can do more than provide escape via mimetic excitement; they can also engage our moral imagination in much the same way that drama and literature can enliven and enrich those same reflective capacities. It is in this vein that Hubert Dreyfus and Sean Kelly describe David Foster Wallace's aim in writing fiction as "the very traditional— some might call it existential—project of writing characters in order to explore the possibilities (and impossibilities) for living well in the modern world."[18] Indeed, Wallace himself noted in a 1991 interview that while really good fiction could sometimes be quite dark in its assessment of the human condition, it would nevertheless "find a way to both depict this dark world *and* to illuminate the possibilities for being alive and human in it."[19]

Thus, in reading a novel or watching a film or a play, we might see characters grapple with challenges that we have never faced and think about what we would do in similar circumstances. Or we might see them in a situation that we have been in ourselves, and consider whether they have done better, or worse, than we have. We see character traits on display that we admire and want to cultivate, and traits that we strive to avoid (whether or not we see them in ourselves). We see, in other words, a range of possibilities for how to make our way through the world.[20]

If the initial appeal of Shakespeare's plays lay in their captivating dramatic tension, their abiding status as great works of literature no doubt results from the way they push us to explore this vast array of human experience. For example, in *Henry V*, we witness the challenges of political leadership juxtaposed with the plight of the common soldier. *Hamlet* is a timeless case study in how one might handle (or not handle) devastating personal betrayal, and the examination of love in *Romeo and Juliet* continues to exercise its hold on viewers (and readers) centuries after it was first performed. In all these cases, viewers are presented with various options for how they might navigate the roadblocks that life puts in their way and are thereby urged to think about how they might navigate similar circumstances for themselves.

Similarly, following the dramatic arc of sporting contests and athletic careers allows us to witness the efforts of athletes to live good human lives—to pursue excellence, victory, fame, and fortune and also to grapple with failure and loss. And while the drama of a play or novel is the scripted drama of the author's creation, the drama of sport is that of real people who must live with the consequences of their decisions. This is one reason why I reject the idea that sports should be sharply separated from "real life." When we watch sports, we are not watching characters. The actor who plays Romeo doesn't die at the end of the performance; he gets to leave the character's plight behind when he goes home. By contrast, injuries that players incur in the pursuit of their goals are not rehearsed, and the quarterback of the losing team does not get to divest himself of the game's result. If these features of sports do not necessarily make them an encouragement to ethical reflection that is superior to drama or literature, I think they at least show that sports are not inferior in this regard. At a minimum, I want to insist that if it makes sense to regard the plays of Shakespeare as legitimate sources for our own thinking about the nature of the good life, then there is no reason to think that sports are less capable of igniting such reflective capacities.

That said, I also think that sports place certain aspects of human nature on display that make them a potentially unique source for this kind of reflection. Wallace thus highlights the distinctiveness of sports' contribution to our understanding of the human predicament in his celebrated essay on Roger Federer where he locates the captivating power of sports in "human beings' reconciliation with the fact of having a body."[21] Many other human pursuits explore various facets of the human condition: our mental capacities and creativity; our ability to form relationships with other human beings; our place in the broader natural world. But sports, perhaps more than any other human endeavor, make sense primarily as an exploration of the capabilities and limits of the human *body*: how fast it can go; how strong it can be; how it can move and manipulate objects in space; how it can coordinate with other bodies to accomplish a shared goal. Stephen Mumford similarly alludes to these features of sports when he suggests that sport "might be a celebration of the body: an arena in which we can admire the body and the extent of its physical capacities, under our rational control."[22]

As Wallace points out, having a body is not always good. There are, for example, "pain, sores, odors, nausea, aging, gravity, sepsis, clumsiness, illness, limits—every last schism between our physical wills and our actual abilities." But in the face of all these problems, or maybe even because of them, "great athletes seem to catalyze our awareness of how great it is to touch and perceive, move through space, interact with matter."[23] To watch athletes perform, then, is to observe individuals who have decided to make an exploration of the body's limits a prominent feature of their lives.

There are, of course, many areas of our culture that are concerned with bodies, but I would argue that the athletic realm is somewhat unique in its emphasis on what the human body can *do*. Activities having to do with food and drink, for example, are heavily tactile and sensory in nature, and there is no shortage of ways for us to confront the fact that our bodies *appear* a certain way to others. Aesthetic ideals bombard us on a near constant basis, whether on magazine covers at the grocery store (and their regular lists of the world's most beautiful people) or in the emphasis on attractiveness that pervades movies and television. Even the fitness industry seems largely organized around getting our bodies to look a certain way (perhaps with a ceremonial nod to the importance

38 Why Sports Are Like Shakespeare

of health). Sports, on the other hand, value the body's performance much more highly than its appearance. Provided you are able to accomplish the task better than your competitors, it doesn't really matter what your body looks like.

Watching sports is thus one of the few contexts in which we are encouraged to reflect on our embodiment vicariously through the actions of others. As Mumford notes, watching someone work at their job might help us consider our own embodiment, but people who are working "might regard that as a private matter for which they do not want an audience." And watching other people have sex might also place the capacities of the body front and center, but it can also be voyeuristic and problematic in other ways. "[T]he case of sport," on the other hand, "is different insofar as it is socially acceptable and often encouraged to watch others perform."[24] Athletes aren't exactly performing for us—at least not in the same way that actors are performing—but they are consenting to watch them play the games they play.

As any observer of sports will know, there can be wide variance in the specific form that an exploration of the body's capacities might take. Despite prodigious natural abilities, some athletes appear to regard athletic pursuits largely as a means to some other end they value, whether it be fame, fortune, education, or a platform for some other cause. Others seem to regard their pursuits as finely nuanced crafts to be perfected for their own sakes. Some athletes are blessed with extraordinary natural talent, such that very little effort seems to be required to achieve success. Others grind away to develop the modicum of ability they have. And no matter how a given athlete chooses to engage with her chosen sport, she also has a life outside the athletic arena—a life with family, friends, and non-sporting interests that she must figure out how to balance with her athletic endeavors.

Observing how athletes navigate these challenges and how they choose to pursue their various goals can therefore give fans resources for their own pursuit of the good life. Watching how someone attends to their craft can lead us to reflect on our own skills and the use to which those skills might be put. Seeing how a professional golfer hones her swing may, of course, inspire a viewer to put a similar kind of effort into her own game. But it might also lead her to think about how she can improve some other ability she has. Perhaps she is a writer and watching a golf tournament leads her to think about all the hours that players spend practicing in order to prepare for competition. She might then think about how many hours she needs to spend on her writing in order to produce something that is fit for public consumption. She might also think about the place that commitment to excellence in a craft might occupy in a well-balanced life or whether balance and excellence cannot be pursued simultaneously. Thinking about what golfers have to sacrifice to achieve competitive glory might lead her to think about what price she is willing to pay in order to obtain a successful writing career. The activities in question are different, but the athletic example may nevertheless inspire reflection on the particularities of her own life.[25]

This aspect of sports fandom may partially explain why many fans are interested in the private lives of athletes and why human-interest stories about what happens to athletes off the field are so captivating. There is, no doubt, an aspect of voyeurism involved in wanting to know how athletes go about their daily lives, and to the degree that these motivations influence the way that fans relate to athletes, I think we should be highly skeptical of their value. Tarver is thus right to be concerned with the way in which an excessive familiarity with the athletes we admire can feed a problematic kind of hero worship. By contemplating "the wonders of individual efforts in lives just like ours," fans thus believe themselves to recognize "something of themselves in those they idolize."[26] In so doing, they paradoxically turn athletes from individual human beings into ideals. Their perceived relatability transforms them into symbols for all that we would like to be.

However, I think it is also possible that a desire to learn more about the lives of athletes can be connected to a desire to place their athletic exploits in a broader context. The fact of having a body can be explored in a variety of different ways, and a maximization of the body's abilities can be balanced with any number of other human capacities. Catching a glimpse of how various athletes engage in this process can, therefore, give our understanding of their efforts greater nuance and detail. As a case in point, after watching the 2019 documentary *Diego Maradona*, I was left with a profound and conflicting set of reactions to Maradona's remarkable life and career. He is often sympathetic, other times less so. His talent is captivating, as is his commitment to success on the pitch, and yet viewers probably want to reach through the screen at various points in an attempt to prevent him from making some of the bad decisions that plagued him. More than anything in the film, what stood out to me was the incredible amounts of pressure (and also chaos) that surrounded Maradona simply because he was one of the best soccer players who ever lived: his face displays the emotional toll in scene after scene. In short, learning about some of the particulars of his life made me appreciate him more as a human being—a phenomenally talented human being, to be sure, but just a human being nonetheless. Making full sense of Diego's exploits on the field thus requires that we grapple with the details of his life as a whole.

Even if we know very little about the broader lives of the athletes we see performing on the field, it is still possible for spectators to regard athletes as valuable resources for their own pursuit of the good life because the observational data we are able to gather allow us to imagine possible roles that those exploits might play in one's life as a whole. The on-field performance can thus be projected into a variety of possible lives that can challenge us to think critically about our own pursuits. Suppose we see a player injured in the course of a game. We might know very little about their private life off the field. But as fans, we might be aware that they are only in the second year of their professional career and that they are playing their first game after recovering from an injury in their rookie season. The specific details of how they have approached the rehabilitative process may not be available to us, but that fact need not prevent us from reflecting on the various possibilities a person in their predicament might confront.

For example, we might wonder if they considered giving up on their athletic career after their first injury. We might think about what other careers are open to them if they are unable to recover from the injury they have sustained. Perhaps they have numerous other options; or maybe they are at a complete loss as to what they will do with their life if they cannot ever play their chosen sport again. Our minds might turn to the hours of rehabilitation that have yielded only a few minutes of playing time—whether they are thinking that all those painful exercises were a big waste of time and whether it is even worth trying again. After all, there is no guarantee that they will never get injured again, and maybe there are more productive things they can do with their life.

Contemplating these various possibilities can then lead us to entertain similar possibilities for ourselves. How have we reacted to similar misfortunes in our own lives? What costs are we willing to pay in order to achieve our goals? Are our goals worth pursuing, even if we are not ultimately able to achieve them? Would we be willing to devote a year of our lives to rehabilitating an injury, knowing that it could all happen again? And what does it mean to navigate the world with a body that is capable of doing impressive things but that sometimes doesn't do what we want it to do? It is by inspiring us to engage in this kind of reflection that I think athletes can provide valuable resources for spectators who are engaged in their own efforts to flourish as human beings whether or not fans know the specific details of those athletes' lives.

Neither Role Models nor Resources to be Plundered

It is important to emphasize here that I am not suggesting that fans should regard athletes as role models.[27] Spectators who have been inspired to reflect on the sorts of questions I have highlighted may decide that the examples set by certain athletes are worthy of emulation or that certain

40 Why Sports Are Like Shakespeare

athletes are role models for particular traits they would like to develop: perseverance, perhaps, or a laudable commitment to community service. However, it is equally possible that the lessons learned from athletes could be negative, and that they have set examples of what not to do. Perhaps they exhibit poor sportsmanship in the heat of competition or give less than full effort when things aren't going their way, or perhaps we know that their success on the field has come at great cost to their family and friends. Seeing this kind of trade-off may lead us to think about our own personal relationships and what we are willing to sacrifice in the pursuit of our own goals, whatever those goals may be.

The overall picture that emerges here is, I think, similar to what John Stuart Mill advocates in *On Liberty* when he discusses the importance of individuality. While Mill thinks it obvious that our lives should not consist in merely copying the examples of others, he also argues that "it would be absurd to pretend that people ought to live as if nothing whatever had been known in the world before they came into it."[28] In other words, we don't give ourselves the best chance at living good lives if we ignore entirely the attempts that others have made to do the same. Rather, we should avail ourselves of their experience and the various "experiments of living" in which people are engaged.[29] Most obviously, this means not resting content in our own points of view or thinking that we have nothing to learn from others. As Mill notes, "people should be so taught and trained in youth as to know and benefit by the ascertained results of human experience."[30] If you think you have all the answers, you are ignoring a valuable body of inherited wisdom, and that seems like a bad way to approach a question as weighty as how best to live your life.

In the context of sports, then, I contend that what fans are offered is an opportunity to see others pursuing their vision of the good life with their own allotment of gifts, talents, and opportunities—gifts, talents, and opportunities that are likely to be different from our own. Particularly when we watch athletes perform at the highest levels of their sport (as we often do when we engage with sports as fans), we are watching individuals who are attempting to navigate the world with extraordinary physical abilities. They are people who can run faster and jump higher than most everyone else in the world. They have exceptional hand/eye coordination (or foot/eye coordination) and can accomplish feats of endurance that most of us would not so much as consider attempting. They have dedicated thousands of hours to improving those abilities in the hopes of achieving victory in the competitive arena and are taking seriously their nature as physical creatures—entities with bodies that can do things in the physical world. Framed in this way, I suggest that spectators can, and should, explicitly view athletes as engaged in their own experiments in living.

Part of the value that Mill saw in allowing individuals to pursue their own lives in the best way they saw fit was that doing so offers everyone more options. Seeing people navigate the world in ways that I had not previously considered might inspire me to pursue a similar path, and in so doing, I might be able to obtain a happiness that would not have otherwise been available to me. But experiments can also deliver negative results and tell us what doesn't work. In the same way that a medical researcher might be able to find a cure for a disease by avoiding the mistakes of other scientists, one individual's pursuit of the good life might benefit from seeing how others have failed to make the most of theirs. This might not be as inspiring as seeing someone do something we would like to emulate, but that does not cancel out the value of negative results as a resource.[31]

It is also worth highlighting that the view I have been developing in this chapter does not entail that we should regard athletes as mere resources to aid us in our own endeavors. In the same way that some philosophers have criticized consequentialist accounts of morality on the grounds that such views might lead people to regard others merely as raw materials for the maximization of happiness in the world, one might argue that relating to athletes in ways that primarily allow us to enhance our own quality of life leads us to think of them merely as means to our own end of individual happiness—"as mere instruments or repositories of general and non-specific value."[32] According to this view, athletes as individuals nearly drop out of the picture as fans consider them only in terms of how their examples can aid serve as an aid to fans' pursuits.

Given the argument of the previous chapter, it is important that the view I am defending not have this kind of implication. If it is possible to be disrespectful to athletes by claiming their accomplishments as one's own, one might worry about a similar kind of disrespect arising from the attempt to plunder the lives of athletes for one's own purposes, no matter how worthy those purposes might be. Moreover, as I will argue in Chapter 4, it is crucial that we avoid objectifying athletes or losing sight of the fact that they are individual human beings—persons who have projects and goals of their own.

However, that caveat in place, I don't think that the approach to sports I am advocating necessarily has this kind of consequence. To begin with, it isn't at all clear that fans who regard athletes as useful in their own pursuit of the good life are at a greater risk for plundering the lives of athletes than are fans who approach sports with a more purely escapist mindset. Indeed, the fan who regards sports as a mere diversion may have an excessively narrow interest in what athletes are able to do. If athletes are not delivering sufficient entertainment value, they may be essentially useless to the spectator. For fans whose interest in sports is explicitly partisan, this might mean that players who are not helping their team win can be safely ignored or, worse, reviled. Fans who want to be entertained by winning may have little interest in those who do nothing to further such an end.

Even fans who do not have particular rooting interests in the outcome of games can still treat athletes simply as a means to their own pleasure. Supporters might, therefore, watch Real Madrid play Barcelona and not really care about the outcome of the contest. To that degree, they may not judge the entertainment value of any given player by their contributions to either team's competitive prospects. Nevertheless, if they merely watch in order to be entertained, their interest in any given player is going to be determined by the entertainment value that player can offer. Players who are not adding to the excitement of the contest can be safely ignored. Players who make the highlight reel will most fully engage the viewer's attention. Everyone else is simply playing a supporting role, the details of which will likely go unnoticed.

By contrast, I would argue that in order to regard someone as providing useful resources for our own pursuit of the good life, we must regard that person as fully engaged in their own pursuit of the good life. That is, we have to see them as doing something that, at least in principle, we could see ourselves doing, and this approach requires a measure of sympathy and respect for athletes as individuals. Even if we regard them as negative examples—individuals who are making a mess of their lives in ways that we think it best to avoid—viewing them in such a way requires seeing them as more than sources of amusement. Only individuals who have lives to ruin can be regarded as negative examples, and thus a measure of sympathy and understanding is required to view individuals in this way. Put differently, a mere means to our pleasure doesn't have a life to ruin; she has no talent to waste or physical abilities to balance with other pursuits. Only individuals who are capable of success and failure in living along a variety of different dimensions can sensibly be regarded in these ways.

I think that adopting this framework for thinking about the athletes we observe has some interesting implications for the experience of watching sports. Keeping the fact that athletes are engaged in their own exploits at the forefront of our minds helps to pay them sufficient respect and thereby avoid the pitfalls of "we" that I discussed in the previous chapter. At the same time, it has the potential to inspire us to reflect on the variety and possibilities of the human experience. Engaging in this kind of reflection may cause us to marvel at what others are able to make of their gifts and talents, and challenge us to develop our own abilities in ways that might not have previously occurred to us.

42 Why Sports Are Like Shakespeare

Moreover, the practice of imaginatively engaging with sports in a way that highlights the humanity of athletes can also shape the excitement of watching sports. On the one hand, we can distance ourselves from the fortunes of athletes in ways that remind us that their wins and losses are not our wins and losses. On the other hand, we can nurture a sympathy for their plight that encourages us to see their efforts as being of genuine significance. Identifying strongly with every turn of fortune in the lives of our favorite teams may yield correspondingly strong emotions in the lives of fans, and the emotional of lives of fans who speak of their team as "we" are likely to be impassioned. But fans who view athletes as fellow participants in an effort to live good lives have the tools of sympathy to enrich their own experience as spectators. They may not be able to regard a loss by their favorite team as their loss, but they will nevertheless be able to appreciate the significance of the emotional cost to the participants.

Sharing Our Awe With Others

Having argued for the potential value of watching sports, I want to conclude this chapter by suggesting one form that group identification might take in this context as a way of responding to Barash's contention that sports fans inevitably devolve into mindless mobs. Barash may very well be correct that the human tendency to organize into groups is rooted in the need to protect ourselves from the dangers of the world and the efficiencies we can obtain from the division of labor. Nor do I doubt that an abiding sense of other groups as a threat to our own well-being can animate the ways in which we identify with the particular groups we do. Indeed, it is plausible to think that the context of competitive sports can sometimes exacerbate the impulse to set ourselves against other groups. If the proceedings on the field produce a winner and a loser, then we want to make sure that our group wins, even if we aren't exactly the ones who are playing. And if members of opposing groups do things that upset us, the emotional intensity of our environment may lead us to respond in combative or violent ways. Group identification plus competition can be a recipe for trouble.

Moreover, it is also true that fans can lose a sense of their own individuality as they become absorbed in both the games they are watching and the group that surrounds them. This dynamic is perhaps most powerful when one is present in the stadium cheering among thousands of other fans. The sheer volume of the crowd—in terms of both its size and the noise it is capable of producing—makes it easy to lose track of oneself, and the behavior of the group can dictate one's own bodily movements. If everyone else is standing, you also stand. If everyone else is singing, you sing too. And if everyone else is yelling offensive things, then perhaps you find words coming out of your mouth that you would never utter in any other context. We should all be wary of the potentially coercive and destructive powers of the crowd.

There are, however, multiple reasons why one might lose oneself in a crowd, and it is clear that not all of them require a mindless abdication of our reflective capacities. As Dreyfus and Kelly suggest, "The sense that one is joined with one's fellow human beings in the celebration of something great reinforces the sense that what one is celebrating is really great."[33] We can, of course, appreciate greatness by ourselves, as when we wander alone through an art museum or read a novel in the silence of our offices. The kind of solitary contemplation that is occasioned by these sorts of experiences can be profound, yet there is something about even these kinds of encounters that urges us to share them with others. We read a compelling book and want to talk about it; we hear a catchy new song and urge others to listen to it; when we revisit the museum, we make sure that our friends see the painting that so moved us. As Dreyfus and Kelly put it, experiences of greatness "take on greater meaning when they are shared with a community of like-minded folks who are experiencing the same kind of awe."[34]

Thus, insofar as the experience of watching sports is the experience of witnessing athletic excellence or of seeing athletes grapple in real time with the limits of the human body, it should not be at all surprising that we enjoy it more in the company of others. Encountering "fully embodied athletic grace—like our encounters with other kinds of fully embodied joys—can give us a genuine kind of religious experience."[35] In this way, Dreyfus and Kelly compare watching sports to riding a wave: "a solid foundation that can support as many riders as will fit upon it" and that can "sweep up more as it runs along."[36] "These moments of sport are like that," they write. "When you are in the midst of them, riding the wave, they carry you along and give meaning to life."[37]

Some might be turned off by the religious overtones of this analysis, but Dreyfus and Kelly are merely pointing to the collective experience of a goodness beyond oneself—something that transcends our individuality even if it is not fully Transcendent (with a capital T). This notion of the sacred is "nothing like the eternal, everlasting kind of certainty and security that philosophers from Plato to Descartes to Kant desired." The experience they envision is "transient and multiple and requires care." Moreover, it does not seem to be an experience that requires one to lose an awareness of oneself as an individual. Indeed, Dreyfus and Kelly suggest that these experiences are *enhanced* when we are consciously aware that they are shared—an awareness that seems to require rather than preclude a simultaneous awareness of oneself. As they put it:

> Whether it is in the church or the baseball stadium, the awesomeness of the moment is reinforced when it is felt as shared by others. When it is also shared that it is shared—when you recognize together that you are sharing in the celebration of this great thing—then the awesomeness of the moment itself bursts forth and shines.[38]

If this kind of response is more likely to be intense in sports stadiums filled with thousands of people, it can still be present when we are watching on television. The energy of the crowd is palpable at live sporting events and the euphoric bursts of emotion are thereby fueled by that energy in a way that cannot be replicated from a distance. Nevertheless, the impulse to share our experience of watching sports frequently extends beyond the confines of the stadium. We gather together in bars and in our homes to watch games with friends because the social environment provides an immediate outlet for our reactions. And technology has made it easier for sports fans to be social even when we are by ourselves. I often check Twitter during games I am watching precisely so that I can see others' reactions as events unfold, and my dad and I have a long-standing habit of texting each other throughout Badger and Packer football games, a pastime largely unthinkable when I was growing up (because as younger readers may be surprised to learn, there were no cell phones in the 1980s and early 1990s).

In this way, watching sports can inspire us to be communal no matter where we happen to be or who we happen to be with, and this communality strikes me as a clear mark *in favor* of the activity. As social creatures who need interaction with other human beings in order to flourish, we can do far worse than be united by our collective love of, and appreciation for, athletic excellence. Provided we are aware of the dangers lurking in the background, becoming absorbed in the collective experience of watching a sporting event can most certainly be a good thing.

Notes

1. David Barash, "The Roar of the Crowd," *The Chronicle Review*, March 20, 2009, www.chronicle.com/article/The-Roar-of-the-Crowd/32744. All quotations of Barash's work in this chapter are from this essay.

2. David Rowe, "Sports and Culture," in *The Blackwell Encyclopedia of Sociology*, ed. George Ritzer, J. Michael Ryan, and Betsy Thorn (London: Blackwell, 2007), 4676.
3. Simon Kuper, "How Books about Sports Got Serious," *The Financial Times*, November 22, 2013, www.ft.com/content/d1d75a48-513c-11e3-9651-00144feabdc0.
4. Robert W. McCabe, "The Rise of American Sport and the Decline of American Culture," in *Sports in School: The Future of an Institution*, ed. John Gerdy (New York: Teachers College Press, 2000), 138.
5. This way of framing my point owes to John Stuart Mill's famous quote: "It is better to be a human being dissatisfied than a pig satisfied; better to be Socrates dissatisfied than a fool satisfied." See *Utilitarianism* (London: Longman's, Green, and Co., 1879), 14.
6. Barash explicitly references Koestler's *The Ghost in the Machine* (London: Arkana, 1989).
7. Erin Tarver, *The I in Team: Sports Fandom and the Reproduction of Identity* (Chicago, IL: The University of Chicago Press, 2017), 26.
8. Ian Plenderleith, *The Quiet Fan* (London: Unbound, 2018), 4–5.
9. Norbert Elias and Eric Dunning, *Quest for Excitement: Sport and Leisure in the Civilizing Process* (London: Blackwell, 1986), 65.
10. Elias and Dunning, *Quest for Excitement*, 65.
11. Elias and Dunning, *Quest for Excitement*, 42.
12. Elias and Dunning, *Quest for Excitement*, 82.
13. Elias and Dunning, *Quest for Excitement*, 58–59.
14. Stephen Greenblatt, "General Introduction," in *The Norton Shakespeare*, ed. Stephen Greenblatt, Walter Cohen, Jean E. Howard, and Katharine Eisaman Maus (New York: W.W. Norton and Co., 2000), 35.
15. Elias and Dunning, *Quest for Excitement*, 43.
16. J. S. Russell, "The Ideal Fan of Good Fans?" *Sport, Ethics and Philosophy* 6, no. 1 (February 2012): 25.
17. Andrei Markovits and Lars Rensmann, *Gaming the World* (Princeton, NJ: Princeton University Press, 2010), 47.
18. Hubert L. Dreyfus and Sean Kelly, *All Things Shining: Reading the Western Classics to Find Meaning in a Secular Age* (New York: Free Press, 2011), 42.
19. Larry McCaffery, "An Interview with David Foster Wallace," *Review of Contemporary Fiction* 13, no. 2 (Summer 1993), 131. Quoted in Dreyfus and Kelly, *All Things Shining*, 28.
20. On the possible relationship between literature and ethical reflection, see Colin McGinn, *Ethics, Evil, and Fiction* (Oxford: Clarendon Press, 1997); Craig Taylor, "Literature and Moral Thought," *British Journal of Aesthetics* 54 (2014): 285–298; and Neera K. Badhwar and E. M. Dadlez, "Love and Friendship: Achieving Happiness in Jane Austen's *Emma*," in *Jane Austen's Emma: Philosophical Perspectives*, ed. E. M. Dadlez (Oxford: Oxford University Press, 2018), 25–54.
21. David Foster Wallace, "Roger Federer as Religious Experience," *The New York Times Magazine*, August 20, 2006, www.nytimes.com/2006/08/20/sports/playmagazine/20federer.html.
22. Stephen Mumford, *Watching Sport* (London: Routledge, 2012), 137.
23. Wallace, "Roger Federer as Religious Experience."
24. Mumford, *Watching Sport*, 132.
25. The ability of sports to engage our moral imagination in these ways is part of the reason I find wholly aesthetic accounts of the value of sports unsatisfying. In my view, sports clearly have aesthetic value, and it is unquestionably fruitful to reflect on how the aesthetic characteristics of sport relate to a broader understanding of art as well as how aesthetic ideals relate to such matters as winning and athletic excellence. As Wallace puts it, "Beauty is not the goal of competitive sports, but high-level sports are a prime venue for the expression of human beauty" ("Roger Federer as Religious Experience.") Nevertheless, because they leave aside almost entirely the manner in which most fans engage with sports, appeals to the purely aesthetic characteristics of sport seem insufficient as accounts of the value of being a *fan* as opposed to an aesthete who sees beauty in the athletic realm. For a brief overview of these issues, see Emily Ryall, *Philosophy of Sport: Key Questions* (London: Boomsbury, 2016), Chapters 17 and 18. Mumford defends a moderate aestheticism in *Watching Sport*. A more robustly aesthetic approach is adopted by Hans Ulrich Gumbrecht in *In Praise of Athletic Beauty* (Cambridge, MA: Harvard University Press, 2006).
26. Tarver, *The I in Team*, 86.
27. On the question of whether athletes should be regarded as role models, see Raldolph Feezell, *Sports, Philosophy, and Good Lives* (Lincoln, NE: University of Nebraska Press, 2013), Chapter 6; Ryall, *Philosophy of Sport*, Chapter 25; Törbjörn Tännsjö, "Is Our Admiration for Sports Heroes Fascistoid?" *Journal of the Philosophy of Sport* 25, no. 1 (May 1998): 23–34; and Christopher Wellman, "Do Celebrated Athletes Have Special Responsibilities to Be Good Role Models?" in *Ethics: An Anthology*, ed. Jan Boxill (London: Blackwell, 2003), 333–336.
28. John Stuart Mill, *On Liberty* (Indianapolis, IN: Hackett Publishing, 1978), 55.

29. Mill, *On Liberty*, 54.
30. Mill, *On Liberty*, 55.
31. If this approach does not advocate regarding athletes as role models, neither does it countenance viewing them as "imagined objects or fictional characters in a drama, whose characters and exploits we admire within this illusory domain, rather than persons whose lives outside of sports are either exemplary, noteworthy, or even interesting" (Feezell, *Sport, Philosophy, and Good Lives*, 150). Regarding athletes as engaged in experiments in living requires that we see them as real people trying to balance the full range of life's concerns.
32. Michael Stocker, "The Schizophrenia of Modern Ethical Theories," *The Journal of Philosophy* 73, no. 14 (August 1976): 460.
33. Dreyfus and Kelly, *All Things Shining*, 193.
34. Dreyfus and Kelly, *All Things Shining*, 193.
35. Dreyfus and Kelly, *All Things Shining*, 198.
36. Dreyfus and Kelly, *All Things Shining*, 199.
37. Dreyfus and Kelly, *All Things Shining*, 200.
38. Dreyfus and Kelly, *All Things Shining*, 193.

3

LOVE 'EM LIKE A BROTHER

In Defense of Partisan Fandom

If the argument of the previous chapter is convincing, then we have reason to think there is potential value in being a spectator—that being an observer of the athletic pursuits of others can provide valuable resources for the observer's efforts to flourish as a human being and that such experiences are enhanced when they are shared with others. However, even if this claim is true, it doesn't follow that all ways of being a spectator are created equal or that becoming heavily invested in the exploits of particular teams is an effective way to obtain the resources in question. For all I have said, dispassionate fandom might be the way to go. Indeed, it might be that trying to enjoy an athletic contest without caring about the outcome allows one to appreciate the efforts of a larger number of players. Fans of particular teams may be highly focused on one side of the contest, but that focus may blind them to half of the game's participants, and in some cases, even lead fans to be hostile to players on the opposing team as well as that team's fans—an attitude that does not seem conducive to exploring the nuances of the good life.

Moreover, while partisan fans may experience great emotional highs when their favorite teams win, they also open themselves up to the possibility of great disappointment. The joy might be more intense for the partisan fan, but so is the misery. By contrast, the odds that one can enjoy an athletic event without supporting any particular team are probably quite high. As long as the game is reasonably competitive and interesting, the experience will almost always be compelling. Much like one can be engrossed in a film or novel, the plotline of the athletic competition can be more than enough to entertain. Think of the way viewers become captivated by such stories during the Olympics and end up transfixed by sports they watch once, at most, every four years. If the sort of group identification that emerges within fan bases of various teams can sometimes lead to violence and mindless animosity toward other fan bases, perhaps it can also undermine the sense of awe in the face of athletic excellence that is worth sharing with others.

Stephen Mumford lends some support for this assessment when he recalls a 2007 soccer match between Real Madrid and RCD Mallorca. Late into the night, Mumford finds himself unable to sleep as he reflects on his experience in the stadium. Ruud van Nistelrooy had scored to cap an enthralling 4–3 victory for Madrid, and Mumford declares it the most sublime soccer he had ever seen. He writes that "[t]he game seemed to have become something else: something that made a profound comment on the human condition."[1] Even though he "had just watched a game with no interest in who won and who lost," Mumford says that "it was nevertheless the deepest emotional moment [he] had experienced in sport."[2] The fact that he was not committed to either team did

DOI: 10.4324/9781003223696-4

not undermine his enjoyment of the game; his disinterested approach seemed instead to enhance the experience. If he had been a passionate fan of Real Madrid, he might have been thrilled by the victory, but he might also have been too preoccupied with the uncertainty of the result to lose himself in the sheer excellence and beauty of the contest. And had he been a Mallorca supporter, he would almost certainly have been overwhelmed by the crushing disappointment of loss. The fact that it had been such an incredible game would have provided little solace.

It was in the wake of this experience that Mumford says he adopted a purist approach to fandom—a mode of following sports that involves "no allegiance to any particular team."[3] While purists may have a deep appreciation for particular sports, and might very well devote large amounts of time to watching and studying them, they do not have a devotion to any specific team or strong preferences concerning the outcome of the games they watch. This sort of detached approach contrasts sharply with the deep attachments that many people have to their favorite teams—attachments exemplified by the relationship to Arsenal that Nick Hornby explores in the pages of *Fever Pitch*. Whereas Hornby surely loves soccer, it's very difficult to read *Fever Pitch* without thinking that he loves Arsenal somewhat more than he loves the game that Arsenal plays. Mumford, on the other hand, cares not so much about who wins the games he watches as about whether excellence is displayed on the field.

Presented in this way, the partisan and the purist are, no doubt, extreme types, and most fans probably incorporate a mix of both partisan and purist commitments in their approach to sports. Purists likely have at least some mild preferences for who wins certain games and thereby develop at least a mild affinity for some teams over time. How many purist soccer fans really don't care *at all* who wins *El Classico* battles between Real Madrid and Barcelona or who might prevail in a World Cup final? There are probably some, but even if preferences shift from year to year—or from *Classico* to *Classico* and World Cup to World Cup—I suspect that very few people watch such games without *any* concern for the outcome. By the same token, many partisans have some broader appreciation for the sports their favorite teams play such that they are able to appreciate contests in which those teams are not involved. Indeed, I am sure that many partisan fans can appreciate high-quality contests in which their teams *are* involved, even when the outcome is not the one they would prefer. For example, in 2018, the Wisconsin men's basketball team played a Big Ten Conference Tournament game against Michigan State. It was a closely fought affair that Wisconsin ended up losing 63–60, and while I was disappointed at the outcome, I remember consciously thinking at numerous points what a good game it was—a thought I was able to entertain in spite of my deeply partisan commitment to the Badgers. The most resolutely partisan among us can still appreciate a well-played game, even when our favorite teams lose.

Theorists of fandom thus acknowledge the simplified nature of the purist/partisan taxonomy, and Mumford explicitly notes "that there are degrees of partisanship and purism on a spectrum."[4] Nevertheless, academic discussion of this debate tends to represent various accounts of fandom as ideals toward which we should strive. Mumford therefore argues that there is "no really compelling argument in favor of being a partisan" and feels comfortable recommending "the more purist stance."[5] Randolph Feezell similarly recommends a moderate purism that allows "some inevitable partisan connections" but also encourages one to "appreciate athletic excellence wherever it occurs." "[C]heer for your team, only mildly, if you do support one of the competitors," writes Feezell. "Losing is not like death, nor is it an occasion for misery, especially for fans."[6] Nicholas Dixon, on the other hand, officially renounces "the attempt to defend the moderate partisan as superior to the purist" while nevertheless arguing that "being a moderate partisan has special value."[7] Dixon thus tries to strike a delicate balance: partisans should not say their approach to sports is superior to that of purists even though there is a value in what they do that is not available to purists. It is, therefore, difficult to read any of these authors without thinking they are recommending their version of fandom as the best way to engage with sports as a spectator.

48 Love 'em Like a Brother

I confess that I find a wholly purist approach to fandom baffling. As one whose introduction to sports came by way of a love for particular teams, it is difficult to put myself in a frame of mind where it makes sense to spend time watching games with no real investment in their outcome or with no favorite team whose efforts throughout the season *matter* to me. Even when I consider my love of soccer—a love that preceded any attachment to particular teams—the fact that I would eventually have some partisan loyalties now seems inevitable. Yes, I can still watch numerous soccer games in which I have no rooting interest, but my affection has nevertheless gravitated to teams that now structure my engagement with the sport.[8]

That said, like Dixon, I would not officially claim that my way of following sports is superior to the purist approach advocated by Feezell and Mumford, nor would I argue that fans who want to watch sports in the best way possible must therefore become partisans. After all, I have a difficult time understanding people who are accountants. From my perspective, spending hours upon hours with numbers and math and paperwork and spreadsheets sounds mind-numbing and soul-destroying. But I happen to know a few people who seem to enjoy being accountants and some of them even claim to love it. Even though I can't exactly understand their point of view—and even though the life of the accountant is not one that I would want for myself—I certainly wouldn't claim that being a philosophy professor is an objectively superior way to live, much less that everyone should strive to be a philosopher instead of an accountant. Similarly, I may not be able to fully understand the purist approach to sports fandom, but I am perfectly willing to acknowledge that my way of being a fan is not necessarily better than a more detached approach.

In this way, I am generally convinced by J.S. Russell's claim that "there is no ideal fan of team sports" and that there are "many other ways of being a fan than being a purist or a partisan as described by Dixon," none of which "is morally superior to the other." Like Russell, as long as fans "meet basic requirements of respect for others and fair play," I'm happy to let a thousand flowers bloom.[9] Indeed, I am inclined to think that purists and partisans can (and should) learn to appreciate alternative ways of engaging with sports and glean whatever insights are available from those who do things differently.

Given all these caveats, my aim in this chapter is not really to argue for the superiority of partisan fandom but rather to examine what, if any, distinctive goods might come from attaching oneself to a particular team. Think of it like a philosopher trying to explain what is good about his job to an accountant (or an accountant trying to explain what is good about his job to a philosopher). If we are to understand the value of watching sports in terms of the resources that such an activity offers for our pursuit of the good life, are there any such resources that can be obtained by partisans? And if so, are there any limits that such a framework might place on our loyalties as fans?

Finding the Right Analogy With Personal Relationships

The debate between purists and partisans has often focused on a comparison between loyalty to sports teams and loyalty to individual persons. Thus, in his canonical defense of partisanship, Dixon suggests that in the same way that "a person in love does not seek to 'trade up' to a different partner who scores higher than her current partner on the most significant evaluative scales," partisan fans remain committed to their teams "despite significant changes in personnel and fortune." As such, the partisan fan is not "tempted to 'trade up' to a more successful, skillful team" except in "unusual circumstances." By contrast, the commitment of the purist is "purely conditional" such that, according to Dixon, the purist "barely qualifies as a fan at all." If "retaining affection for one's partner despite changes and disappointments is essential to love," he likewise thinks that "a certain amount of unconditional loyalty" is "essential to genuine support of a team."[10]

Russell, on the other hand, denies that the parallel between romantic love and partisan devotion establishes the points that Dixon wants to make. He therefore contends that if romantic love justifies this kind of commitment, it would be on the sort of basis advocated by defenders of the *union account of love*.[11] According to this view, "the motive to romantic love reflects an intention to create a new entity, a we, that each partner regards as an extension of himself (or herself) and with whom each identifies his (or her) interests and fortunes."[12] When lovers remain committed to each other, it is to this *we* that they are committed because leaving one's beloved destroys the newly created entity. As Russell puts it, "In the case of romantic love, someone who trades up or simply abandons their partner destroys the *we* entity they have created and also therefore a part of the extended self of the other now ex-beloved."[13]

There is, however, no comparable *we* in the case of fans and the teams they support. In Russell's estimation,

> it makes no evident sense to say that a partisan who opts to switch allegiance destroys a part of the team she leaves, to say nothing of destroying a joint person their attachment has helped create. The reasons for this are straightforward. Relations of romantic love are so profoundly personal, immediate and reciprocal that they are fundamentally different from a partisan fan's abstract and distant connections with a particular team.[14]

Without the *we* that justifies the commitments of romantic lovers, the analogy between romantic love and partisan fandom starts to fall apart. And rather than being similar to the laudable commitments of interpersonal love, partisan fandom begins to look pathological.

Given the argument of Chapter 1, I am obviously sympathetic with Russell's claim that invocations of "we" in the context of fandom should be greeted with a heavy dose of skepticism. But I am also skeptical of the union account of love more generally because I don't think that loving someone or something ever requires an identification with the object of love. In other words, we can love people (and things) such that it matters deeply to us what happens to them and not think that we are a part of the thing that we love.

For example, it seems clear (at least to me) that I can love my wife without appealing to some third entity—a "we"—that the two of us constitute. To be sure, my wife and I are partners who do all sorts of things together, have shaped each other's lives in innumerable ways, and it would be silly to deny that all sorts of things happen to *us*. We have moved multiple times, bought and sold houses, and are in the process of raising our children. My happiness is deeply affected by her well-being, and I express my love for her by trying to promote that well-being in various ways. As such, I am clearly invested in her happiness.

But for all that—for all the ways our lives are entwined—we are separate entities: two people who love each other and have decided to make their way through the world together, but two people nonetheless. She does all sorts of things that I do not. For example, as I write, she is working on her master's degree as well as completing her first year in a new job as an elementary school librarian. I am doing neither of those things (even as I support and am fiercely proud of her accomplishments). And I do all sorts of things that she does not, such as coach youth soccer and watch a lot of sports on television. (The former probably occasions some pride in her; the latter, not so much.) Investment in another may be a necessary condition for loving that other, in that we only love people or things if it matters to us what happens to them. But that sort of investment doesn't require that we identify with them in a way that generates a "we" whether the object of our love is a sports team, a partner, a child, or a friend.

Having registered my disagreement with the union account of love, however, I want to argue that the dispute between partisans and purists does not primarily suffer from invoking that account.

50 Love 'em Like a Brother

Rather, I think the discourse has been skewed by taking romantic love more generally as its central paradigm, no matter how, exactly, such love is to be understood at the level of theory. Love takes many forms, and it may be that romantic love is not the best lens through which to understand the attachments that fans develop to the teams they support. In the remainder of this chapter, then, I want to press the idea that familial love—love of the sort that parents, children, and siblings have for each other—better captures the way in which many fans feel connected to their teams than do ideals of romantic love. If this idea is plausible, I think it also frames the distinctive value of partisan fandom in a potentially useful way.

Familial Love and the Contingency of History

A key assumption lying in the background of the purist/partisan debate is that any attachment of love is properly grounded, at least initially, in an assessment of a beloved entity's objective characteristics. In other words, it is taken for granted that the reason we love the people (or things) we do is that they score well when judged by some criteria of excellence. Dixon invokes this idea when he suggests that our love "for our partners begins with an appreciation of their good qualities." We come to love the people we do because we esteem them highly with respect to some traits they possess, most likely some feature of their personality or appearance. Over time, such an attachment "becomes less dependent on our partners' qualities and fixes instead on their unique instantiation of those qualities: in other words on their special identity."[15]

Thus, while I may have first been attracted to my wife because I admired various of her characteristics, and rated them highly with respect to other people in the world, over time it is *her* that I have come to love—not some amalgamation of traits considered in abstraction. As a result, my love is not dependent on a continually high assessment of the qualities that first engaged my affections. Rather, as Robert Nozick puts it, "a romantic mate eventually comes to be loved, not for any general dimensions or 'score' on such dimensions but rather for his or her own particular and nonduplicable way of embodying such general traits."[16] The characteristics may provide the initial basis for attraction, but love eventually settles on the person who possesses those characteristics.[17]

If we carry this framework into the debate between partisans and purists, both parties seem to agree that an assessment of a team's characteristics is an appropriate basis for admiring or attaching oneself to that team. Where they disagree is in whether that attachment should change in light of corresponding changes to the team. The partisan invokes the analogy with romantic love to argue that once fans become attached to a team, it is the *team* they love, rather than some combination of the team's characteristics viewed in abstraction. Thus, in the same way that a person will remain committed to her beloved through various changes in that beloved's characteristics, the partisan fan will "stick with her team despite significant changes in personnel and fortune." And just as lovers tend to strongly resist exchanging their beloveds for individuals who better exemplify certain traits, most fans are not "tempted to 'trade up' to a more successful, skillful team, except in unusual circumstances."[18]

The resolute purist, on the other hand, will not think that fans should really attach themselves to teams at all. That is, they should not emotionally invest in the performance of any given team over an extended period of time, in the way that I am invested in whether the Badgers win or lose. What they may countenance instead is something like admiration. Fans might, therefore, admire certain characteristics that teams exhibit: a particular style of play, for example, or a commitment to sportsmanship and fairness. But unlike the partisan, the purist will think that such admiration should consistently track the characteristics that ground a fan's initial support. If a fan likes a team's style of play, and the team no longer plays that style, then the fan should look for different objects of admiration. In the same way that customers are under no compulsion to continue patronizing a restaurant whose food they no longer enjoy, fans shouldn't be attracted to teams who no longer exemplify the traits they previously found admirable. Indeed, given the ethical and idealistic nature of the traits that purists believe to warrant fan attraction to a team, they seem to support a corresponding ethical *obligation* to abandon any allegiance to teams that no longer exemplify traits that are worthy of such devotion. You are not only permitted to admire a different team; you should most definitely redirect your affections.

Some fans, no doubt, become attached to teams by assessing that team's objective characteristics, and insofar as they do, I suppose their attachments give credence to this way of framing the debate. But far more often, I suspect that the objects of fans' attachments are not chosen at all, or if they are chosen, they are not chosen in the manner suggested by an analogy with romantic love. Consider my love of the Wisconsin Badgers—one I have had as long as I can remember. I am quite sure that I did not select the Badgers for any aesthetic reasons, because the play of Wisconsin's football and basketball teams in my youth was far from beautiful. Nor did they exhibit any particular excellence on the field. Indeed, until my last couple of years in high school, Badger teams did a lot more losing than winning. And as for ideals of sportsmanship, I suppose it is possible that they rated well in that regard, but if they did, I was completely unaware of it as a child. In other words, if they were exceptionally well-behaved either on or off the field, that fact played no part in my developing love of Wisconsin sports.

What did serve as a basis for that love was simply the fact that my dad loved them: I liked sports and found my affections being directed to the teams he supported. It was not as though I selected the Badgers from among the many possible teams I might root for, much less rated them on any supposedly objective scale of excellence. They were a part of my family life such that my attachment grew organically out of that relational experience. I was certainly not forced to become a Wisconsin fan, but neither did my dad and I have any conversations about what other teams I might support. The Badgers were simply where my affections landed, and having landed there, it became inconceivable to me that they might be transferred to another object.

As readers of *Fever Pitch* know, Nick Hornby's support of Arsenal followed a similar trajectory. After a three-week dalliance with Manchester United, based on a love for Bobby Charlton and George Best "that had taken [him] completely by surprise,"[19] Hornby's father took him to the Arsenal game that began his lifelong devotion to the club. He even recognizes that if he'd "gone to White Hart Lane or Stamford Bridge the same thing would have happened, so overwhelming was the experience the first time."[20] Similarly, in *Rammer, Jammer, Yellow Hammer*, Warren St. John notes that the only real explanation for why he is a fervent supporter of Alabama football is that he grew up in Alabama. Sure, the Crimson Tide's impressive run of victories in his childhood meant that, for the most part, he was largely spared from most fans' experience of "losing at least once a season." But St. John doesn't cite winning as the basis of his devotion. Rather, success has been a pleasant (and lucky) feature of a relationship that was probably sealed the day he was born.[21]

I suspect that many, if not most, fans arrive at their sporting loyalties via some such means. Rather than selecting teams from the vast array of options—the way one might decide what to order off a restaurant menu—they simply find themselves attached to the teams that garner their affection. They get caught up in the excitement for the hometown team, or they have a parent or friend who has strong loyalties that they inherit by default, or they attend a school and develop a corresponding connection to that school's sports programs. Thus, while most sports fans can tell some story about how they became attached to their objects of devotion, it will, in most cases, be a story that is contingent on the particularities of their personal history—not the identification of some putatively objective set of excellences.

If we are looking for a parallel for this kind of attachment in the realm of human relationships, it seems that fan devotion is much more akin to parental love or the love that family members develop for each other than romantic love. Unlike our romantic partners whom we select (albeit mutually), we don't select our parents, kids, siblings, or extended family. After all, in the normal course of events, we are more or less stuck with the family we have. Selecting our parents, at least biologically, is impossible, and when we are born we inherit any number of family connections that we did not choose. If we have older siblings, we certainly weren't able to select them, and those of us who have younger siblings were probably not consulted about that development before it happened. (My parents certainly didn't ask me how I felt about having a baby sister, at least not until the matter was already decided.) And while most people make a conscious choice about whether they want to have children, once that decision is made, they do not get to select the particular kids they end up having. Children simply come out how they come out.

Nevertheless, despite the fact that we do not choose our family members, such individuals often end up as significant objects of love. We love our siblings and our parents and our grandparents simply because they are family. And the idea that the love of our children is based on their objective characteristics is, upon some reflection, likely to strike many parents as odd, even perverse. We might admire certain of their traits—some talent they happen to have or some virtue they have developed over time—but these characteristics don't ground our love for them. Harry Frankfurt thus describes parental love as follows:

> The fact is that I loved [my children] even before they were born—before I had any especially relevant information about their characteristics or their particular merits and virtues. Furthermore, I do not believe that the valuable qualities that they do happen to possess, strictly in their own rights, would really provide me with a very compelling basis for regarding them as having greater worth than many other possible objects of love that in fact I love much less. It is quite clear that I do not love them more than other children because I believe they are better.[22]

We love our children because they are our children, not because we esteem them highly according to some independent measure. And whatever attachments we develop with other family members grow out of similarly historical developments. We don't choose our families. We are thrown together with them, and yet some of the deepest bonds of affection in human life arise in just such contexts.

Even in cases of adoption, where it might seem more plausible to say that parents have chosen their children, it is almost never true that such choices are made because parents assess their adopted children highly on some putative scale of excellence. Occasionally, prospective parents will have some prior acquaintance with a child and decide to pursue adoption on the basis of that relationship. But even in such instances, their decisions are not based on a conviction that the child is objectively superior to other children or that they possess certain properties that make them somehow more worthy of being adopted than other available kids. Indeed, far more often, adoptive parents have almost no control over which particular child they adopt as they work through adoption agencies who match them up with children they have never previously met. Having made the choice to become parents, creating a family via adoption thus involves many of the same dynamics as creating a family via other means: parents get the kids they get; siblings have little say in the matter; and the bonds that develop are rooted in these familial dynamics rather than an objective assessment of each other's strengths and weaknesses.

All analogies have their limits, but I think that highlighting some of the ways in which familial love can differ from romantic love shows that fans' love of sports teams is often better captured by the former model than the latter. In other words, the love that fans have for their teams is more like the love they have for their parents or siblings or children than the love they have for romantic partners. We are often thrown together with our favorite teams much like we are thrown together with other members of our family, and the attachments that result can thus occupy a similar place in our lives.

I grew up with the Wisconsin Badgers in much the same way that I grew up with my younger sister. And while I certainly love my sister more than I love the Badgers—and while the fact that she is a person entails that the relationship I have with her is clearly different from any relationship I could have with a sports team—I think the similarities in these relationships make it inapt to explain the ground of either love by appealing to certain objective characteristics. To be sure, my sister has many qualities that make me admire her—she is a really talented musician and has a killer sense of humor—and the Badgers might also exemplify certain traits that even non-fans can appreciate. However, I don't love my sister because she is a talented musician any more than I love the Badgers because of any particular excellences they happen to exemplify. I love them because they are the team I grew up with, just as I love my sister because she is my sister.

My attachment to Tottenham admittedly came about somewhat differently, but in ways that I think still follow the basic pattern of familial attachment rather than romantic love. My father was not a soccer fan, so I didn't inherit my love of Spurs from him, and I didn't have the kind of semester abroad experience that would have allowed me to spend time at White Hart Lane (in the way that a lot of American fans of Fulham seem to have fallen in love with that club by seeing games at Craven Cottage). Rather, as my love of soccer was developing, I found that I wanted to develop a connection with a particular team, as opposed to remaining an observer uninvested in the proceedings. Spurs happened to be on television a fair amount in that period, and the American Clint Dempsey was playing for them, and at some point, I simply found myself rooting for them. I don't think I ever made a conscious decision to adopt them, but the pattern of adoptive parenting is nevertheless an accurate enough description of how things unfolded. Having opened myself up to the possibility of attaching myself to a particular team, the world threw me together with Spurs, and now the thought of "upgrading" to another team is more or less unthinkable.

The Value and Lessons of Love

The mere fact that we often become attached to individuals or teams in this way does not, by itself, show that it is good for us to do so or that such attachments are worth preserving. Some explication of the distinctive benefits of this kind of love is therefore appropriate as is some discussion of whether these benefits can be derived when our attachment is to a team rather than a person. In other words, what value is there in succumbing to this kind of love? And does it make any sense to direct such love toward sports teams?

One simple but important answer here is simply that such attachments satisfy a deep-seated human need to love. Frankfurt highlights what is at stake in this regard when he argues that loving is an essential component of our well-being. While the things we love may be important, what Frankfurt has in mind is that the fact of our loving them is similarly crucial. As he puts it, "Quite apart from our particular interest in the various things that we love, we have a more generic and an even more fundamental interest in loving as such." Thus, Frankfurt suggests that while his children are important to him for their own sakes, there is "the additional fact that *loving my children* is important to me for *its* own sake."[23]

He continues:

> Whatever burdens and distresses loving them may in the course of time have brought me, my life was notably altered and enhanced when I came to love them. One thing that leads

people to have children is precisely the expectation that it will enrich their lives, and that it will do this simply by giving them more to love.[24]

A life devoid of the things we love would certainly be an impoverished life. It is also possible to contemplate a world in which those things are present, but our attachments to them are not. Everything would be the same in this world: all the same people would exist with all the same traits doing all the same things. What would be different is simply that we would have no investment in them, or anything else for that matter, and it is difficult to see how that kind of world is superior to the one in which we live: a world where the things we love exist *along with our love for them*.

To be sure, a life without love would likely be free of the pain that relationships can cause us. Absent loving attachments, there would be no particular reason for us to be upset when bad things happen to our friends and family or to be emotionally scarred when they do things that disappoint or wound us. But even leaving aside the fact that doing so would put us at odds with tendencies that seem fairly hard-wired in human beings—just try to not care about what happens to your friends or family—a life devoid of real attachments would also deprive us of all the pleasures that come from caring about people. If we aren't particularly invested in what happens to our friends, then we aren't going to experience joy when good things happen to them. We won't be particularly moved when they get a new job or have children. And if our attachments to our children render our emotions vulnerable to their misfortunes, they also enable us to feel joy when things go well for them: when they score their first soccer goal; when they succeed in mastering a difficult task in school; when they grow up and have families of their own.

At the extreme, Frankfurt thus thinks that a life without love would simply be a life of boredom—one in which "we have no interest in what is going on" and our "responsiveness to ordinary stimuli flattens out and shrinks." In this way, people who are bored are unable to make distinctions of any significance and their "conscious field becomes more and more homogeneous." And when boredom becomes extreme, Frankfurt contends that "there is an end to all psychic movement or change." Unable to differentiate things they care about from things they do not, boredom is "tantamount to a cessation of conscious experience" as bored people cease to live a life that we recognize as distinctively human.[25]

Thus, one of the functions of loving anything is that it opens up the possibility of enjoyment in life. In the context of the family, this is important because we spend so much time around them, especially when we are young. Healthy relationships with family members can provide us many things: food, shelter, clothing, education, wisdom, life advice, and so on. And attachments of love to those same family members can make the significant amount of time we spend with them enjoyable. Put differently, without such attachments, our interactions with the people who nourish and sustain us would be almost incomprehensibly monotonous.

Applying this point to the realm of sports, it seems fair to say that a world in which no one cared about the outcome of sporting events would be a world in which sports are exceedingly boring. The love that fans have for particular teams enriches the experience of all spectators, even those who may not be overly invested in the outcome. To be sure, we can all appreciate spirited contests between two teams that we do not support. For example, the most thrilling game of the 2018 World Cup was, in my view, Belgium's 3–2 victory over Japan, and I found myself gripped by the match even though I didn't have a strong preference for either team. But the intensity of my experience watching that game was no doubt heightened by the knowledge that there were millions of people who had *very strong* preferences regarding the outcome. The drama on the field was framed not simply by the investment of the players; it also unfolded against the backdrop of millions of Belgians and Japanese around the world watching the game on the edge of their seats.

Indeed, after the game ended, I went immediately to Facebook to check on the status of a Belgian friend who I knew had experienced the game as a diehard partisan. Knowing *he* was invested in the game only added to *my* enjoyment.

When Mumford writes of watching the match between Real Madrid and Mallorca that converted him to a purist view of fandom, I can't help but think that his experience would have been markedly different if the stadium had been filled with thousands of purist fans who only wanted to see a quality game of soccer. Such fans might very well have cheered impressive displays of skill and teamwork, and they may have thought that their time was well spent in the way that people feel that their time is well spent after a trip to an art museum. However, it is exceedingly unlikely that the vibrancy of the atmosphere in the stadium—the cheering, the singing, the jumping up and down—would have been anything approaching what, in fact, surrounded Mumford and no doubt contributed to the aesthetic quality of his experience. Without the love that the fans expressed for their favored teams, it would have been a much quieter, less transfixing, affair. In this way, I would argue that purist fandom is compelling, at least in part, because of the existence of robustly partisan fans.

There is, of course, no particular reason why sports teams *must* be the object of our love. Billions of people are not sports fans, and their lives are not necessarily deficient because of this fact. They simply direct their affections to other things. But neither is there any reason to demean or dismiss the idea that sports teams can be legitimate objects of love. If playing sports constitutes a worthwhile human pursuit—that is, if they have the capacity to enhance the lives of those who play them—and if, as I have argued, it is possible for those who watch sports to regard athletes as providing valuable resources for their own pursuit of the good life, then it is not at all clear why we should think it inappropriate to love sports teams. We do not balk at the idea that someone can love a particular band or artist, and if someone claims to love an author with whom one has no real personal relationship, we do not think that their affections have landed on something trivial. If sports are a worthy human activity—like music or literature—and if we can derive benefit from those who play them—in the way that we derive benefit from artists, writers, and musicians—then attaching ourselves to sports teams is certainly no more questionable than attaching ourselves to those who are engaged in other worthwhile human activities.

I think that a second benefit of this kind of love is that, in Michael Sandel's phrase, it teaches us to be open to the "unbidden."[26] Whether we like it or not, many of our emotional attachments outside the realm of sports are to things over which we have very little, if any, control. If we are resistant to this view, I suspect it is because we have a tendency to overestimate the degree to which we are responsible for the things in which we are invested. Parenthood springs most immediately to mind as an example of this phenomenon. Parents are, if nothing else, invested in the well-being of their children. They tend to be happy if their children are doing well and distressed when their kids are struggling. Of course, this emotional investment can be skewed in all sorts of ways. Parents often have their own criteria for well-being that they project onto their children in ways that create conflicts between differing visions of the good life. Kids may be perfectly satisfied with lives that are very troubling to their parents, and vice versa. But even if we acknowledge these sorts of challenges, it remains the case that most parents are emotionally invested in how their kids are doing.

It is also the case that how one's kids are doing is very often beyond their parents' control. If people could guarantee the path that their kids' lives would take, and the emotional states that would attend their circumstances, it is hard to imagine that anyone would be unhappy, much less anyone who suffers unfortunate tragedy, troubled relationships, unsatisfying careers, financial difficulty, or serious illness. Were parents able to insulate their children from the worst of life's struggles—to guarantee them a satisfying life filled with engaging pursuits with good companions—most of them surely would do so. That, after all, is what loving parents want for their kids.

56 Love 'em Like a Brother

As everyone knows, however, this is not how life works. One doesn't need to have children in order to see that we can long for these sorts of things for ourselves and those we love even though they might never materialize. Some people work their entire lives to overcome poverty, and the idea that they might find careers that are meaningful and satisfying is the furthest thing from their minds. They would be satisfied with a regular job that pays the bills. Others struggle to maintain stable and healthy relationships, and still others suffer tragic accidents or confront debilitating illnesses. If we are unable to guarantee desired outcomes in our own lives, we have even less control when we consider the challenges faced by our loved ones.

This lack of control extends not only to the paths our kids' lives will take but also to the kinds of people that our kids will end up being. As much as we might want to, we cannot control their personalities, their appearance, their interests, or abilities. They come out kicking and screaming with whatever color hair they happen to have and turn into individuals we cannot predict in advance. Investment bankers have kids who are performance artists. Math professors have children who are professional athletes. Pastors have children who become atheists, and atheists have children who become pastors.[27]

While our initial impulse may be to lament this lack of control over how our loved ones turn out, Sandel has argued that there are some unappreciated benefits of recognizing our comparative helplessness. He writes that in

> a social world that prizes mastery and control, parenthood is a school for humility. That we care deeply about our children and yet cannot choose the kind we want teaches parents to be open to the unbidden. Such openness is a disposition worth affirming, not only within families but in the wider world as well. It invites us to abide the unexpected, to live with dissonance, to rein in the impulse to control. A Gattaca-like world in which parents became accustomed to specifying the sex and genetic traits of their children would be a world inhospitable to the unbidden, a gated community writ large. The awareness that our talents and abilities are not wholly our own doing restrains our tendency toward hubris.[28]

If our tendency is to think that we can exercise firm control over the trajectory of our lives, Sandel thus argues that parenthood should not only disabuse us of these notions; raising children also has the capacity to open us up to new possibilities—to make us recognize the value in appreciating a future we cannot predict. In so doing, Sandel contends that we are able to develop the virtue of humility. If recognizing that we are not entirely responsible for how our lives or the lives of our loved ones turn out forces us to confront the uncomfortable reality that we cannot guarantee the happiness of those we care about, it also helps us to appreciate when things go well—to be thankful that fortune has smiled upon us and to look forward to what unforeseen possibilities might lie in the future.

If it seems tenuous to draw a connection between sports and the cultivation of this sort of openness and humility, I want to suggest that the realm of partisan fandom is a remarkably fertile ground for the development of such traits. As a case in point, there is a scene in *Fever Pitch* where, right after humorously describing his first encounter with a dead body, Hornby talks about what he has learned from the game of soccer. In addition to European geography, and some rudimentary sociology based on his observation of hooligans, Hornby writes that "he has learned the value of investing time and emotion in things I cannot control, and of belonging to a community whose aspirations I share completely and uncritically."[29] Though he only hints at exactly what kind of value he has in mind here, I would argue that a love of sports teams has the potential to teach us the kind of humility and openness that Sandel discusses in the context of familial love.

When I watch Tottenham play, I care about the outcome of the game. This concern is not a mild preference, in the way that I might prefer to have an apple fritter rather than a plain glazed donut on those mornings when I indulge my desire for sugary baked goods. It is a concern that will affect my emotions into the future. If no apple fritters are available, I might be mildly disappointed. But I like plain glazed donuts just fine, so I'll forget the absence of fritters minutes after I've finished breakfast. By contrast, if Tottenham wins, my mood will be lifted, not only in the immediate aftermath of the victory, but every time I think about that occasion. And should they lose, I will be disappointed—rolling over the various missed opportunities and mistakes in my head. If the game is against a rival—Arsenal or Chelsea—these emotions will only be heightened. I'll think about the celebrating fans of the opposition and my blood will boil.

What is also true is that I have zero control over whether Tottenham wins or loses any game they play. Perhaps fans in the stadium can exercise some influence on the outcome of soccer matches (though, as I noted in Chapter 1, the precise nature of this influence is disputed). And perhaps my purchase of Tottenham shirts and hats puts money in the club's accounts that can be used to improve their team. But I live in North Carolina and have only ever seen Spurs play on television. When I yell during their games, the only people who hear me are my family who, incidentally, don't care one iota about the outcome of the game. And even if it is the case that overall sales of Tottenham merchandise do have some impact on their competitiveness, the value of my purchases in that regard has to be vanishingly small. I therefore seem to be in exactly the predicament that Hornby describes: I am emotionally invested in the outcome of events over which I have no control.

Of course, most sports fans are keenly aware of this dynamic, even as we have trouble coming to grips with it. There is no more helpless feeling than watching your favorite football team line up to attempt a game-winning field goal knowing there is nothing you can do to ensure that the ball goes through the uprights. Indeed, our inability to fully accept this helplessness probably explains the elaborate game day rituals that many fans go through. We might not be able to block, tackle, or throw and catch the ball, but if we fly our team's flag and wear our favorite jersey and drink beer from our lucky mug, maybe, just maybe, the universe will respond to our yearning for victory. I doubt very many people really believe that these efforts have any effect on the outcome of games. But fully accepting that we are passive observers is just too difficult; we want to *do* something—anything—that might help our teams win. Recognizing that we are helpless in the face of this desire is, therefore, an important step in a fan's process of maturation.

From Fandom Back to "Real Life" (Or Why Your Kids Probably Aren't Better Than Other Kids)

Obviously, there is no guarantee that the lessons of fandom will translate to other parts of our lives. But let me conclude by noting a few ways in which fans might work to cultivate these kinds of connections. First, thinking of our love of sports teams along the lines I have suggested forces us to recognize that we do not love our teams because they are objectively superior to other teams and that, as a result, the attachments that other fans have to their teams are not to objects that are objectively inferior. A particularly egregious form of this is when fan bases carry on about how their teams "do things the right way" when rhapsodizing about the love they have for those teams. Implicit in this rhetoric is the conviction that their teams' commitment to "do things the right way" is the basis for such love, and that other teams are importantly lacking in this crucial measure.[30]

Now it may or may not be true that the teams these fans support "do things the right way," however one might want to measure such a trait. What is important for my purposes is the fact

58 Love 'em Like a Brother

that these teams "do things the right way" is not the basis for the attachments such fans have to those teams any more than the fact that my sister has a great sense of humor is a basis of my love for her. If most fans support the teams they support because they have inherited their parents' attachments or because they happen to live in the city where the team plays, then representing their attachments as resting on another basis is nothing but sanctimony: a way to morally criticize, and feel superior to, rival fans and teams.

Many of the negative aspects of group identification that concern some critics of fandom can, therefore, be minimized when we recognize (and even appreciate) the contingent nature of our attachments to teams. As a fan of the Packers, I might really dislike the Dallas Cowboys (as, indeed, I do). But I must also recognize that, had my dad grown up in Texas instead of Wisconsin, I might very well have been a Cowboys fan myself, and so there is no objective basis for animosity toward Cowboys fans. Put differently, my love for the Packers doesn't mean that there is anything deficient about the love that Cowboys fans have for their team.

In the same way, I think we can recognize that we do not love most of the people we love because they are somehow objectively superior to other people. If the tendency to indulge this fiction is rampant in sporting circles, it seems that it is equally prevalent in familial circles, particularly when it comes to parenting. The love that parents have for their children slides easily into a sense that our children are better than other kids in any number of ways: academically, athletically, morally, or artistically.[31] And while this tendency might simply be annoying to outsiders, it can also be corrosive in any number of ways.

For example, such beliefs can fail kids who grow up thinking they are better in all sorts of respects than they really are. When this fiction collides with reality, the results can be problematic. Seeing students and athletes regularly confront the fact that they are not as smart or athletic as they have been told has convinced me that they would be much better served by more accurate assessments of their abilities. Moreover, this tendency can also lead children to think that the love of parents rests on their parents' high estimation of their abilities. While I have no doubt that children need to think they have genuine strengths and weaknesses, the idea that the love of others rests on those strengths and weaknesses can be a recipe for insecurity and anxiety. Thus, one of the great struggles of parenting is to give children an utterly secure sense that they are loved *while also* helping them discover and develop their talents.

Fans who strive to recognize the nature of their attachment to their teams may, therefore, be able to cultivate habits for thinking about such attachments more generally, and perhaps clear-eyed reflection on the relationships we bear to our favorite teams can help us improve our relationships with loved ones and grapple with the vulnerability that is inherent in all such attachments. Alternatively, explicitly reflecting on the love that one has for particular persons can help fans to put the commitment they have to their favorite teams in proper perspective.

It is in this way that thinking about the love of teams as analogous to familial love can also help us reflect on the limits of what such love might require of us. One of the motivations that seems to drive purist accounts of fandom is that resolute partisans end up supporting teams that are not *worthy* of support—teams that conduct themselves in unsportsmanlike ways or who do not exemplify the highest ideals that sport has to offer. But if we reflect on the love we have for our family members, it should be clear that notions of desert in this context are somewhat out of place. I don't love the Green Bay Packers because they deserve my affection any more than I love my parents or my sister or my kids because *they* deserve it. As a result, my love is likely to persist even when the objects of that love do things of which I disapprove because desert was never the basis for my attachment in the first place. If such persistence is appropriate in the case of familial love (as it surely seems to be), then there is no reason to think it untoward when the object of one's love is a sports team.

However, to invoke this comparison is not to suggest that fans should support teams no matter what those teams do any more than a love of one's brother requires that one support him no matter what he does. Unfortunately, many of us have experiences with family members who do terrible things or who treat us (or themselves) in ways that make it unhealthy to continue in any kind of substantive relationship. Sometimes, the choice to cut off interactions is for the sake of one's own well-being; other times, it is because doing so is in the best interest of one's beloved. Think here of the addict who is consistently enabled by their family. At a certain point, no matter how much one loves such a person, continuing the relationship might not be good for any party involved.

In the same way, it is possible that the teams we love might behave in ways that make it unwise to continue our support. Perhaps they treat their fans in ways that are exploitative or start to exemplify traits that corrode fans' wider moral sensibilities. In such cases, a fan might very well be justified ending whatever relationship she has with the team: ceasing to watch games or refusing to buy tickets and team apparel. Determining exactly where to draw the line on such cases may be difficult, just as it can often be difficult to decide when to sever ties with family members. But drawing on the model of familial relationships might be able to help fans identify when remaining devoted to a team is no longer healthy. Love might justify commitment to deeply flawed entities— whether persons or sports teams. It doesn't necessarily require that we be committed to them no matter what.

Notes

1. Stephen Mumford, *Watching Sport: Aesthetics, Ethics and Emotion* (New York: Routledge, 2011), vii.
2. Mumford, *Watching Sport*, ix.
3. Mumford, *Watching Sport*, 10.
4. Mumford, *Watching Sport*, 18.
5. Mumford, *Watching Sport*, 18.
6. Raldolph Feezell, *Sports, Philosophy, and Good Lives* (Lincoln, NE: University of Nebraska Press, 2013), 91.
7. Nicholas Dixon, "In Praise of Partisanship," *Journal of the Philosophy of Sport* 43, no. 2 (May 2016): 236.
8. I am inclined to think my willingness to watch as much soccer as I do is explained by my interest in the game as a coach. When Spurs or the Crew are not playing, I mostly watch soccer as a student, trying to gain whatever tidbit of knowledge I might file away for future use with my players.
9. J. S. Russell, "The Ideal Fan or Good Fans?" *Sport, Ethics and Philosophy* 6, no. 1 (February 2012): 18.
10. Nicholas Dixon, "The Ethics of Supporting Sports Teams," *Journal of Applied Philosophy* 18, no. 2 (January 2001): 152.
11. For a discussion of the union account, see Bennett Helm, *Love, Friendship, and the Self* (Oxford: Oxford University Press, 2010), 13ff.
12. Russell, "Ideal Fan or Good Fans?" 19.
13. Russell, "Ideal Fan or Good Fans?" 19.
14. Russell, "Ideal Fan or Good Fans?" 20.
15. Dixon, "The Ethics of Supporting Sports Teams," 151.
16. Robert Nozick, *The Examined Life* (New York: Simon and Schuster, 1989), 82. Quoted in Dixon, "The Ethics of Supporting Sports Teams," 151 (with, as far as I can tell, an incorrect page reference).
17. I explore this dynamic more fully in "Irreplaceability and Identity," *Social Theory and Practice* 38, no. 1 (January 2012): 33–54.
18. Dixon, "The Ethics of Supporting Sports Teams," 152.
19. Nick Hornby, *Fever Pitch* (New York: Riverhead Books, 1998), 15.
20. Hornby, *Fever Pitch*, 21.
21. Warren St. John, *Rammer, Jammer, Yellow Hammer* (New York: Three Rivers Press, 2005), 2.
22. Harry Frankfurt, *The Reasons of Love* (Princeton, NJ: Princeton University Press, 2004), 39.
23. Frankfurt, *Reasons of Love*, 51.
24. Frankfurt, *Reasons of Love*, 51.
25. Frankfurt, *Reasons of Love*, 54.
26. Michael Sandel, "The Case Against Perfection," *The Atlantic*, April 2004, www.theatlantic.com/magazine/archive/2004/04/the-case-against-perfection/302927.

60 Love 'em Like a Brother

27. A profound reflection on what it means for parents to have children who are markedly different from them is Andrew Solomon's *Far from the Tree* (New York: Scribner, 2012).
28. Sandel, "The Case Against Perfection."
29. Hornby, *Fever Pitch*, 70.
30. At my father's strong urging, I have removed any reference to fan bases that are, in my estimation, particularly guilty of flying the "We Do Things the Right Way" banner. However, dear reader, if you and I ever share a beer, I'll be more than happy to offer some examples.
31. Interestingly, my anecdotal evidence would suggest a kind of inverse relationship in this regard. The better that a parent thinks their kid is, the worse they probably are—especially when it comes to morality and various personality traits. The need to think that our love rests on some objective basis can make us blind to all sorts of faults.

4
AVOIDING THE PITFALLS OF OBJECTIFICATION

On January 16, 2018, Washington State University quarterback Tyler Hilinski was found dead in his apartment, having suffered a self-inflicted gunshot wound to the head.[1] The outpouring of grief from teammates and coaches in the Washington State community was exactly what one would expect in the wake of such a tragedy, as the people who knew Hilinski attempted to process the loss of their friend. The anguish was gut wrenching on a human level, but not at all surprising. On Twitter, various tweets and retweets referencing the incident popped up in my feed, and I couldn't help but think of the impact of Hilinski's death on his teammates who would somehow have to carry on with football and classes. I found myself reflecting on the possibility that one of my students might contemplate a similar course of action—as some of them probably have—and hoping that they would be surrounded with enough institutional and relational support to save their life. And as a parent, I thought about the unimaginable pain of losing a child.[2]

These feelings were all fairly predictable—or at least I hope they would be for anyone with a modicum of human empathy. However, two additional thoughts occurred to me that were occasioned by comparatively recent developments in our sporting culture. The first was to wonder almost immediately whether the game of football had contributed to whatever psychological challenges led Hilinski to contemplate taking his own life. After all, the high-profile suicides of football players like Junior Seau and Dave Duerson, and their subsequent diagnosis of chronic traumatic encephalopathy (CTE), have raised serious questions about the health consequences of playing the game. We've long known that football can cause joint and muscle problems for players well after their playing days are over, and that anyone who steps onto a football field risks breaking a bone and perhaps even losing consciousness. What we are only beginning to appreciate are the effects of the game on football players' brains. Hilinski was much younger than Seau and Duerson and had, therefore, taken many fewer hits to the head. But maybe he was nevertheless just one more in a growing line of casualties the game has produced.[3]

The second thought was occasioned by a tweet (or, more precisely, a retweet) that surfaced in my feed. Two days after Hilinski's death, Justin Reid, then a Stanford University student and safety on the Cardinal football team who now plays in the NFL for the Houston Texans, wrote the following:

> Student-athletes and athletes in general are more than just your entertainment. We're people who go through anxiety, depression, and difficulties just like everybody else. Please remember that when you're tweeting at us like we're animals.[4]

DOI: 10.4324/9781003223696-5

I don't remember who retweeted the comment, because I don't follow Reid on Twitter. What I do remember is being immediately struck by the profundity of Reid's statement. Here was a player on a rival team[5] pleading with anyone who might listen to remember that athletes are people too. It was a simple remark, one that *should* go entirely without saying. And yet it clearly needed to be said, perhaps more than ever in light of Hilinski's sacrifice.

I will address questions about the ethics of watching football and other violent sports in the next chapter. What I want to discuss here is the more general phenomenon of objectification and the sometimes subtle ways in which fans objectify the athletes they claim to support. My discussion in the remainder of the chapter thus proceeds as follows. I first motivate the idea that the concept of objectification is useful for identifying some distinctive problems with the ways that fans relate to athletes—problems that may not show up when viewed thorough other conceptual lenses. I then locate this topic in the broader scholarly debate about objectification before turning to some specific applications of the analysis I develop. If Reid's tweet shows us anything, it is that the experience of feeling objectified may be more widespread among athletes than many of us think. Hopefully, the process of thinking through the particular forms that objectification might take in the realm of sports will enable fans to avoid some of its distinctive pitfalls.

The Significance of Objectification

Invoking the concept of objectification in the context of sports might seem odd, because it is a notion that seems to imply that the objectifier somehow diminishes the individual they objectify. Indeed, at least part of what concerns certain feminists about pornography is the way that the agency of women is reduced by men who view women simply in terms of their ability to satisfy their sexual urges. In a widely cited paper, Martha Nussbaum has thus suggested seven ways in which it seems possible to objectify something:

1. *Instrumentality*: one treats it as a tool of one's own purposes
2. *Denial of autonomy*: one treats it as lacking in autonomy and self-determination
3. *Inertness*: one treats it as lacking in agency and activity
4. *Fungibility*: one treats it as interchangeable (a) with other things of the same type, and/or (b) with things of other types
5. *Violability*: one treats it as lacking in boundary-integrity, as something that is permissible to break up, smash, break into
6. *Ownership*: one treats it as something that is owned by another, can be bought or sold, etc.
7. *Denial of subjectivity*: one treats it as something whose experience and feelings (if any) need not be taken into account.[6]

While Nussbaum does not regard this list as a set of necessary and/or sufficient conditions for objectification, what is important for my purposes is that each possible mode of objectification is a reduction of those who are being objectified. They are regarded only in terms of their ability to satisfy the desires of another. They are not unique in any particular way, can be easily exchanged for someone else who can serve the same function, and are not treated as though their thoughts or feelings about their predicament need to be taken seriously.

I think it is fairly easy to see how this dynamic can be at work in pornography as people are regarded solely in terms of their ability to provide sexual pleasure for others. It may be less clear how such a reduction can be at play in the world of sports. After all, most sports fans probably wanted to be high-profile athletes at one point in their lives. Every sports-loving man I know wanted to play professional baseball, basketball, or football in his childhood, and many of them continue to satisfy their desire for athletic competition on the golf course or weekly over-40 games of basketball or soccer. If anything, athletes would seem to be *inflated* in the estimation of fans rather than reduced. By contrast, I suspect that consumers of pornography rarely think wistfully of missed opportunities to pursue a career in the field. They may imaginatively project themselves into the sexual scenarios they are watching, but they probably aren't longing for a career in the pornographic industry (at least not if they are thinking clearly about what work in that industry involves).[7]

However, plenty of sports fans do want to experience what it would be like to get a key base hit in the World Series or score the decisive goal in a Champions League final. They wonder if they might have been able to achieve more athletic glory had they put in a bit more work and received a few more lucky breaks. I suspect that sports fans often wish they were high-profile athletes in ways that consumers of pornography don't really wish to be porn stars, and this can make it difficult to see how objectification is at issue when it comes to their engagement with sports. One can almost hear fans protesting, "How can I be objectifying them? I admire them—I want to *be* them—and you can't objectify someone whose life you would like to have."

While there are, no doubt, important differences between the relationship that sports fans have to athletes and the relationship that consumers of pornography have to workers in that medium, I don't think the mere fact that many fans would like to be high-profile athletes entails that they are incapable of objectifying the individual athletes they seem to admire. To begin with, wanting to have something that you do not, in fact, have can easily lead to feelings of jealousy or envy—neither of which tend to promote healthy attitudes toward their objects. The man who is jealous of his ex-girlfriend's new lover may not regard him as much of an individual at all, instead thinking of him almost solely as "the new guy." Indeed, such jealousy might lead to hatred and disdain, even as he wants to be in the position the new guy happens to occupy. In the same way, sports fans might be consumed with a jealousy unconstrained by admiration. Perhaps they think that particular athletes do not deserve to be where they are or are not making the most of the opportunities they have been given. Such fans might think that they would perform and behave much differently if they were in a similar position, and, as a result, might regard athletes with something bordering on contempt.

Moreover, fans can be exceedingly fickle in the ways they dole out their approval. When athletes are performing well and helping their teams win, fans will lavish them with affection, only to turn on them the moment things head south. Just ask Bill Buckner how quickly fans' attitudes toward players can change.[8] Thus, despite the love that fans have for their favorite teams (or perhaps because of it), it is clear that we cannot brush aside concerns about those very same fans having less than ideal attitudes toward players.

Fair enough, one might reply. But why think that *objectification* represents a particularly serious danger for fans? Why not worry that disdain, contempt, or simple hatred—emotions that are familiar and easily identifiable in the realm of sports—are the real problem?

Part of my reason for invoking the language of objectification is that I think there are fairly innocuous versions of these other feelings that fans experience on a regular basis. We often talk of "hating that guy" in reference to a player on a rival team and may very well be frustrated to the point of contempt with players on teams we support whose performances routinely make us want to gouge out our eyes with kitchen utensils. Often, these feelings are simply by-products of our emotional investment in the game and do not, I suspect, represent our considered views. Even as such feelings are intense in the moment, I think most fans can hold them at an ironic distance. For example, I remember numerous times in the late 1990s and early 2000s when I expressed my hatred for Randy Moss during his tenure with the Minnesota Vikings. But did I really *hate* Randy Moss? Of course not. I just hated how well he tended to play against the Packers and no doubt would have adored him had his jersey been green and gold instead of that hideous purple.

64 Avoiding the Pitfalls of Objectification

This is not to deny that feelings of hatred or contempt can manifest themselves in problematic ways. Overtaken by such emotions, fans may hurl unacceptable insults at players, whether in person or on social media. Anyone who has been to a high-profile sporting event knows that fans are capable of yelling some pretty remarkable things at players, both on the opposing team and their own. And scrolling through the social media accounts of athletes after a game—whether it is a win or a loss—can be a jarring experience. Feelings of hatred can certainly lead to vicious behavior. Nevertheless, I want to suggest that the notion of objectification better identifies what is problematic about these sorts of actions than does a simple appeal to negative emotions. On the one hand, invoking the concept thus helps us to distinguish innocuous expressions of hatred and contempt from those that are more troubling. (As a case in point, by employing the notion of objectification, we can see why it was not necessarily a big deal when I expressed my hatred of Randy Moss.) On the other hand, when we regard the objectification of athletes as something to avoid, we can see some of the more subtle and insidious consequences that such an attitude might have.

What Is Objectification?

As I've noted, the most common application of the concept of objectification is to the realm that tends to concern feminists who write about the phenomenon, namely, sex. Working through Nussbaum's list of the ways that it is possible to objectify something, it is fairly easy to see how women (in particular) might be objectified in everyday sexual encounters, media portrayals, and pornography. In being regarded simply as means to the sexual gratification of men, they can also be regarded as inert or lacking subjectivity. Men who are solely interested in their own desires might regard women as fungible in various ways as well—each just as good as another, provided they are able to adequately "do the job." And in pornographic contexts, to say nothing of the media more generally, women are frequently regarded as nothing but beautiful bodies. If they are sufficiently attractive to arouse men's sexual interest, there is really no need to be concerned about what they think or feel, or even to acknowledge that they think or feel anything at all.

While these examples of sexual objectification are likely to strike many of us as morally problematic, one of Nussbaum's more interesting claims is that we do not always wrong others by objectifying them. For example, she notes that treating someone "as lacking boundary integrity, may well be consistent with treating-as-autonomous, and it is a prominent claim of defenders of consensual sado-masochism, for example lesbian and gay writers Gayle Rubin and Richard Mohr, that this is so."[9] Similarly, she argues that "the kind of apparent fungibility that is involved with identifying persons with parts of their bodies need not be dehumanizing at all, but can coexist with an intense regard for a person's individuality."[10] In these and other ways, Nussbaum thinks that certain aspects of objectification can be "either necessary or even wonderful features of sexual life."[11]

Lina Papadaki has recently argued that this implication of Nussbaum's view is problematic because it renders the category of objectification unreasonably broad, and her primary concern along these lines is that it is a mistake to embrace a "distinction between benign and negative objectification."[12] For Papadaki, cases of the sort that Nussbaum describes as innocuous or positive objectification do not, in fact, deserve the label at all because they are not really cases in which the autonomy and subjectivity of others is denied. She writes:

> We treat objects as not having any autonomy or subjectivity whatsoever. We do not treat objects as lacking in autonomy and subjectivity the one moment, and then go on treating them as autonomous subjects the rest of the time. Furthermore, since objects clearly do not have humanity, we do not at any time acknowledge, respect or try to promote their humanity. Doing so would be absurd, and even problematic.[13]

Thus, for Papadaki, the idea that objectification could occur in a context where the autonomy and subjectivity of another is deeply respected is contradictory. If one's autonomy and subjectivity are being respected, then one is not being objectified, no matter what things might look like to an external observer.

Papadaki's counter-proposal is to accept the basic structure of Nussbaum's account but to suggest that a particular way of treating another person as an object only counts as an instance of objectification if that treatment also denies an individual's humanity. In this way, it does not count as objectification to treat someone as fungible, provided that an attribution of fungibility does not also deny that person's humanity. Similarly for instrumentality, inertness, and the rest of the items on Nussbaum's list.[14]

Papadaki is not overly expansive on what constitutes an individual's humanity, referring to it in different places as one's "autonomy and subjectivity" and one's "rational capacities."[15] Nevertheless, the examples she offers as clear instances of objectification seem to highlight the significance of being able to direct one's own course of life (i.e., autonomy) and the importance of simply having thoughts and feelings (i.e., subjectivity). Thus, as a supposedly illustrative example, she offers a case of paternalism in which a man locks his friend in her room to keep her from going ice-climbing, and notes that "the paternalistic friend has not fully acknowledged his friend's rational capacities; he has not respected her humanity."[16] This, it seems to me, is clearly a case of autonomy denial. But when she notes that a man might objectify his wife in not taking account of her thoughts and feelings because he was "brought up to think that women are too emotional to think rationally," it seems that she is instead pointing to a denial of subjectivity.[17]

I am inclined to agree with Papadaki (and thus to disagree with Nussbaum) that the notion of objectification is inherently negative. To my ears, it sounds odd to speak of innocuous instances of objectification, and I think that if one's autonomy and subjectivity are being respected, then any apparent objectification is only pseudo-objectification. Thus, where Nussbaum sees benign or even positive instances of objectification, I would argue that the object-like treatment in question does not really qualify as bona fide objectification precisely because it is not morally objectionable; the autonomy and subjectivity of another person are being respected and, hence, they are not being wronged. It may be that we sometimes want to be treated in ways that are ordinarily regarded as inappropriate, but the fact that we want to be treated in such ways makes an important difference and, in my view, rules them out as instances of objectification.

At a certain point, this dispute is probably a linguistic one about the appropriate use of the term "objectification," and as such, it may not be entirely resolvable. That said, Papadaki's counter-proposal does not appear to solve the problem that she identifies in Nussbaum's account, namely, the undue expansion of the category of objectification. For in arguing that to objectify someone is to deny a person's humanity, Papadaki may be committed to the view that *all* instances of wronging another individual are instances of objectification. After all, it is not wholly implausible to think that all cases of wronging someone are such precisely because they constitute denials of that person's humanity. And if that is the case, then what Papadaki is offering is not really an account of objectification as much as it is an account of all moral wrongness.

I think this feature of her account shows itself in the examples I have already mentioned. Thus, locking one's friend in a room to prevent them from doing something that might cause them harm may very well be an instance of wrongness, and it may be wrong because the friend's autonomy has been denied. But is it thereby an instance of objectification? The friend would be right to complain that they had been denied the ability to make their own choices. However, if they also complained that they had been objectified, I think we would take them as registering a different sort of complaint. In that case, we would characteristically want to know what *else* had been done to them in addition to having their ability to make their own choices taken from them.

66 Avoiding the Pitfalls of Objectification

Similarly with the husband who thinks his wife is too emotional to make rational choices. Such a stance is, no doubt, condescending. Nevertheless, I suspect that the wife's typical complaint in that context would not be that she has been objectified, or even that she had been treated like an object. Rather, I take it that the more common reaction would be that she has been treated like a *child*. This, again, may very well be grounds for thinking that the husband has wronged his wife, because she is not, in fact, a child. But the specific complaint of objectification does not seem to be especially on point. Objectification has been extended to instances of wronging that seem more adequately and illuminatingly explained in other terms.

Rae Langton has put forward her own proposal regarding objectification, which seems to overcome some of the problems latent in both Papadaki and Nussbaum's views. Responding directly to Nussbaum, Langton thus asks whether there might be "aspects of the idea of an 'object' that are relevant to feminist thinking, but absent from Nussbaum's proposal" and proceeds to suggest three possibilities:

8. *Reduction to body*: one treats it as identified with its body or body parts
9. *Reduction to appearance*: one treats it primarily in terms of how it looks, or how it appears to the senses
10. *Silencing*: one treats it as silent, lacking the capacity to speak.[18]

According to Langton:

> [T]he relevant idea of an "object" turns out to be of something lacking in subjectivity and autonomy, something inert, something that is an appropriate candidate for using as a tool, exchange, destruction, possession, all as Nussbaum suggested; and in addition it is something that is *silent*, something that is just an *appearance*, just a *body*.[19]

What seems to unify these particular facets of objectification is that they highlight the ways in which our interactions with other human beings might focus on certain of their characteristics to the exclusion of others. As Carolyn McLeod puts it when discussing her own experience of being objectified as a teenager, "They treated me as if a part of me could represent me, which is one element of objectification," and it is this kind of reduction that Langton points to as the essence of objectification.[20]

Moreover, Langton's emphasis on individuals' bodies—in both their appearance and their capacities to perform certain tasks—helps to distinguish the kind of wrong at stake in objectification from other ways in which it is possible for one human being to wrong another. In this view, objectification is problematic not simply because it focuses on the bodies of others; it is problematic because the objectifier focuses on the bodies of others to the exclusion of their subjectivity. As Langton puts it:

> We can do things with people in just the same way that we do things with flour and chocolate, when making a cake; or do things with rocks, when building a house. We can think of people as human resources.[21]

Problems thus arise when we ignore the fact that human beings are parts of the physical world *that also have a point of view on that world*—that they are capable of having preferences, forming plans, and expressing opinions. And when our interactions with others fail to take sufficient account of these capacities, things have gone awry in a specific way: one individual has objectified another.

Nussbaum and Papadaki might agree with much of this. After all, Nussbaum includes a denial of autonomy and subjectivity on her original list, and Papadaki might contend that denying that others have a point of view on the world is what it is to deny their humanity. Nevertheless, in appealing to the significance of bodies and appearance in conjunction with silencing, I think Langton rightfully highlights that objectifying others centrally involves viewing them with a certain kind of detachment. If I reduce someone to their appearance, it will not matter to me at all what they think about their place in the world. I might simply regard them as a visual specimen whose only value lies in the aesthetic experience they are able to offer me.

Similarly for the possibility of reducing someone to their body. This kind of reduction might overlap with a reduction to appearance, insofar as it seems possible to be only concerned with another's body in terms of how that body looks. But one might also be concerned solely with what that body is able to do. Sometimes, those functional capacities will benefit me directly, and the sexual contexts that most concern feminists in discussions of objectification can clearly fall into this category. One might, therefore, objectify someone by being concerned only with the ability of that person's body to satisfy one's sexual appetites. However, the reduction of someone to their bodily capacities does not require that those capacities benefit one quite so directly. In this way, a business owner might relate to their employees simply in terms of their ability to lift a particular amount of weight and move objects from point A to point B. Surveying a warehouse floor, they might evaluate the workers' abilities at a distance, entirely uninterested in what they look like or what they happen to think about their predicament. In so doing, I think it is plausible to conclude that they are objectifying their employees.

The Objectification of Athletes

I thus contend that it is some combination of the reduction to appearance and reduction to body, taken together with a commitment to silencing, that most plausibly characterizes objectification. And in the context of sports, it seems that Langton's particular focus provides valuable resources for understanding some of the ways that athletes can be objectified. For example, female athletes are often appreciated for their appearance rather than their athletic prowess. Such women may very well be playing their respective sports autonomously and observers may be genuinely horrified at the prospect of women being forced to engage in athletic activity (or any other activity, for that matter) against their will. Nevertheless, the objectifier isn't particularly interested in the various ways that female athletes—at least the female athletes he is watching at the moment—might exercise that autonomy. He just wants them to look nice.

This sort of objectification is very much of a piece with the objectification of women in other lines of work. Rather than being evaluated or esteemed because of their ability to do their jobs well, they are regarded in terms of their ability to look pleasing in the eyes of others, primarily men. Anna Kournikova becomes the most famous woman tennis player in the world, not because of her phenomenal success on the court—success that didn't quite correlate with her level of fame—but rather because of her sex appeal and her corresponding status as the most searched for woman on the internet. And men may be happy to watch beach volleyball players compete in bikinis or converse about the physical appearance of the starting lineup of the USWNT, even as they cannot begin to analyze the performance of the players on the field (perhaps because they have never really watched the team play).

But this script can also be flipped in the context of sports, not because fans ignore the on-field performance of athletes but rather because they focus on that performance to the exclusion of everything else. The reductive approach to women that has often focused on their appearance or sexual function can equally attach to an individual's physical prowess on the field of play. The

68 Avoiding the Pitfalls of Objectification

specific characteristic or capacity that is being targeted may be different. But to the degree that one thinks that such prowess is all that matters about an individual—and to the degree that fans look to silence athletes and marginalize their subjectivity—then it would seem that one has engaged in objectification.

Examples of such an attitude are not overly difficult to find. Consider as a central ease, the way that fans often respond to athletes who speak out on controversial social issues. During the 2016 NFL season, San Francisco 49ers quarterback Colin Kaepernick chose to kneel during pre-game renditions of the national anthem in protest of incidents of police brutality against black Americans.[22] While Kaepernick drew support for this protest from some quarters, he was also greeted with more than his share of criticism. Some simply disagreed with the substance of his views, arguing that his allegations of racial oppression were not well-founded.[23] Others took a more comprehensive stance against his actions and urged Kaepernick, and all other athletes, to "stick to sports."[24]

Such an attitude does not seem to be confined to the United States. When former Liverpool striker Stan Collymore (who now works as a soccer analyst on television) expressed his support for the Labour Party in advance of a 2019 election, he received the following response on Twitter from the Shrewsbury & Atcham Conservative Association:

> DEAR LUVVIES
> INC. ACTORS, SINGERS, TV CHEFS
> SPORTS PRESENTERS/CRISP SALESMEN
>
> WE SPEND OUR HARD EARNED CASH
> TO LISTEN TO YOUR MUSIC AND TO
> WATCH YOU DRESS UP AND PRETEND
> TO BE SOMEONE ELSE IN FILMS AND ON TV.
>
> YOUR JOB IS TO TAKE US AWAY
> FROM REALITY AND ENTERTAIN US.
>
> YOUR PERSONAL OPINION
> MEANS NOTHING TO US.
>
> YOU ARE SIGNIFICANT AND INFLUENTIAL
> ONLY IN YOUR OWN MIND.
> TO THE REST OF US, YOU ARE
> NOTHING MORE THAN A PUPPET.
>
> SING. ACT. COOK.
> MAKE CRISP ADS.
>
> SHUT UP![25]

Collymore is here being told to confine his expressions to a limited array of topics—to shut up and do only that which the audience finds acceptably entertaining. That Collymore is being called out here in his capacity as a TV personality (even as he is lumped together with actors, singers, and TV chefs) does nothing to undermine the point. After all, can we imagine the Shrewsbury & Atcham Conservative Association criticizing a former footballer in this way, but responding any differently were England football captain Harry Kane to express similar opinions?

The "stick to sports" position is, then, a straightforward attempt to silence athletes. Coercion is not at issue, because no one is forcibly preventing them from speaking. Indeed, one might urge athletes to stick to sports while vigorously asserting that they have a *right* to speak their mind. Nevertheless, even though expressing the desire for someone not to speak has no power to guarantee the desired silence, I think it constitutes an important kind of objectification. After all, the motivation for such a view seems to be a belief that the real job of an athlete is to excel in their particular sport, not opine about political or social matters—to just shut up and perform on the field. And implicit in this attitude is a reduction of athletes to their physical capabilities. The right of athletes to speak may officially be acknowledged, but one's interest in them really only concerns their ability to perform. It is the athletic equivalent of a man telling a woman to just stand there and look pretty, which, as a reduction to appearance, seems to be a paradigm case of objectification. In this case, even though the objectifier wants athletes to just shut up and play (and may not really care at all what they look like), the core features of objectification are still present.

Nor does money fundamentally change this dynamic. It may be true that a handful of professional athletes are exceptionally well-compensated for their work. Nevertheless, even if we confine our attention to the most highly paid athletes and leave aside the many players who have short careers with salaries at the league minimum, it doesn't follow that highly paid athletes cannot be objectified. If highly compensated porn actresses can be objectified, as certainly seems possible, then there is no reason why athletes cannot be objectified despite their high salaries. The level of compensation may change the willingness of some individuals to subject themselves to objectification, but money does not, by itself, do anything to eliminate the phenomenon.

Indeed, there is a counterintuitive way in which the fact that some athletes are well compensated may exacerbate the tendency to objectify them. For example, one might appeal to the high salary of a particular athlete as justification for a particular view of that athlete's off the field behavior. After all, if one is getting paid to perform on the field—and getting paid more in one season than most people earn in a lifetime—then one should be solely devoted to that task. Any other interest, pursuit, or relationship should be pushed into the background, and highly paid athletes who give the slightest appearance of letting their off-field lives interfere with their on-field performance can come in for especially harsh scrutiny. In this way, an athlete's wealth can easily become a justification for viewing him as nothing but a body—a body that is being paid a lot of money to perform.[26]

Moreover, confining one's attention to the fact that some athletes are well-compensated can make it easier to ignore the significant costs that certain sports impose on those who play them. It is one thing to witness an individual enduring significant physical punishment against his will. Most reasonably empathetic people would be rightly troubled by this scenario, and the willingness of certain athletes to endure similar trials can, therefore, assuage some of our moral concerns on the grounds that at least no coercion is taking place.

However, this lack of moral concern can easily slide into a lack of appreciation for the punishment or costs in question. In this way, the thought that the physical punishment being witnessed is not morally problematic can quickly become the thought that such punishment doesn't really matter. After all, those enduring it are doing so willingly and are being well paid. Following this train of thought, wealthy autonomous athletes who are voluntarily choosing to subject themselves to a large amount of physical suffering become the wealthy bodies that are being paid to perform—bodies whose pain does not register with fans precisely because they can be dismissed with the observation that they are well-paid bodies that could have done otherwise. Thus, even if we leave aside questions about whether the pursuit of monetary rewards can undermine the autonomy of individuals who are in difficult financial circumstances by pressuring them into doing

70 Avoiding the Pitfalls of Objectification

things they would not otherwise do, it does not seem that paying athletes a lot of money eliminates the possibility of objectifying those same athletes.

The Downstream Effects of Objectifying Athletes

Reacting to athletes who are speaking out on controversial issues and demanding, in various ways, that they keep quiet constitutes an instance of objectification that is explicitly public. Fans who respond in this way are overtly indicating that they only care about athletes' performance on the field. As I argued in Chapter 2, an exploration of the limits of the human body is central to our interest in sports, and so there is certainly nothing problematic if the capacities of athletes' bodies are primarily why we are interested in them. Nevertheless, regarding athletes solely in terms of their physical capacities—and thereby reducing them to those capacities—is problematic for at least two reasons.

First, when we objectify others, we cut ourselves off from a fuller picture of them as individuals and thereby miss out on an appreciation of the various forms that a pursuit of the good life can take. Indeed, reducing individuals to any single capacity or characteristic makes it impossible to regard those individuals as pursuing the good life at all, because it is not capacities or characteristics that live good lives but rather human beings who have many different capacities and characteristics. If part of the value of sports is that we are able to benefit from athletes' experiments in living, objectifying athletes leaves us with little justification for our fandom: such an outlook deprives us of the very thing that makes the time we spend watching sports worthwhile.

Second, the tendency to objectify high-profile athletes can affect the way we relate to athletes with whom we are more directly related, particularly children. The concern here is one that feminists have often made about pornography, namely, that the objectification of women in pornography affects the view that men have toward women *in general*. As such, the tendency to objectify women they will never meet leads men to objectify women they will meet, and it is in these interactions where the real problems lie. Men who objectify women in general may, therefore, be inclined to treat them simply as sexually arousing aesthetic objects or possible tools for their own sexual gratification. In this way, they may be inclined to disregard their other talents and abilities in academic and professional contexts, to say nothing of friendships, family life, and everyday interactions with strangers.

Applying these concerns to the realm of sports, one might worry that objectifying people we are watching on television will lead to the objectification of people we meet in real life. And because we may be inclined to treat individuals differently when we objectify them, the objectification of people we will never meet can thereby lead to the improper treatment of those with whom we do come into contact. In this way, it is not the objectification of high-profile athletes that is primarily at issue. Rather, it is the effect that such objectification has on the encounters we have with people we see every day that is troubling.

I find this argument fairly compelling in the case of pornography, and while it may initially seem difficult to identify similar features of our relationships to athletes, there are more parallels between these cases than we might initially assume. In particular, I think the effect that the objectification of high-profile athletes can have on youth sports should be enough to spur reflection on the ways we view athletes more generally.[27] (And if this sounds like a precious plea to "do it for the children," I'll happily admit to the charge.)

As someone who has been around youth sports for years as a player, parent, and coach, I could write volumes on the problems that infect this part of our sporting culture (and I might very well do that some day). However, if I were to summarize all of these problems and identify their underlying source, it is that far too many adults treat kids like they are professional athletes. Because so many sports parents are also fans, they often approach youth events much as they do the college and professional games they watch. And as a result, any tendency that adults have to objectify high-profile athletes can certainly infect the ways they relate to the children they cart to practice every Wednesday and watch in games on the weekend.

This objectifying attitude toward children can manifest itself in many ways. It can lead to an inordinate emphasis on results, as fans whose happiness depends on whether their favorite football team is winning can view a youth recreational league basketball game in similar terms. It can lead parents to view their children's bodies as performance machines that operate in abstraction from all the other academic, leisure, and social pursuits in which children like to engage. And it can lead adults to reduce their children's value to their athletic performance, just as fans often regard players simply in terms of what they are able to accomplish on the field.

If these sorts of attitudes are problematic when directed at the athletes we watch perform on television and in sold-out stadiums, they are doubly so when applied to children. Youth sports should be, above everything else, a venue for kids to explore the capacities and limits of the human body *in the broader context of their pursuit of the good life*. The last thing they need is to have the expectations of others foisted upon them or to be treated like the adults they have yet to become. They must be allowed to engage in their own experiments in living and not be used as guinea pigs in the experiments of others. Adults in all sorts of roles—parents, teachers, coaches, and administrators—should, of course, guide and encourage kids who have the desire and ability to work at improving their athletic abilities. But this guidance should always keep the full humanity of these children firmly in view.

To the degree that the objectification of high-profile athletes feeds these sorts of problems, it would seem that fans have good reason to be careful about the ways in which they view all athletes and to avoid the pitfalls of objectification in all its guises. I think the primary way for fans to accomplish this is to continually remind ourselves that athletes are not simply bodies that perform for our benefit; they are individual human beings whose efforts in the competitive arena are but one part of their broader pursuit of the good life. Or, if that formulation is not quite catchy enough, I might suggest the following slogan: athletes are people too. Their lives are not ours to manipulate, and they don't owe any particular allegiance to our agendas. How they choose to balance their athletic pursuits with everything else they might care about in life is, ultimately, up to them. And while we may be right to think that some athletes squander their talent or otherwise make choices that undermine their well-being, we should recognize that their lives are the ones most affected by these decisions, not ours.

Some Less Obvious Forms of Objectification

If the response that fans have to athletes who speak out on controversial social issues is one clear example of objectification, there are other genres of fan behavior that also fuel (or are fueled by) an objectifying attitude. For example, I think the popularity of fantasy sports has made it easier for fans to think that they have a certain kind of ownership of athletes—that athletes' primary value is in their fantasy point production rather than whether they help their (actual) teams to win or exercise any other sort of excellence on or off the field. The very act of drafting players, trading them, and evaluating them solely based on their stat line can lead one to forget that there are real people behind the names on one's fantasy roster. Thus, when former NFL tight end Martellus Bennett said on Twitter, "I'd much rather have fans of Martellus Bennett the man than Martellus Bennett the TE," I think we can read him as expressing a desire to be regarded as a human being rather than a stat machine.[28]

More traditional forms of gambling can also lead fans to be concerned with athletes only insofar as they are able to help them win money. The anger I have heard expressed at players whose

72 Avoiding the Pitfalls of Objectification

performance means that a team fails to cover the spread—even if that team wins the game—sometimes reflects the idea that a player's job is to help a bet deliver. Gamblers obviously know that this is not, strictly speaking, true. Nevertheless, it seems that viewing sports through a gambling lens has the potential to significantly change the way that athletes are regarded.

My point is not that gambling is necessarily bad, or that fantasy sports are inherently corrupting. I gave up fantasy football several years ago, not because of any moral qualms about objectification, but rather because it changed the way I watched real football. I would find myself conflicted about what I wanted to happen on the field: one set of desires motivated by fantasy considerations and one set motivated by my partisan rooting interests. Rather than simply try to live with the conflict, or manage my fantasy team with an eye to avoiding all such problems (which is nearly impossible, if you want to be at all successful), I just dropped fantasy football and have never regretted it. Similarly for gambling. I'm not very good at separating what I want to happen from what I think will happen, which is very bad for a gambler. So I just don't bet on games. Problem solved. However, these aren't particularly moral justifications, and while I have registered my concerns about the degree to which fantasy sports and gambling might promote the objectification of athletes, I leave open the possibility that some fans are able to manage their attitudes successfully.

Moreover, fans don't have to gamble or play fantasy sports in order to succumb to objectifying attitudes. Plenty of the trappings of run of the mill partisan fandom also create some of the pitfalls of objectification. I have already discussed at various points how fans can regard the successes and failures of their favorite teams as their own successes and failures. This kind of emotional investment can make fans feel like they are the primary beneficiaries and victims of results on the field. In these scenarios, the athletes as individuals may drop out of the equation as they are regarded simply for their ability to secure wins that benefit the fans, rather than perform in ways that fit in with an athlete's broader pursuit of the good life.

It is also true that some of the language that fans and media use when talking about players has the distinct ring of objectification about it. If drafting and trading players in fantasy sports allows fans to think of athletes as commodities, endlessly breaking down possible trades and drafting possibilities for the teams one supports can probably have a similar effect. I think the language of world soccer is even worse in this regard with its explicit (and seemingly endless) discussion of which players teams need to buy and sell. If the treatment of players as mere assets always lies below the surface, this kind of talk makes it explicit in a way that should be somewhat disconcerting, at least if we want to avoid the pitfalls of objectification.

Language that refers to players as property is all the more disconcerting when predominantly white fan bases and management teams are discussing players of color. Particularly in the United States, where the legacy of slavery continues to structure many of our social interactions and justice for ethnic minorities is much more aspiration than reality, the idea that human beings can be bought and sold for the services they are able to provide should, at an absolute minimum, make us uncomfortable.[29] And though I don't have any data to support this contention, it strikes me that the reaction that fans have to black players who want to speak out on controversial issues is often different than the reaction they have to white players who want to make similar kinds of statements. Perhaps because players of color may be inclined to address issues that draw the public's attention to racial injustice, and thereby challenge entrenched white supremacy—it seems that black players in particular are expected to just shut up and play. They force white fans to look in the mirror and evaluate what they see. It is far easier to simply zone out and enjoy the game than to be bothered with such discomfiting thoughts.

As I have argued, the fact that fans may go on to cheer wildly for players does not undermine the possibility of objectification, and just because you cheer for a black player on your favorite team doesn't rule out the possibility of objectifying that player any more than it rules out the possibility of being racist. It is in this connection that Erin Tarver has written insightfully about the phenomenon of mascotting:

> To treat an athlete as a mascot is to relate to him or her as an instrument for one's own benefit as a sports fan and thus as an object existing primarily to serve the ends of the constitution and reproduction of one's own social identity. . . . [M]ascots are viewed and treated as one-dimensional entities, not full persons with desires, goals, or aspirations beyond those that are part of their given role; they are, moreover, required to be nonthreatening and to exist for the benefit or amusement of the mascotting person or group—to be, in other words, like a pet.[30]

Tarver points out that the mascotting relationship allows fans to ostensibly support athletes even as that support is confined to a rather narrow sphere. For example, white baseball fans may, therefore, embrace "Latino players to the extent that they help their teams win, but it is far from clear that the same fans treat these players as representatives of their communities or as anything other than mascots."[31] And through the medium of a Gatorade ad starring Michael Jordan, white "audiences are able to fantasize about occupying a space they would not likely inhabit in real life—an inner-city basketball court with a black man who can leap several feet at a standstill."[32]

As with other instances of objectification, the mascotting relationship may be problematic in its own right. But what I think Tarver points to is the fact that objectifying athletes in this particular way allows fans to engage in a form that is all the more corrosive because of its self-deceptive character, and white fans who profess their love for athletes of color even as they persist in objectifying those same athletes risk exacerbating racism rather than combating it. "I can't be racist," they might think to themselves. "Donald Driver is my favorite Green Bay Packer of all time!" Taking such support as an indication of their enlightened views on race, it can be easier for fans to ignore their own biases and prejudices and all of the ways they continue to deny others the full value of their humanity. One who appreciates an athlete solely for what they are able to provide with their athletic ability has not moved far beyond the mindset of the slave owner who appreciates the labor that his slaves are able to provide. And celebrating the athletic accomplishments of those you would never have over for dinner does not make you a champion of racial equality.

This danger is clearly illustrated in a scene in Warren St. John's *Rammer, Jammer, Yellow Hammer*. Alabama football fans, who have just witnessed a Crimson Tide victory in which any number of black players have played a crucial role, are watching highlights on ESPN when news breaks of a potential scandal involving Alabama wide receiver Shamari Buchanan. The allegation is that a state trooper has been fixing speeding tickets for various Alabama players and that Buchanan may have benefitted from the scheme. The transgression could pose legal problems for Buchanan and the state trooper, but the more pressing concern is that it might threaten Buchanan's athletic eligibility. St. John then relates the following exchange:

> "It's the stupid niggers," a woman snarls.
> *What?*
> "Stupid niggers are always getting us into trouble."
> Silence, then:
> "She's got a point," a man at her side says. "Them niggers always doin' sumpin' stupid."[33]

The free use of such racist language is likely startling to many readers, but one suspects that many other fans respond with equally troubling thoughts that they keep to themselves. To the degree that cheering for racially integrated teams from the stands allows them to paper over such impulses

74 Avoiding the Pitfalls of Objectification

in their minds, we might question whether they have made the problem worse by making it more difficult to identify.

As I hope is clear, none of this precludes the objectification of white athletes. Fans can reduce their value to the ability of their bodies to perform no less than athletes of color, and we may care as little for what Aaron Rodgers has to say about social justice as we do Colin Kaepernick's thoughts on the subject. Nevertheless, in a world that continues to struggle with racism, it is worth asking whether our tendency to objectify athletes is itself tinged with the prejudice to which we believe ourselves immune.

What Do Athletes Owe to Fans?

Let me conclude by considering one objection to the concerns about objectification that I have raised. One might grant the possibility of objectifying athletes along the lines I have suggested but nevertheless think that athletes on the competitive stage owe fans something more substantial than I have allowed thus far. Yes. Their lives are theirs to live. But the fact that fans give up time and money to watch them play imposes an obligation on athletes to live up to certain standards of performance or, at the very least, to try their best to live up to those standards. They can lead their lives as they see fit, but having chosen to devote part of those lives to competitive athletics, fans have a right to expect certain things of them.

This objection is fine, as far as it goes, because it really amounts to nothing more than the claim that certain jobs have certain requirements. Firefighters can do whatever they want with their lives, but if they are going to be firefighters, they have to be willing and able to fight fires when called upon. That is simply what it is to be a firefighter, and individuals who do not want to be required to fight fires when called upon should pursue a different line of work. By the same token, my pursuit of the good life can take any variety of different forms, but given that I have opted for a career as a philosophy professor, I can't rightfully claim that I shouldn't have to teach classes because doing so conflicts with my right to live my life as I please. If I don't want to teach classes, that's fine; I just shouldn't be a philosophy professor.

I take it that some complaints of athletes can be characterized in a similar way. A professional basketball player whose body is exhausted from a long competitive season may very well not feel like playing on a given night (in much the same way that I might not feel like teaching class on a given morning). But it would be a mistake for them to claim that they have no obligation to play in the game because it is their life to lead in whatever way they choose. That may be a good reason for even the most talented basketball player in the world to decline to pursue a career as a professional athlete. It is not, however, a very good reason for those who have chosen to be professional athletes to decline to play in a game. Playing games, after all, is their job.

It is, however, a mistake—and, I contend, a serious one—to think that this obligation is imposed entirely by a fan's investment in the proceedings and that fans thereby have a special claim on an athlete's abilities. Athletes might take on certain responsibilities when they step into the competitive arena. But there is no reason to think that they give themselves over entirely to the desires, whims, opinions, and judgments of fans. I owe my students well-prepared lessons, engagement during classes, assignments that are graded in a fair and timely fashion, and (probably) some measure of enthusiasm for the subjects I teach. However, I do not owe them my undivided attention 24 hours a day, seven days a week. They have no say in what I do in my family life: how I choose to raise my children, what we do on our summer vacations, or where I take my wife to dinner for her birthday. They have a right to express their concerns about my teaching to me and those in my university's administration. But they certainly do not have a right—in the sense of a moral right—to lambast me on social media or call me terrible names because they do not think I am good at my job. Their tuition dollars make it entirely legitimate for students to have certain expectations of their instructors, and yet those expectations have clearly justifiable limits. Any student who thinks their opinion about what a professor does in his free time should carry any weight at all has made an error in judgment.

In the same way, fan investment in the teams they support may give them a right to expect that athletes are putting forth effort in competition and off the field in preparation for that competition. In exchange for that effort, it seems to me that they probably have a right to express both their pleasure and disappointment in the results that teams are able to secure. This is, roughly, the fan's analogue to a student's course evaluation. If fans like what is going on, they can cheer; if they don't, they can boo. And performance can justify either continuing to support the team or deciding to spend one's time doing something else. If you don't like a professor's class, you don't have to take another one.

It seems to me that fans who go much beyond these basic expressions of commitment have fallen into the grips of an objectifying attitude, one that leads them to think they have the kind of rights that one might have over a body whose job was merely to perform to the fan's own satisfaction. Nor does a legitimate interest in the lives of athletes off the field (of the sort I discussed in Chapter 2) entail that fans can exercise any legitimate control over those lives. We may benefit in all sorts of ways from others' experiments in living, but we do not get to determine how those experiments are run.

Perhaps, then, it is largely as a result of objectification that fans engage in abusive behavior toward athletes, both in person and on social media. Objectification is what leads fans to opine confidently about what athletes do in their private lives, as though the price of their ticket bestows control over the entirety of an athlete's existence. And it is the commitment to silence the people they objectify that makes fans think that athletes should really just shut up and play. If we are troubled by an objectifying attitude toward people generally, then we should be equally troubled by it in the context of sports.

Notes

1. Kyle Bonagura, "Police: Washington State QB Tyler Hilinski Found Dead in Apparent Suicide," *ESPN. com*, January 17, 2018, www.espn.com/college-football/story/_/id/22125232/washington-state-qb-tyler-hilinski-found-dead-apparent-suicide-police-say.
2. Greg Bishop, "A College QB's Suicide. A Family's Search for Answers," *Si.com*, June 26, 2018, www. si.com/college-football/2018/06/26/tyler-hilinski-suicide-washington-state-qb-cte.
3. Hilinski was eventually diagnosed with CTE, though because our understanding of the relationship between CTE and depression continues to evolve, we should be cautious in attributing a direct link between football and his suicide.
4. Justin Reid (@jreid_viii), "Student-athletes and Athletes in General Are More than Just Your Entertainment," *Twitter*, January 18, 2018, https://twitter.com/jreid_viii/status/954055280312033280 (at last check, Reid's Twitter account had been deleted).
5. Washington State and Stanford both play in the north division of the PAC 12 Conference.
6. Martha C. Nussbaum, "Objectification," *Philosophy & Public Affairs* 24, no. 4 (Autumn, 1995): 257.
7. My point here is not necessarily that entire pornographic industry requires that its workers endure horrific workplace conditions (though I have no doubt that is a problem in many cases). Nor is it to deny that some performers very much like their jobs. Rather, my point is the much more mundane one that working in porn is a job much like every other jobs, and that those who glamorize it from the outside are probably distorting what the work actually involves. See, for example Aurora Snow, "This Is What It's Really Like to Work in Porn," *Fortune*, February 5, 2016, https://fortune.com/2016/02/05/this-is-what-its-really-like-to-work-in-porn.
   One further clarification. Whether all pornography is objectifying is a question I leave aside, as is the question of whether pornography is ethically problematic only to the degree that it promotes or engages in objectification. Thus, I don't intend to take a stand here on whether pornography is, all things considered, ethically permissible or whether the production and consumption of pornography can be part

76 Avoiding the Pitfalls of Objectification

of flourishing human lives. The view I present only commits me to the much more modest claim that pornography is ethically problematic to the degree that it promotes objectification.

8. For readers unfamiliar with the history of baseball, Bill Buckner was the Boston Red Sox first baseman whose error in the 1986 World Series likely cost the Red Sox the championship. A well-liked player before the incident, fans directed vicious anger toward him in the years that followed. As it happens, Buckner died while I was working on this book. For an informative obituary, see Daniel E. Slotnik, "Bill Buckner, All-Star Shadowed by World Series Error, Dies at 69," *The New York Times*, May 27, 2019, www.nytimes.com/2019/05/27/obituaries/bill-buckner-all-star-shadowed-by-world-series-error-dies-at-69.html.

9. Nussbaum, "Objectification," 261. In support of this claim, Nussbaum cites Richard D. Mohr, *Gay Ideas: Outing and Other Controversies* (Boston: Beacon Press, 1992) and Gayle Rubin, "Thinking Sex," in *The Lesbian and Gay Studies Reader*, ed. Henry Abelove, Michèle Aina Barale, and David M. Halperin (New York: Routledge, 1993), 3–44.

10. Nussbaum, "Objectification," 276.

11. Nussbaum, "Objectification," 251.

12. Lina Papadaki, "What is Objectification?" *Journal of Moral Philosophy* 7, no. 1 (January 2010): 36.

13. Papadaki, "What is Objectification?" 28.

14. Papadaki, "What is Objectification?" 32.

15. Papadaki, "What is Objectification?" 32.

16. Papadaki, "What is Objectification?" 32.

17. Papadaki, "What is Objectification?" 34.

18. Rae Langton, *Sexual Solipsism* (Oxford: Oxford University Press, 2009), 228–229. Langton's numbers in this quote are a continuation of the list proposed by Nussbaum.

19. Langton, *Sexual Solipsism*, 231.

20. Carolyn McLeod, "Mere and Partial Means: The Full Range of the Objectification of Women," *Canadian Journal of Philosophy Supplementary Volume* 28 (2002): 221.

21. Langton, *Sexual Solipsism*, 204.

22. Billy Witz, "This Time, Kaepernick Takes a Stand by Kneeling," *The New York Times*, September 1, 2016, www.nytimes.com/2016/09/02/sports/football/colin-kaepernick-kneels-national-anthem-protest.html.

23. Clay Travis, "Colin Kapernick Is an Idiot," *Outkick the Coverage*, August 27, 2016, www.outkickthe coverage.com/colin-kaepernick-is-an-idiot-082716.

24. Mark W. Sanchez, "Mike Ditka to Colin Kaepernick: Get the Hell Out," *New York Post*, September 24, 2016, http://nypost.com/2016/09/24/espns-mike-ditka-to-colin-kaepernick-get-the-hell-out.

25. Shrewsbury & Atcham Conservative Association (@Conservativeshr), "Dear Luvvies," *Twitter*, December 12, 2019, https://twitter.com/conservativeshr/status/1205132402361851905 (At last check, the account of the Shrewsbury & Atcham Conservative Association had been suspended).

26. Compare, in this vein, Langton's very compelling discussion of the ways in which autonomy attribution in pornography can actually undermine women's autonomy in *Sexual Solipsism*, 237ff.

27. This line of thought was inspired by a comment made by Allison Gray at a talk I delivered at Davidson College.

28. Martellus Bennett (@MartysaurusRex), "I'd Much Rather Have Fans of Martellus Bennett the Man than Martellus Bennett the TE," *Twitter*, September 1, 2017, https://twitter.com/MartysaurusRex/status/903662352779927552 (At last check, the tweet had been deleted).

29. For similar reasons, the British habit of referring to young soccer players as "boys" (even when they are young men) always makes me cringe.

30. Erin Tarver, *The I in Team: Sports Fandom and the Reproduction of Identity* (Chicago, IL: The University of Chicago Press, 2017), 97.

31. Tarver, *The I in Team*, 102.

32. Tarver, *The I in Team*, 108.

33. Warren St. John, *Rammer, Jammer, Yellow Hammer* (New York: Three Rivers Press, 2004), 149.

5
A CAUTIOUS DEFENSE OF FOOTBALL

That football players routinely endure bone-jarring collisions is not news. Anyone who watches a game for even a few minutes will see grown men hitting each other in ways that would leave most human beings unable to move for days. Observe a college game at field level (as I have had the opportunity to do) and you will come away surprised that deaths are not routine, such is the force with which players throw themselves into each other play after play. Nor is it a surprise to football players that these collisions sometimes have cognitive effects. Having one's "bell rung" or being dazed after a particularly vicious tackle is commonplace for anyone who has played the game for any length of time.

What has become news over the last 15 years or so is the growing realization that for at least some players, the cumulative effect of playing football can lead to a degenerative brain disease called chronic traumatic encephalopathy (CTE). Long thought to be confined to boxers (and therefore known as dementia pugilistica or "punch drunk syndrome"), the symptoms of CTE include "memory loss, confusion, impaired judgment, impulse control problems, aggression, depression, and, eventually, progressive dementia."[1] If a robust connection were established between playing football and developing this kind of condition, it would contravene the long-standing view of many medical professionals that the effects of concussions are temporary, non-cumulative, and reversible.[2] Adding the risk of long-term brain damage to the chronic physical pain that most ex-players already experience could significantly change the cost/benefit analysis for those contemplating whether or not to play the game or in any other way participate in the culture of football.

For football fans, then, the question posed by these developments is whether we can, in good conscience, continue to watch a game that systematically destroys the brains of many of the men who play it. I have been at pains throughout this book to highlight the respect that fans should pay to the sacrifices made by the athletes they watch perform, but in my view, the sacrifice that some football players are making considerably raises the stakes. It is one thing for fans to keep in mind that major league pitchers are putting their arms under tremendous strain every time they throw a curveball—stress that may leave them in considerable pain throughout the baseball season and even into their decades-long retirement. It is something altogether different to ponder the fact that playing football left Junior Seau and Dave Duerson in such a debilitated mental condition that they felt their best option was to take their own lives with gunshot wounds to the chest. If the pleasure of the crowd is obtained at such a cost, can any fan with a modicum of human empathy continue to cheer?

DOI: 10.4324/9781003223696-6

78 A Cautious Defense of Football

I've had my doubts, and over the past few years my relationship to football has grown increasingly complicated. When, in March of 2015, San Francisco 49ers linebacker (and University of Wisconsin standout) Chris Borland announced that he was retiring from football after an impressive rookie season in the NFL, I nearly gave up the watching the game. Foregoing much of his $2.35 million contract, and whatever future earnings he might have accrued in his very promising career, Borland decided the risk to his future health was no longer worth it. Invoking comparisons that are often made between football and war, he said:

> Getting a TBI [traumatic brain injury] and having post-traumatic stress from war, well, that's a more important cause. Football is an elective. It's a game. It's make-believe. And to think that people have brain damage from some made-up game. The meaninglessness of it, you draw the line at brain damage.[3]

A growing list of players seem to agree. In April of 2016, New York Jets offensive lineman D'Brickashaw Ferguson and Buffalo Bills linebacker A.J. Tarpley, both otherwise healthy and productive, joined Borland in ending their careers early due to concerns about CTE.[4]

If these were merely isolated cases of overly cautious players deciding to sacrifice their athletic careers for the sake of their brains, they might be easy to dismiss. However, the potential scope of the problem seems to be much greater. A recent study published by the *Journal of the American Medical Association* showed that 177 of 202 brains of deceased football players showed signs CTE, and of the 111 NFL players examined, 110 were diagnosed with the disease.[5] These numbers are, no doubt, skewed by the self-selection of the study subjects. The brains that were examined came from athletes who had experienced problems or had suspicions they might have had CTE. Nevertheless, the regularity with which CTE has been found in the brains of former football players is alarming and could potentially transform the way in which fans relate to the game of football. Viewers might be willing to tolerate a game in which there is a small chance that a handful of players could suffer significant brain damage; they may be somewhat less committed to one they know will systematically destroy the brains of a majority of its participants.

In my view, the facts about CTE rates—facts on which researchers are only beginning to get a firm handle—matter. Is it a problem that a small, if significant, minority of players will have to deal with? Is it a more rampant side effect of playing the game that will affect the majority of players? Are there genetic factors that predispose individuals to brain trauma? Are the dangers exacerbated by the use of performance-enhancing drugs? And when is most of the damage sustained? At the youth and high school level, or in colleges and the NFL? Watching football in the absence of such information can be a somewhat disorienting experience. The ethical stakes are unclear because we don't know in precise detail the nature of the sacrifices that players are making.

Borland's retirement affected me at a surprisingly personal level. I had followed his college career at Wisconsin closely, and even though I am decidedly *not* a 49ers fan, I was extremely pleased that his time in the NFL was off to a good start. Somewhat undersized as a linebacker in big-time football, he had always played the game with a tenacity and intelligence that elicited deep admiration. Coupled with thoughtful interviews and off-the-field service projects with his Badger teammates, he seemed to be everything that idealistic fans might want in the players they support: a personally engaging solid citizen who could exhibit excellence on the field. For him to step away from the game—and to be so straightforward and thoughtful in explaining his decision—made it incredibly difficult to ignore.

An additional factor complicating my thoughts about football has been a growing recognition that with the flood of new information about the potential health consequences of the game, there would be no chance that I would let my son play. Mind you, this was never a real possibility anyway. He is a soccer player who has never shown even the slightest interest in playing football. Nevertheless, this recognition was (as it continues to be) uncomfortable for me. I have to acknowledge that I am happy to have others sacrifice their mental health for my enjoyment even as I regard my son's brain as too precious to expose to the punishment football can mete out. This tension was thrown into even sharper relief the fall my son entered high school and began attending football games in which his friends and classmates were playing. Now, the social highlight of his week (as it is with many high school students in the United States) revolves around an activity in which I sort of wish his classmates weren't engaged. I don't know if my cognitive dissonance makes me a hypocrite, exactly, but it certainly doesn't exonerate me from such a charge.

Perhaps other people are grappling with a similar experience, but it isn't at all clear what effect that reflection is having on our practices. For this reason, Chuck Klosterman has suggested that our relationship to football currently

> operates as two parallel silos, both of which are shooting skyward and gaining momentum. One silo reflects the overall popularity of the sport, which increases every year. The other silo houses the belief that the game is morally reprehensible, a sentiment that swells every day. Somehow, these silos never collide.[6]

If we are troubled by what we are watching on the football field, many of us seem to be watching anyway.

Given my overall aims in this book, my primary goal in the remainder of this chapter is to offer a defense of *watching* football. However, because I think that the ethical challenges of watching football centrally involve questions about what happens to players on the field, my focus will be organized around a defense of playing the game. In considering the potential value of being a sports fan, I have assumed to this point that the activity being observed is not ethically problematic in its own right. In other words, if watching basketball or soccer is not a particularly laudable way to spend one's time, that isn't because there is anything wrong with playing basketball or soccer. By contrast, the challenge being posed here is whether ethical questions about playing the game of football unavoidably contaminate the ethics of watching it. If there is no defense of a sport that poses a serious risk to the long-term mental health of those who play it, then it seems unlikely that there is any serious case to be made for the ethical acceptability of watching that same sport. Exonerating the value of watching football thus requires a vindication of playing football in ways that don't seem as pressing with, for example, basketball and soccer—sports that we do not have any ethical qualms about playing.

In light of these concerns, my contention is that it can make sense for athletes to risk serious injury in the pursuit of goods that (a) cannot be obtained without that risk and (b) they regard as valuable enough to their own pursuit of the good life to be worth incurring any potential costs associated with that pursuit. I thus attempt to articulate the ways in which football players might sensibly arrive at such conclusions about the dangers of playing their sport. I then consider how this framework applies to the question of whether children should be allowed to play football and conclude by considering whether there is any distinctive value in watching football or other violent sports like boxing or MMA. If this overall case is compelling, I think it is one that requires us all to address some of the more troubling features of American life concerning race, socioeconomic status, and equality of opportunity (or the lack thereof). If football fans should be worried about the brain damage that the sport may cause, they should also be concerned about the conditions under which boys and young men decide to play it. Put differently, if you are going to watch football with anything like a clear conscience, you should be committed to making sure that those who play the game do so in as autonomous a manner as possible.

80 A Cautious Defense of Football

Football as a Threat to Autonomy

Calls for the abolition of football date to the beginning of its development as a quasi-organized sport in the late nineteenth century. As David Dayen points out, the early game was far more vicious than it is today:

> Protective equipment was virtually non-existent; players wore leather caps and almost no padding. Lasting injuries were commonplace. Roughnecks were admitted into Ivy League schools as ringers to beat up on the opposition. Physicians stood ready on the sidelines. Punching, kicking and choking were common strategies ("I saw a Yale man throttle—literally throttle—[a Harvard player], so that he dropped the ball," recalled one observer of the 1902 Harvard-Yale game). Players leaped on downed ball-carriers, and endless pileups featured slugging and eye-gouging.[7]

Indeed, in 1905, "19 college football players died from injuries sustained while playing the sport; with five times as many college players participating today, the modern equivalent would be 95 on-field deaths."[8] It's hard to imagine a sport with that kind of death rate surviving now, much less beginning its ascent to the top of our country's pyramid of sporting popularity.[9]

In suggesting that the game is morally problematic because of the threat it poses to its participants, arguments against the moral permissibility of football that straightforwardly invoke the dangers of the game have a distinctly paternalistic ring. But for precisely this reason, such arguments are not, by themselves, entirely convincing. All sorts of activities are dangerous or potentially bad for those who engage in them. They are not, for that reason alone, immoral, nor does it follow from their dangerous nature that they should be banned.

For example, it would be inappropriate to launch a distinctively moral crusade against donuts even though eating donuts is not particularly good for your health. One who eats donuts is not thereby a bad person, and even if public health initiatives that emphasize the importance of good eating habits are worthwhile enterprises, it would be a bridge too far to suggest an absolute ban on donuts. By the same token, free solo rock climbing—climbing without the aid of ropes or a harness—is extraordinarily risky, because the consequences of a mistake in such a scenario are nearly always fatal. Nevertheless, the level of risk assumed by free climbers does not entail that the activity is immoral or that individuals should not be permitted to engage in it. If eating donuts and free climbing are not immoral, it is not at all clear why we should conclude that there is something morally problematic about football simply on the grounds that it is dangerous.

For this reason, I think the most plausible arguments against football invoke what Nicholas Dixon has called preemptive paternalism: "restrictions on autonomous actions in order to preserve greater future autonomy."[10] According to this line of thought, the problem with football is not that it is bad for players in some straightforward way. The problem is rather that playing football can undermine one's future health such that, even if one decides to play the game of one's own accord and in light of all the best information, the brain damage that some endure as a result of their participation in the sport will leave them in a position where they are no longer capable of genuine autonomy. Thus, in the same way that many people think it is wrong to place oneself into slavery because it is wrong to give up one's autonomy, one might also think it wrong to engage in *any* activity that will significantly undermine one's autonomy in the future.

Dixon thinks that these considerations justify intervening to protect the health of boxers—athletes long known to be at serious risk for brain damage—and Pamela Sailors and Patrick Findler have recently applied Dixon's general approach to football.[11] Indeed, according to Sailors, preemptive paternalistic considerations are even more pressing in the case of football because it is a game

A Cautious Defense of Football **81**

that is often played by children who have not yet developed into fully autonomous agents. She thus denies that football is "just another case where we should allow people to make seemingly bad choices in the name of liberty" because "even if competent adults should be afforded the freedom to make such choices for themselves, the choice to play football is forced long before adulthood."[12]

If fully autonomous adults want to play a game that will leave them without autonomy in the future, perhaps there is nothing morally problematic about that choice, and they should be allowed to make it. However, precisely because they are not yet fully autonomous agents, it is wrong to let children engage in similar kinds of behavior. Findler thus argues that the risks of football simply outweigh whatever benefits may attend children's participation in the game. Because "parents have an obligation to promote their child's well-being," they have a corresponding "prima facie obligation to prevent their children from engaging in activities that threaten the acquisition" of the "skills and capacities they will require as adults in order to make autonomous choices."[13] The fact that CTE threatens those very capacities therefore entails that children should not be permitted to engage in activities, like football, that significantly increase the risk of developing such a condition. Given that the sport has a deep grounding in participation at the youth and high school levels, Sailors therefore concludes "that the sport, as currently constituted, is morally unacceptable."[14]

I think questions about the participation of children in football are more profitably handled separately from questions about the ethical permissibility of the game in general. Invoking the legitimacy of preemptive paternalism raises the question of whether it is *ever* morally acceptable to engage in an activity that undermines one's future autonomy, no matter one's age. It is, then, a secondary question what to do with children—people who are not yet fully autonomous but who may nevertheless be in a position to do things that undermine their future autonomy.

As I've noted, the impermissibility of choosing to place oneself in slavery is often invoked to demonstrate the impermissibility of giving up one's autonomy, and examining the differences between voluntary slavery and football is therefore a useful way to determine whether arguments against football that appeal to preemptive paternalism are generally successful. The structure of this comparison is straightforward. Voluntarily deciding to put yourself in a position where you no longer have any control over your life is wrong because it is a sacrifice of one's future autonomy. And if that sacrifice is what makes instances of voluntary slavery morally wrong, then consistency requires that we judge other instances of such sacrifice to be wrong as well.[15]

But even if one agrees that it would clearly be wrong to voluntarily enslave oneself in nearly every conceivable circumstance, it isn't clear that the reasons that justify that conclusion generalize in a way that renders impermissible any action that undermines one's future autonomy. To begin with, such comparisons are not sufficiently attentive to the difference between wholly abdicating control of one's own life (as in the case of slavery) and engaging in activities that may reduce one's capacities in the future. After all, as Jessica Flanigan points out, people "reliably hinder [their] autonomous capacities" when they "stay up late, ride roller coasters, stand on their heads, watch reality television, or fall in love," and we do not think that such activities should be prohibited on to protect their future autonomy.[16] Where, exactly, playing football might fall in this mix depends on facts about the mental health consequences of the game that researchers have yet to determine. For some, the results of playing football may be like the results of eating too many donuts or not getting enough sleep. For others, their predicament may be more like those who are incapable of living dignified lives. Either way, Flanigan would seem to be right that valuing our ability to choose cannot be entirely inconsistent with doing things that might hamper our future ability to choose.

From my perspective, however, a more fundamental problem with the comparison between voluntary slavery and football lies elsewhere, namely, in a failure to press deeply enough into the nature of the potential sacrifice that individuals are making when they give up their autonomy in different cases. Voluntarily entering into slavery is not morally problematic only because it constitutes a sacrifice of autonomy. It is problematic because slavery is a relationship between individuals that is clearly immoral on other grounds. Human beings should not own other human beings—or buy, sell, or trade them as property—no matter how much freedom they allow such individuals to exercise control over their own lives. For this reason, there is nothing in the condition of slavery that is worth sacrificing one's autonomy to obtain—no conception of a good human life that includes such a choice. To put it in slightly more technical terms, there is no good internal to the condition of slavery that might justify the pursuit of such an arrangement.

There may, of course, be other goods that one could only obtain by enslaving oneself to another. For example, one can envision a scenario in which the lives of one's children are threatened and the only way to save them is to agree to be someone's slave. In that case, the decision to enter slavery might be justified, but not because there is anything at all worthwhile in slavery. The goods to be obtained in that case—saving the lives of one's children—would be external to the enslaved condition and, in this case, the sacrifice might be justified only because of the threat being posed.

The fact that such a decision would be made under threat—and, as a result, would not be entirely autonomous—does not undermine the point I am trying to make. Indeed, I would argue that it highlights the fact that slavery is not a condition that can be justifiably chosen for its own sake. We can imagine non-ideal scenarios in which choosing to be a slave is morally permissible because it allows one to obtain something else of value—an unfortunate calculation that individuals might have to make because of the evil intentions of others. But this is very different than simply volunteering to be the property of another human being. Justifying that kind of choice would require the identification of some distinctive good that could only be obtained by being a slave, and because no such good exists, neither does any such justification.

Compare another case where people tend to worry about the loss of autonomy: addiction. Our understanding of the psychology and physiology of addiction is still developing, and as a result, conceptualizing addiction from the armchair should be done with caution. Nevertheless, part of the concern that people have about addiction is that addicts seem to have lost their ability to govern their own lives. They have sacrificed a reasoned control of their desires and impulses for the momentary satisfaction provided by their particular addictions, and as a result, they may no longer be autonomous.[17]

But while the sacrifice of autonomy here is rightfully concerning, the reasons why it is sacrificed seem to be doing a lot of work in making addiction the problematic condition it is. In calling the aim of the addict "momentary satisfactions," I have been deliberately pejorative. Such terminology presents what addicts get out of their addiction in a way that makes it not worth the sacrifice of anything important and certainly not the sacrifice of one's autonomy. We all need momentary satisfactions, and a life devoid of them is not among the best lives that humans can live. But given that we can obtain pleasure in any number of ways that still enable us to control our own lives, the sacrifice of autonomy for base pleasures seems like a way to ruin one's life rather than enhance it. So even in cases that are sometimes thought to be paradigm examples of when it is wrong to sacrifice one's future autonomy, the mere sacrifice of autonomy doesn't tell the whole story. Some understanding of what autonomy is sacrificed *for* is always lying in the background and doing a fair bit of work in shaping our understanding of the ethical stakes involved.

What a defender of violent sports wants, then, is some specification of what athletes in such sports might be pursuing that could possibly justify a loss of autonomy—goods that can be uniquely obtained in such a context and are, crucially, *worth* obtaining as part of a flourishing human life. What are individuals who play such sports pursuing? What is the distinctive value of an endeavor that places one's mental and physical health at such risk? And can the sacrifices made to obtain such goods possibly be worth it?

The Attractions of Dangerous Sports

I've never played a down of proper tackle football in my life (just the backyard variety that parents probably don't let their kids play anymore). I've never boxed or wrestled. And I would never consider any kind of high-risk mountain climbing, cliff diving, or BASE jumping. So for me, any exploration of why people are attracted to such activities comes via the first-personal accounts of others, and though they are not presented systematically by the athletes who talk about their experiences, what draws people into dangerous or violent sports seems to fall into three broad categories.

First, many athletes are attracted to the intricacies of these sports that do not have any direct connection with danger or violence. It is in this way that Laila Ali talks about how she loves "the give and take of boxing, anticipating a punch before it's thrown." She says, "I see the footwork, the motion, the dance in my dreams. I love the subtle play between defense and offense, jabbing and ducking, moving ahead, maintaining position, giving ground, gaining momentum."[18] There is obviously combative language in this description. Ali is not papering over the fact that boxing involves two people who are trying to hit each other. But when she talks about her love of the sport, she doesn't talk about what it feels like to punch another woman in the face. She talks about the complexity and nuance of the movements involved and the thought that necessarily goes into a well-executed fight.

Former NFL defensive back Dominique Foxworth writes in a similar way about the complexities of football—the multiple games within the game that he thinks are unique to the sport.

> The NFL will never be positionless like basketball. No single player will ever lead his team in tackles, passing yards, rushing yards, sacks and interceptions. Football is made up of hyper-specialized players in distinct positions, playing several different games, which makes for a dependence that is not seen in any other sport and rarely seen in life. Interconnectivity and complexity that you can't find anywhere else.[19]

Even though Foxworth grants that the violence of the game "contributes to the high stakes that are needed to create its accelerated Darwinian atmosphere," it is not the violence itself that Foxworth discusses when he talks about what he loves about football. The violence is part of the equation, but it is the intricacies of 11 men doing their individual jobs in the service of the offensive or defensive unit's goal that truly captivates him.

One more example to illustrate this dynamic. Though anyone who has watched the mesmerizing film *Free Solo* has to acknowledge that the possibility of dying is an inherent part of rock climbing (or at least climbing without the aid of ropes or any other protective equipment), that danger doesn't appear to be the primary attraction for people interested in the sport. It seems instead that rock climbers are captivated by mountains as compelling problems to solve. "I'm down here, and I want to get up there," they think to themselves. "How do I do it? What help do I need? What help can I do without?"

Jon Krakauer invokes this kind of thought when describing the challenge of climbing Meru Peak in the Indian Himalayas—a feat not accomplished until 2011 and documented in the extraordinary film *Meru*. He says:

> Meru is not just hard. It's hard in this really complicated way. You can't just be a good ice climber. You can't just be good at altitude. You can't just be a good rock climber. You've

84 A Cautious Defense of Football

gotta be able to ice climb, mix climb. And you've gotta be able to do big wall climbing at 20,000 feet. It's all that stuff wrapped in one package that's defeated so many climbers and will probably defeat you and will maybe defeat everybody for all time. That, to a certain kind of mindset, is an irresistible appeal.[20]

Of course, climbers are keenly aware that getting to the top of any challenging climb is dangerous; that is part of the problem to be solved. But it is the problem-solving that attracts many of them, not the danger. The danger is something to be managed and, as much as possible, avoided.

Second, some athletes do have a genuine attraction to the explicit physicality of certain sports: the hitting and being hit; the close proximity to other human beings; the contest of wills to see who is tougher. Binnie Klein, who writes about taking up boxing in her mid-50s, thus describes her first sparring session:

> I jab several times. It's familiar and reliable. I'm thinking about my feint. When can I try it? How can I put it all together onto this constantly moving target? Suddenly I'm ready, and I jerk forward a bit as if to jab with my left and then bam! I've thrown my right and hit John right on his nose, right in the middle of his face.

The experience is surprising, but pleasantly so. "I'm dazzled," writes Klein. "I hit this man. I have made contact. It feels amazing."[21]

Jonathan Gotschall similarly notes that people at his MMA gym "struggle for words that are huge enough to describe the feeling of winning a fight, and like soldiers, they generally fall back on comparisons to sex or drugs."[22] In his own training, Gotschall—an English professor whose journey into MMA started in his late 30s—does not immediately take pleasure in hitting other human beings, but eventually comes to appreciate the experience. He notes that there have been a few

> times when I've hit guys too hard and seen their eyes lose focus—seen them stagger to one side or plop down like babies on their butts. When I've hit someone this hard, I've felt bad and apologized. And always, secretly, I've felt a little good, too. It felt a little good that night when I opened my friend Mike's nose, then watched my gloves paint his face red. To physically dominate another man is intoxicating. It's a deeply satisfying feeling. And I can see how real fighters, who are usually nice men outside the cage, can acquire a fondness for that feeling and want to experience it again and again.[23]

Such an admission likely makes some readers uncomfortable—at least those of us who tell ourselves that violence is never the answer to our problems or that drawing blood from another human being is barbaric and beneath the dignity of the more evolved members of our species. And yet, the fact remains that the experience of such contact is meaningful for some people.

Importantly, this love of violent contact need not include any real animosity toward the individual with whom one is fighting. When Gotschall describes the satisfaction of opening Mike's nose, he's talking about his friend. And when Klein says that it feels amazing to hit a man in the face, that face belongs to her trainer, John, a man she clearly adores. What is being envisioned is not, then, the indulgence of a generalized hatred or anger. It is rather a focused aggression taking place in the context of clearly defined rules that promote restraint and respect for one's opponent. Not everyone may see the attraction, but many participants in these kinds of activities certainly do.

A third form of attraction to violent or exceptionally dangerous sports is simply the deep love that many athletes have for the sports in which they participate—a love that doesn't allow them to find contentment apart from that pursuit. It is tempting to describe this love as an obsession. But "obsession" has, to my ear, a negative connotation to it that I don't think is fair in this context. It is rather that individuals see the possibility of a life without their chosen endeavor as a significantly impoverished existence. They know the risks they are taking, and decide that living without the rewards of their sport is not a life they want.

Here again, climbers are particularly thoughtful on the potential trade-offs they are making, and many of them seem to have explicitly thought through this issue in a way that, perhaps, athletes in other sports have not. Jimmy Chin, after witnessing the near death of his friend and climbing partner Renan Ozturk and, in a separate incident, surviving a catastrophic avalanche himself, thought seriously about what he wanted the rest of his life to look like. He had seen firsthand how dangerous a life in the mountains could be. And yet, he says that after "some time off, and some serious contemplation, the idea of not skiing and not climbing and not being in the mountains was too much to imagine. I just wasn't ready to give it all up." Similarly, Jon Krakauer describes the mindset of his friend and fellow climber Conrad Anker as

> this constant dialectic. He needs the mountains to climb, but it's like, am I taking too many chances? Can I control the risk? Of course you can't control the risk. Well then why am I doing this? Because I have to do it, or I go fucking crazy![24]

I cannot relate to a love of mountain climbing so strong that a life without it seems scarcely worth living. I am much too afraid of heights—or, more specifically, much too afraid of falling from such heights—to take up climbing. But I suspect most people know what it is to love something in this way—to be attached to it such that you do not really want to contemplate life without it. That one happens to love something that is dangerous, and exposes one to the risk of death or losing one's future autonomy, doesn't make it a different kind of love than one who spends every waking moment thinking about how to improve their golf game or whose favorite moments are the time spent on a daily 10-mile run. They are, to be sure, loves of different things, with different stakes and different costs and benefits. But, even if we would judge that the risks are not worth it in a particular case, we can acknowledge that other people are wired differently. The golfer might think that the mountain climber is dumb to court death as much as he does. The climber might think that the golfer is just wasting time walking around and whacking a ball with a stick.

I'm not sure how to run this calculation in any straightforwardly objective way; perhaps, given their own loves, they are both right. I don't think the pleasures of climbing or boxing or football would, for me, be worth the risks involved, because I am not particularly inclined to participate in these sorts of activities. But whether those are good trade-offs for me shouldn't be the standard. The standard should be whether it is a good trade-off for the ones who are making it.

If this framing of the choice to risk one's own health and future autonomy is plausible, then I think it can make sense for athletes to trade some of the costs imposed by their respective sports for the distinctive benefits that they derive from those very same sports. If you love mountain climbing, there is really no other way to obtain the goods that mountain climbing can provide—goods that come with a significant risk of serious injury or death. And if you love boxing, whether because of the intricacies of the sweet science or the primal exchange of hitting and being hit, choosing another combat sport is really the only way to approximate that kind of experience. You certainly aren't going to get it on the golf course. Same for those who are captivated by either the complex teamwork and strategy of football or its brute physicality. If you enjoy playing football, you probably aren't going to be satisfied with sports that involve markedly less contact. And if the benefits of football are important enough to you, then perhaps it is worth risking significant injury or long-term brain damage that will undermine your future autonomy.

86 A Cautious Defense of Football

There are, of course, other takes on the costs of playing football, and it is crucial not to under-estimate the punishment that some athletes endure. In his memoir *Out of Their League*, Dave Meggyesy details how the game "kept him from responding and communicating on a human level with other people."[25] After seven years as a linebacker for the St. Louis Cardinals, Meggyesy could no longer tolerate what he regarded as the dehumanizing aspects of the game and quit football to join "forces with those individuals and groups trying to change society"—a project he regards as incompatible with a professional football career.[26] In a similar vein, Hall of Fame linebacker Harry Carson writes that he "would not play the game again knowing what I know now" about the dangers of brain damage that football poses.[27] While acknowledging that football "has made me to some degree the person I am today," Carson closes his own memoir by noting that "any recognition of what I did in football is long forgotten or means absolutely nothing to me."[28] Carson simply regards any potential benefits of the game as not worth the costs paid to achieve them.

That significant caveat in place, the fact that some people question the worthiness of such trade-offs does not mean that they are inappropriate for everyone. And there are certainly football players saying that they would play all over again even knowing what they know now about the consequences of the game.[29] What voices like Meggyesy and Carson emphasize, however, is the importance of making sure that the decision to play football or other dangerous sports is as informed as possible. A theme that pervades Carson's memoir is the lack of information offered to players of his generation. They simply did not know what the game might be doing to their brains, and that fact understandably bothers a significant number of players who feel that they were robbed of making a choice about what risks they wanted to take with their mental health. Thus, despite all that we still don't know about the exact relationship between football and CTE, anyone contemplating playing the game today should be made aware of all the information that is available. Expanding the informational basis on which such a decision is made is a crucial way to pay sufficient respect to those who are making it.

Sacrificing for Money and Fame

One might reply to my argument thus far by pointing out that while the sort of trade-off I have described is comprehensible, it doesn't represent the trade-off that many athletes in these sports actually make. Rather than pursue goods internal to the sports they play—goods that are only obtainable via participation in those sports—many athletes are trying to obtain much less idealistic goods like money and fame. Thus, most boxers aren't boxing because they have a deep love for the sweet science. They are boxing because they want the financial rewards that a successful career in boxing can bring. And a lot of football players don't like either hitting or getting hit. They are simply using their abilities to get a college scholarship and, perhaps someday, an NFL contract that can give their families some financial security.

Critics of dangerous sports might, therefore, worry that while trading one's future autonomy for the internal goods of sport can be part of a good human life, executing such a trade for fame and fortune is not similarly noble. Moreover, to the degree that those seeking the financial benefits of various sports tend to be poorer, concerns about exploitation might begin to arise. If the poor are, in effect, mortgaging their future autonomy for the enjoyment of the rich and doing so largely because of the financial enticements they are being given, one might worry that they are not making a fully autonomous choice. The lure of money is pressuring them to do things that they would not otherwise do, and because there are significant costs associated with that choice, such a scenario should make us uncomfortable.

However, this objection does not, strictly speaking, constitute a direct challenge to the arguments I have made in defense of violent sports. Rather, it is an objection to the conditions under which those sports are often played. In a world where no one had to do anything for money that they did not otherwise want to do, there would be comparatively few worries about exploitation. And yet, if the argument I have been developing in this chapter is compelling, it could still be a world in which people decided to participate in dangerous sports. Correct the conditions that make exploitation a possibility, and the financial rewards of football no longer threaten to exploit athletes who come from disadvantaged backgrounds.

Thus, insofar as these considerations serve to push society as a whole toward greater socio-economic justice, no defender of dangerous sports should find them at all troubling. The less frequently that people have to make decisions out of financial desperation, the better. And if the financial desperation of certain athletes draws our attention to the need to address the societal conditions that impose this kind of pressure, then I think we should be open to learning from their experience and using what we find to improve the lives of all our fellow citizens.

Moreover, I think it is worth acknowledging that money plays varying kinds of roles in each individual's pursuit of the good life. I am comfortable asserting that the pursuit of money for its own sake is empty, in large part because money has no intrinsic value; in my view, it is a paradigm example of a good that has value only because of what it can get you: food, shelter, clothing, cars, houses, peace of mind, power, etc. Nevertheless, the mere fact that someone engages in an activity largely for financial reasons does not, by itself, invalidate that pursuit as worthwhile. Perhaps the individual is not simply looking to enrich herself or to spend her money on frivolous things but is instead looking to devote much of her wealth to philanthropic causes she cares about. Or perhaps she is not looking for anything more than long-term financial security for her loved ones. Money may not have any intrinsic value, but the quality of one's life is certainly undermined if one is mired in poverty. Sacrificing one's own future well-being in order to improve the future well-being of others is not generally a course of action that we criticize; it is not clear why it should be dismissed as unworthy when the course of action is playing a dangerous sport.

Even when the financial benefits primarily accrue to the athlete herself, it is not clear why such a fact should fundamentally change the ethical equation. Many people do work they don't particularly enjoy because the financial rewards of that work allow them to do all sorts of things they *do* enjoy. Their work is a job, rather than a calling.[30] But that doesn't invalidate the work. It simply means that they derive their primary enjoyment in life from other things: time with family and friends, various leisure pursuits, traveling the world, hiking the mountains, reading great literature, and listening to great music. And the more money they have, the more freedom they have to engage in these sorts of activities. Perhaps the significant financial rewards that come from a successful athletic career enable individuals to enjoy their lives in ways that make them willing to accept the potential costs of those same careers.

Finally, there is a something unseemly about denying a chance to improve one's socioeconomic status to the very people who most need to improve that status. As I've noted, it would certainly be preferable if no one were pressured by financial considerations to do things that they would prefer not to do absent those considerations. Nevertheless, given the clearly non-ideal nature of our current societal arrangements, it is odd to tell financially insecure people that they cannot engage in an activity because of the financial rewards that it brings. Surely it is better for the financial rewards to go to the poor rather than the rich in such a scenario. At the very least, it is not any worse for poor people to do things for significant financial reward even if we are justified in lamenting their need to do so.

It is, of course, highly relevant here that very few people actually obtain significant financial rewards from participating in sports. For example, according to the NCAA, only 6.8 percent of high school football players end up playing in college. And of those who play in college, only 1.5

percent end up playing at a major professional level.[31] Even if a football player makes the NFL, the financial benefits are not nearly as great for most players as the public might think. The median NFL salary in 2018 was $860,000 (meaning that half the players in the league make less than that). And when you factor in the fact that an average NFL career lasts about three years, you end up with a lot of football players making something much closer to the league minimum of $465,000 for a job that is over before people in many other careers have really gotten started.[32]

$1.5 million is nothing to scoff at. I certainly wouldn't turn it down. But given that the chances of getting even that amount of money are significantly less than 1 percent for any high school football player, is it enough money to justify the punishment that players take on the field or the long-term brain damage that might result? Aaron Rodgers might be able to respond with an unequivocal "yes" to this question because his career has lasted over a decade and his current salary is around $20 million. The answer might be very different for the vast majority of football players who put on a helmet. Thus, in the same way that the possible health consequences of football need to be made clear to those who are considering playing the game, the realities of earning a living in the sport need to be made plain as well. Anyone thinking of risking their future mental health in the hopes of fame and fortune should know that the likelihood of achieving such a goal is quite low. They may, of course, still decide to take that chance. Or they may have other reasons to play, of the sort I discussed previously. But whatever the basis of their decision, they should be as informed as possible when the stakes are as high as they are here.

What About the Kids?

Even if everything I have said about the potential sacrifice of one's future autonomy is correct, there still remains the problem of how to think about the participation of children in an activity that has the potential to affect their mental health in serious ways in the future. If adults want to risk brain damage, either because of their deep love of the sport or because of the financial rewards it may bring, that is one thing. It is quite another when the person making that choice is a 13-year-old boy who is not yet allowed to drive a car and whose values and sense of self are still developing right along with the brain he risks damaging by boxing or playing football.

The short answer to the question that heads this section is, in my mind, fairy simple. Children shouldn't engage in activities that threaten the long-term health of their brains. Thus, in the same way that parents manage any number of other behaviors in order to protect their children's well-being in the future—from restricting the foods they eat to providing them with a well-rounded education—they should also make sure that kids do not do anything that threatens their ability to manage their own lives when they get older.[33] Because worries about the effect of tackle football on the developing brains of young children strike me as exceedingly well justified, I think eliminating the sport in this form for kids aged 15 and under is appropriate. Flag football and other skill development activities that avoid contact with the head are clearly unproblematic, but we should get the younger kids out of helmets and pads.

That said, I think a more comprehensive response should acknowledge that there are important differences between 8-year-olds and 16-year-olds, and that while it may not be appropriate to grant 16-year-olds full control of their own lives, these difference are nevertheless relevant to the question of whether it is wrong for them to decide to play dangerous sports. After all, we think it appropriate—even essential to good parenting—to give children greater amounts of latitude in decision making as they get older. Some of these decisions are fairly trivial. My wife and I gave the barber explicit instructions about how to cut my son's hair when he was very young (and didn't really care what his own hair looked like). But as he moved into his pre-adolescent years and developed more clearly defined opinions about his appearance, he began to take the lead. Similarly with his clothing choices. I can still remember dressing him from head to toe when he was in kindergarten; now, at the age of 17, he wears what he wants.

Aside from a social media post that he might find embarrassing a decade from now, these choices aren't likely to affect his future autonomy all that much. They are, as I've stipulated, not all that important. However, other choices that we let kids make have the potential to affect their future lives in a more robust way. My parents made me take piano lessons starting in kindergarten, and I continued to do so until my sophomore year in high school. At that point, I preferred to devote time to improving my golf game instead of practicing scales and chord progressions, so my parents let me quit. While I was certainly never going to be a world-renowned concert pianist, the decision nevertheless affected my future in certain ways; when I quit taking lessons, I more or less stopped playing the piano altogether—something I periodically regret as I get older.

Similarly, I opted (of my own accord) not to take AP Calculus in high school, not because I was bad at math—I was actually pretty good at it—but simply because I didn't like it. My parents could have forced me to take the class, on the grounds that doing so would have been good for me in the future. The calculus teacher at my high school was excellent, and I'm sure having the knowledge would have kept open a wider variety of options for me than did my decision to take as few math classes as possible. Even now, I occasionally think a basic knowledge of calculus would be useful in my career as a philosopher. Nevertheless, as a high school senior, my parents decided that I should make my own academic decisions, and even though I am not sure that I made the best choice, I think they were right to let me make it.

Even concerning such weighty matters as medical decisions, standard medical practice is to allow children an increasing voice in their own care, sometimes invoking the "rule of sevens." For children under 7 years of age, parents are consulted exclusively about medical care; children have essentially no voice in the process. When children are between 7 and 14, "doctors seek parental permission and their patient's assent to treatment." When children in this age range refuse treatment, "there is a strong ethical presumption against forcing treatment unless the child's life is at stake and treatment cannot be deferred without substantial risk." And the American Association of Pediatrics maintains that children over the age of 14 "have the same decisional capacities as adults" and therefore have the same rights concerning informed consent as any other patient.[34] Even if one thinks it is inappropriate for 15- and 16-year-olds to have full control over their medical decision-making, it seems that the desires of children at this age should be given significant weight in determining the best course of action. Put differently, a parent who decided on a course of treatment for a 15-year-old of typical mental capacity without seriously considering the wishes of that child would, in my view, be acting wrongly.

If we grant older adolescents a significant voice in their own medical care, it is not obvious why our thinking should be different when it concerns a child's interest in playing sports. Being committed to the idea that young children should not be able to risk their long-term mental health does not require that one make similarly blanket prohibitions regarding older children. In the same way that a 15-year-old's strong desire to refrain from a medical treatment should be given significant weight in a parent's decision about what course of action to pursue, it seems that a 15-year-old's strong desire to play football should be given significant weight when determining whether to allow him to play. Those desires should not necessarily be rubber stamped; they should be probed and discussed to ensure that the child understands their stakes as much as possible. But we should listen to an older child who feels drawn to a sport for the same reasons that certain adults are drawn to it. If it is appropriate for a child to be able decide that he wants to discontinue life-sustaining medical treatment, perhaps, after thoughtful discussion of the potential risks involved, it is also appropriate for a child to be allowed to play football.

90 A Cautious Defense of Football

If someone counters that the whims of even 15- and 16-year-olds are constantly changing such that they should be given little weight, I am inclined to concede the point. Nevertheless, while many 15-year-olds change their deepest passions frequently, there are some whose desires and goals in life stay remarkably stable even into adulthood. Some people who have dreamt of being doctors since they were 5-year-olds end up having very successful careers in medicine. My mother grew up wanting to be a teacher, which is exactly what she became. And while some professional athletes no doubt discover their passions somewhat later in life, my guess is that the overwhelming majority of them have been pursuing their athletic goals since long before they could reflectively contemplate the full implications of their life choices.

Other significant decisions are similarly affected by adolescent desires and experiences. I first dated my wife when we were 16, and our relationship became more serious toward the end of our senior year in high school. Our desire to be together certainly constrained our future possibilities. We dated long distance for three years in college and passed up opportunities we might have pursued had that not been the case. For example, neither of us studied abroad (which we both would have liked to do, all else being equal) and my wife took summer classes so she could graduate a semester early and move to Wisconsin (where I was living). We were, no doubt, sacrificing a certain amount of future freedom in opting for this course of action. But the heart wants what it wants, and after 23 years of marriage, neither of us regrets the choices we made, even as we recognize that they came with certain costs.

Debra Satz has explored another complexity involved in weighing the future costs and benefits of our decisions under the heading of weak agency. In her discussion of whether or not we should have markets for the sale of human kidneys, she thus points out that because "it may be difficult to imagine what it means to lose a kidney before one actually experiences the loss," the idea that people who sell their kidneys are doing so in a robustly autonomous manner is thereby undermined.[35] People may have all the information and statistics about what life is like with only one kidney, but until they try to live in that sort of condition, they won't be able to fully appreciate the sacrifice they are making. In the same way, one might argue that the full ramifications of risking one's mental health cannot be appreciated until one is living with brain damage. The theoretical comprehension of such costs may be in place, but an inability to really know what it's like skews the cost/benefit analysis—a feature of these kinds of decisions that may be especially prevalent among adolescents who may not be good at appreciating risk in the first place.

It is easy to see how one might apply similar concerns to the decision to play football. In the same way that we can give people information about what it is like to live with one kidney, we can give teenagers all the information we have about the possible effects of playing the game—how they may have aches and pains for the rest of their lives and their brains may not function the way they are supposed to by the time they are 40 years old. And yet, just as people might not really be able to appreciate the reality of living with one kidney, even as they intellectually comprehend the risks, 16-year-old kids might not really be able to appreciate the consequences of playing football. As a result, we have reason to think that they are not making such decisions autonomously and a presumption against allowing them to do so.

But if we look at the wide array of decisions that we make in life, in adolescence and even into more mature adulthood, it isn't at all clear how much weight should be accorded to this worry. We make choices all the time whose effect on our lives is not something we can fully appreciate until years in the future—sometimes many years. When I was deciding whether to go to graduate school in philosophy, many people told me about how difficult it would be to land a good job when I was done, and at one level, I most certainly understood what I was getting myself into by pursuing a career in the field. That said, I don't think anything could have really made me appreciate what it would be like to seek secure employment for six years after receiving my Ph.D.

I stopped taking Spanish in high school knowing that it would be difficult for me to continue to learn the language without the formal requirements of an academic setting. But I most certainly did not fully appreciate how frustrating it would be as an adult to know some Spanish but not be able to use the language in any meaningful way (and find it incredibly difficult to devote time to mastering it in middle age). And people have kids all the time, and as a general rule, we don't think there are moral problems with such decisions even though it really is true that you can't fully appreciate what it is like to be a parent until you are one.

The point here is not that weak agency does not exist or even that it does not present serious challenges for us as we try to live our lives in the best way possible. My point is rather that weak agency is such a pervasive feature of our lives that, by itself, it is unclear how much weight to accord it when ethically evaluating our decisions. Can 16-year-olds really appreciate what it will mean to them in the future to be paying the price for playing a game in their youth? Probably not. But 25-year-olds probably can't appreciate that either, nor might they be able to appreciate the regret they could feel if they choose not to play and thereby miss out on the positive benefits that can be accrued from the game. At some level, every choice we make is a gamble concerning how things will turn out, and try as we might, we always run the risk of making the wrong decision. The best we can do, it seems to me, is give people as much information as possible and work to make society as just as possible so that they do not feel inordinate pressure to make decisions they would not otherwise make.

The Potential Value (and Potential Dangers) of Watching Football

One of my working premises throughout this book has been that the value of playing sports does not justify the value of watching those same sports. If acknowledging this fact puts pressure on any account of the general value of watching sports, I think that pressure is particularly acute in the case of dangerous sports like football, especially given the fact that many fans would not be willing to take the same risks as the athletes they are supporting. Is there anything we can get from watching such sports that we cannot get from watching less risky endeavors (or, indeed, from engaging in any number of non-sports-related activities)?

Perhaps not. In Chapter 2, I made the case that the value of watching sports is very much like the value of watching a theater production or reading a work of literature. If it has any unique value, it is perhaps in terms of the emphasis that sports place on an exploration of the limits of the human body and the fact that athletes are real people engaged in that exploration in real time. But despite my deep love of sports, I am not a sports exceptionalist, and thus I don't think that being a sports fan is the only way that one might obtain various goods that are essential for a well-lived life. My claim is more modest—that watching sports has much the same value as a number of other activities that we generally consider worthwhile.

That general view in the background, it seems that if it is permissible to play football, there is no obvious reason why it would be impermissible to watch others play it or to be a fan of football teams in the same way that one might support a baseball or soccer team. Nor is it clear why fans would not be able to obtain the same sorts of benefits from watching football that they obtain by watching baseball or soccer. In other words, if my argument for the permissibility of playing football has been successful, it seems that the conclusions of Chapters 2 and 3 should apply to football just as they apply to other sports.

That said, as I have grappled with the potential health consequences of playing football, I think my own reflections on the game have moved in directions that illustrate some of the potentially distinctive ways in which fans might be challenged by dangerous sports. Perhaps it is just a function of my move into middle age, but I have found that watching football over the past few years has

92 A Cautious Defense of Football

occasioned some fairly regular reflection on mortality. And if, as I have argued, sports in general allow us to reflect on what it means to have a body (and the limits of what that body is able to do), violent sports place front and center questions about what sorts of punishment the human body is able to endure. Thus, when I watch a football game, I not only appreciate the accuracy of an Aaron Rodgers pass or the agility and hands of Larry Fitzgerald. I also marvel at the continuous barrage of hits unleashed on all participants, the consistent ability of players to continue playing despite these hits, and their willingness to pursue their goals despite the risks they are taking with their bodies and brains. In this way, I've been challenged to think about the fragility of my own life and what kinds of suffering I would be willing to undergo in the pursuit of the things I most care about.

I have also been prompted to think a fair amount about the notion of sacrifice—about how much I am willing to risk death or confront fear and the regular experience of pain in the pursuit of my goals. Sitting behind a desk as I write, I think about how far removed my experience is from 300-pound men who repeatedly collide with other 300-pound men for a living, and because of that difference, I am forced to contemplate a much wider range of human experience. Moreover, while I do not think that courage requires the presence of physical danger, I find myself awed every time a wide receiver stretches for a ball knowing they are going to be punished by a defensive back who is preparing to unload a teeth-clattering hit. The wide receiver's job *requires* such displays of courage on a regular basis. I don't think I could expose my body to that kind of punishment, and that very fact presents me with significant material for reflection.

Or, taking a non-football example that has run along similar lines for me, consider the famous 1974 fight between Muhammad Ali and George Foreman: the so-called "Rumble in the Jungle."[36] The bout is famous for many reasons, but from a purely tactical perspective, it is notable as the fight in which Ali employed the notorious "rope-a-dope" strategy to neutralize Foreman's prodigious punching power. For the better part of eight rounds, Ali absorbed a constant barrage of punishment from Foreman. Doing his best to bounce himself off the ropes in order to minimize the damage that Foreman was able to inflict, Ali nevertheless withstood a remarkable number of hits, any one of which would land most human beings in the emergency room, or worse. The result was that Foreman exhausted himself and Ali was able to respond with a flurry of his own in the eighth round to earn a technical knockout. That strategy may very well have been the only way for Ali to win the fight. But given the cost he paid for victory, I find myself returning to that fight as I contemplate the nature of sacrifice. Was it worth it? And if not, what could possibly have made it so?

The danger in these cases is an unavoidable piece of the puzzle, and one that I do not think we should shy away from. We should not pretend that football is not really dangerous, or that many boxers will not suffer greatly for their achievements in the ring. We should instead make these features of the respective sports an explicit part of our reflection as we think about the remarkable capacities of the human body and the sacrifices some people are willing to make in the pursuit of their goals.

Of course, as with other sports, there is no guarantee that fans will direct their thoughts to these matters, and provided they avoid objectifying the athletes they watch and refrain from problematic behavior while supporting their teams, that may be perfectly fine. Here, as elsewhere, I don't want to begrudge anyone their escapist pleasures (provided those escapes are kept in their proper perspective). And yet, I think that football fans must always be clear-eyed about the punishing nature of the sport, no matter the mode of their engagement with it. They must appreciate the role that violence plays in the games they are watching and the lives of the athletes who play them without glorifying or luxuriating in that violence. The worry here is that fans will not only accept the risks involved in football as a necessary cost of doing business; they will exalt those risks and view them as the only real mark of genuine courage. Klosterman characterizes this mindset as follows:

The contemporary stance on football's risk feels unilateral, because nobody goes around saying, "Modern life is not violent enough." Yet this sentiment quietly exists. And what those who believe it say instead is, "I love football. It's the last bastion of hope for toughness in America." It's not difficult to imagine a future where the semantic distance between those statements is nonexistent.[37]

The potentially damaging nature of this kind of rhetoric should be easy to see, as contributors to online discussion forums respond to efforts by the NFL to limit serious blows to the head by posting such comments as the following:

> This is not good. Freaking women organs running this league.
> The NFL is turning into a touch football "Nancy Boy" League. Steer your kids that have talent into baseball, basketball or any other sport that will still have dignity left in 2 years. . . .
> The pussyification of the NFL continues. Every single goddam year the rules get more and more VAGINIZED.[38]

Accepting the legitimacy of certain kinds of violence should not lead us to disparage those who want to minimize the harm such violence can cause, much less invoke clearly sexist ideas to do so. There may be a fine line between admiring the physicality of the sport (and even acknowledging the violence as one of its central attractions) and celebrating the destruction of the human beings who choose to play it, but conscientious fans should go to considerable lengths to walk that line successfully.

Notes

1. "Frequently Asked Questions about CTE," *Boston University CTE Research Center*, Accessed May 31, 2019, www.bu.edu/cte/about/frequently-asked-questions.
2. See David Orentlicher and William S. David, "Concussion and Football: Failures to Respond by the NFL and the Medical Profession," *Florida International Law Review* 8, no. 1 (September 2012): 23–36.
3. Steve Fainaru and Mark Fainaru-Wada, "Why Former 49er Chris Borland Is the Most Dangerous Man in Football," *ESPN.com*, August 20, 2015, www.espn.com/nfl/story/_/id/13463272/how-former-san-francisco-49ers-chris-borland-retirement-change-nfl-forever.
4. Lindsay Gibbs, "2 More NFL Players Retire Early as Evidence Linking Football and CTE Mounts," *Think Progress*, April 8, 2016, https://thinkprogress.org/2-more-nfl-players-retire-early-as-evidence-linking-football-and-cte-mounts-f170cbe5f4f1#.5nxtm86es.
5. Jesse Mez et al., "Clinicopathological Evaluation of Chronic Traumatic Encephalopathy in Players of American Football," *JAMA* 318, no. 4 (July 2017): 360–370.
6. Chuck Klosterman, *But What If We're Wrong?: Thinking About the Present as If It Were the Past* (New York: Penguin, 2014), 184.
7. David Dayen, "How Teddy Roosevelt Saved Football," *Politico*, September 20, 2014, www.politico.com/magazine/story/2014/09/teddy-roosevelt-saved-football-111146.
8. Dayen, "How Teddy Roosevelt Saved Football."
9. It has been suggested that while the evolution of football equipment has lowered the death rate in the sport, it has also contributed to the current crisis of brain injuries. The modern football helmet may protect the skull from the risk of fracture, but it notably fails to prevent the brain from jostling around inside the skull. Indeed, precisely because their heads are encased hard plastic for the duration of the game, players may now be more likely to use those heads as weapons in the course of play, thus increasing their risk of brain damage. Without claiming any special expertise, I largely find this argument convincing.
10. Nicholas Dixon, "Boxing, Paternalism, and Legal Moralism," *Social Theory and Practice* 27, no. 2 (April 2001): 332.
11. Pamela R. Sailors, "Personal Foul: An Evaluation of the Moral Status of Football," *Journal of the Philosophy of Sport* 42, no. 2 (May 2015): 269–286 and Patrick Findler, "Should Kids Play (American) Football?" *Journal of the Philosophy of Sport* 42, no. 3 (May 2015): 443–462. Dixon's specific recommendation is that boxing should not permit blows to the head. See Dixon, "Boxing, Paternalism, and Legal Moralism."

12. Sailors, "Personal Foul," 273.
13. Findler, "Should Kids Play (American) Football?" 448.
14. Findler, "Should Kids Play (American) Football?" 270.
15. David Velleman has objected to arguments for the right to die that appeal to the importance of individual autonomy on similar grounds. See "A Right to Self-Termination?" *Ethics* 109, no. 3 (April 1999): 606–628.
16. Jessica Flanigan, *Pharmaceutical Freedom* (New York: Oxford University Press, 2017), 72.
17. For an account of the way that addiction can undermine autonomy that I find compelling, see Neil Levy, "Autonomy and Addiction," *Canadian Journal of Philosophy* 36, no. 3 (September 2006): 427–447.
18. Binnie Klein, *Blows to the Head: How Boxing Changed My Mind* (Albany, NY: SUNY Press, 2009), 19–20.
19. Domonique Foxworth, "Why I Love Football," *The Undefeated*, August 12, 2016, https://theundefeated.com/features/domonique-foxworth-why-i-love-football.
20. Jimmy Chin, Elizabeth Chai Vasarhelyi, Shannon Ethridge (Producers), and Jimmy Chin, Elizabeth Chai Vasarhelyi (Directors). (2015). *Meru* [Motion Picture]. United States: Little Monster Films.
21. Klein, *Blows to the Head*, 141.
22. Jonathan Gotschall, *Professor in the Cage: Why Men Fight and Why We Like to Watch* (New York: Penguin, 2015), 201.
23. Gotschall, *Professor in the Cage*, 205.
24. Chin, Vasarhelyi, and Ethridge, *Meru*.
25. Dave Meggyesy, *Out of their League* (Berkeley, CA: Ramparts Press, 1970), 231.
26. Meggyesy, *Out of their League*, 257.
27. Harry Carson, *Captain for Life* (New York: St. Martin's Press, 2011), 316.
28. Carson, *Captain for Life*, 318.
29. "We Asked 14 Retired NFL Players: Would You Do It Again?" *Deadspin*, March 17, 2015, https://deadspin.com/we-asked-14-retired-nfl-players-would-you-do-it-again-1691919600.
30. I owe this particular way of framing the distinction to Michael Lewis in an essay that, even after multiple attempts, I can no longer find (but which was, I believe, originally published by *Bloomberg*).
31. National Collegiate Athletic Association, "NCAA Recruiting Facts," *NCAA.org*, March 2018, www.ncaa.org/sites/default/files/Recruiting%20Fact%20Sheet%20WEB.pdf.
32. Gary Klein, "NFL Myths: Some Players May be '$10-million Guys,' But Not All of Them Are Rich," *Los Angeles Times*, January 26, 2018, www.latimes.com/sports/nfl/la-sp-nfl-myths-20180126-story.html.
33. Even some advocates of the idea that children should be accorded a degree of autonomy think that paternalistic intervention to protect *future* autonomy is justified. See, for example, Amy Mullin, "Children, Autonomy, and Care," *Journal of Social Philosophy* 38, no. 4 (Winter 2007): 536–553; Amy Mullin, "Children, Paternalism, and the Development of Autonomy," *Ethical Theory and Moral* Practice 17, no. 3 (June 2014): 413–426.
34. Flanigan, *Pharmaceutical Freedom*, 42. This basic framework is endorsed by the American Academy of Pediatrics' Committee on Bioethics. See "Informed Consent in Decision-Making in Pediatric Practice," *Pediatrics* 138, no. 2 (August 2016): 1–7.
35. Debra Satz, *Why Some Things Should Not Be for Sale: The Moral Limits of Markets* (Oxford: Oxford University Press, 2012), 195ff.
36. The masterful 1996 documentary *When We Were Kings* is the source for most of my knowledge about the fight and the events leading up to it.
37. Klosterman, *But What if We're Wrong?*, 186.
38. Jeanne Marie Laskas, "The People V. Football," *GQ*, February 21, 2011, www.gq.com/story/jeanne-marie-laskas-nfl-concussions-fred-mcneill.

6

EGALITARIAN FANDOM

A few years ago, I started a soccer outreach program at a local elementary school. My aim was simple—to offer the chance to play organized soccer to kids who might not otherwise have the opportunity—and I began by putting together a boys team, mostly because the immediate pool of players was quite large. The school already had an intramural soccer program up and running, and of the students who were participating, probably 75 percent were boys. It didn't take long to find 12 of them who were willing to have me as their coach.

But even as I started with the boys, I made a decision that the number of boys teams would never be more than one greater than the number of girls teams. In other words, I wouldn't add a second boys team before I had a girls team, and there would have to be a second girls team before we ever had a third boys team. My reasons for this commitment were also simple: girls should have the same opportunity to enjoy playing soccer as boys. Even if more boys had prior experience with the game, and therefore may have already had a desire to play in a competitive environment, it didn't follow that the girls would not enjoy the opportunity once it was presented. Teach them the rudiments of the sport, provide them with a fun environment in which to learn, and they would come to love soccer every bit as much as the boys.

I would guess that these days, a sizable majority of sports fans would endorse these basic commitments. Unlike a couple of generations ago, fathers now encourage their daughters to play sports, and girls increasingly have mothers who themselves played sports growing up. Of course, women have always played sports, but in the United States, the passage of Title IX legislation in 1972 inaugurated a sweeping cultural change regarding the participation of girls in athletics. The federal statute makes it impermissible for an educational institution to exclude anyone from participation in, or denied the benefits of, "any school-based program, including athletics." The practical consequences of this law are that

> any educational institution receiving federal funding (virtually all the country's colleges and public K-12 campuses) must allocate equal resources to male and female participants, from locker rooms to tutoring. Violating the law puts an institution at risk of having its federal funding cut.[1]

The results of this legislation have been fairly clear. More scholarship money for women to play sports in college has led to more girls playing sports at nearly every level of competition. When

DOI: 10.4324/9781003223696-7

Title IX was passed in 1972, only about 30,000 women played college sports.[2] According to the NCAA, the number of women playing college sports during the 2017–2018 academic year was 216,378.[3] At the high school level, over 3.14 million girls now participate in athletics.[4] And while there have been some downward trends in youth sports participation over the last decade, the number of 6–12-year-old girls playing sports is unquestionably higher than it was 50 years ago. Overall, according to the Women's Sports Foundation, before Title IX, "one in 27 girls played sports. Today that number is two in five."[5] About 52.3 percent of girls aged 6–12 reported playing a team sport at least one day in 2017.[6]

However, while more girls than ever are participating in athletics, and while most sports fans likely applaud this development, this support has not yet led to large numbers of fans embracing women's sports *as fans*. For example, Game 3 of the 2018 WNBA Finals between the Seattle Storm and the Washington Mystics attracted 519,000 viewers.[7] Despite being the least watched NBA Finals since 2014, the 2018 series between the Cleveland Cavaliers and Golden State Warriors averaged 17.7 million viewers—a gap in viewership also seen at the collegiate level.[8] The 2018 NCAA men's basketball championship game averaged 16.5 million viewers.[9] That number was down 28 percent from 2017, but was still markedly higher than the 3.5 million viewers who tuned in for the women's championship.[10]

One outlier in this trend was the 2015 Women's World Cup final between the United States and Japan. Watched by 25.4 million people, it was the most viewed soccer game ever in the United States.[11] (For comparison, France and Croatia's 2018 World Cup Final drew a television audience of 11.8 million American viewers.[12]) However, it is hard to avoid concluding that nationalistic sentiment was driving those numbers as much as any genuine support for women's athletics. When players from the US Women's National Team take the field in the National Women's Soccer League (NWSL)—arguably the most competitive women's professional league in the world—they do so in front of crowds that average 6,000 fans.[13] Major League Soccer, which lags behind European soccer leagues in terms of quality (and other American sports leagues in terms of popularity), averages crowds of around 21,000. The best women soccer players on the planet regularly play in front of crowds smaller than those who pay to watch the Toledo Mud Hens play minor league baseball.[14]

To be clear, I'm no better than most fans in this regard. Despite my demonstrable support of girls' participation in sports, I rarely watch women play on television. I don't remember the last women's basketball game I watched, and while I follow the USWNT in their World Cup campaigns, I do not set aside time to watch them play in friendlies or less prestigious tournaments in the way I do for the men's team. At Wake Forest, I have been to a number of men's athletic events but as of this writing, I do not believe I have seen any of the women's teams compete. Nine years into my tenure here, that's not a great record for someone who claims to be committed to gender equality in the athletic realm.

Interestingly, anecdotal evidence suggests that the viewing habits of female sports fans are not markedly different from those of men when it comes to women's sports. When I talk to students about their support of women's sports, hardly anyone says that they have watched a WNBA or NWSL game in the past year, and even the female athletes in my classes rarely report being dedicated supporters of any women's teams. (In fact, I don't recall anyone self-identifying as a fan of a women's professional team.) And it's not that they aren't interested in sports. I rarely have anyone in my class on sports and society, regardless of gender, who is not a sports fan of some sort, and the course regularly attracts both male and female athletes. The issue rather seems to be that as fans, the viewing habits of women pretty much mirror those of men. They watch the NFL, college football, men's college basketball, and perhaps the NBA. Occasionally, they are fans of hockey teams or devoted to European soccer. But while they will wholeheartedly support women's participation in athletics, that support does not translate to women's teams unless, perhaps, the US women are playing in the World Cup.

As a straightforward report on the preferences of sports fans, one might deny that these numbers have any normative significance. Some people like basketball; others like hockey. Football is the most popular spectator sport in the United States, even though it is scarcely played anywhere else in the world. In Australia and England, millions of people tune in to watch The Ashes on television, while I suspect that many American readers of this book will have to quickly google "The Ashes" in an effort to know what I'm talking about.[15] Preferences vary, and there is no immediate reason to think that a preference for watching men play sports rather than women is a fundamentally different sort of preference.

However, this response strikes me as unsatisfactory for anyone who is genuinely concerned about gender equality. To argue that gendered hierarchies should be dismantled while being content with a sporting landscape where men receive a massively disproportionate amount of attention and money may not be a straightforwardly hypocritical, but it seems like an argument that is difficult to carry out in good faith. In this chapter, then, I want to present an alternative way of thinking about the support of women's sports—one that regards such support as a way to undermine patriarchal structures and attitudes and promote the full inclusion of women in our shared social spaces. As a longtime stronghold of masculinity, I would argue that sports fandom has the potential to move the needle significantly in terms of how we work toward gender equality more broadly, and fans who support women's sports may justifiably regard their fandom as an overt expression of their commitment to equality. In this way, being a fan of women's sports offers a double benefit: the chance to make a political statement while also enjoying everything else that sports are able to provide.

I begin by outlining some of the ways in which women's sports are consigned to a second-class status in much of the world, and I argue that this consignment reinforces troubling social inequalities that are based on gender, primarily by marginalizing the athletic talent and labor of women. I then consider some common objections to the idea that women's sports deserve our attention and suggest that all of them fail. As a result, those who love sports have no real reason not to support female athletes or women's teams. While I am reluctant to suggest precise rules for the form that this support should take, I am nevertheless willing to argue that there is genuine normative force to these considerations: sports fans *should* support women's sports. I thus conclude with a few thoughts about the force of this "should" and what it may, or may not, require of fans.

The Gendered Landscape of Professional Sports

The idea that boys may grow up to be professional athletes is unlikely to strike many people as strange. Sure, the odds are long—much longer than many boys with such a dream may recognize— and few of us know anyone personally whose livelihood comes from playing sports. Nevertheless, some men do climb to the highest levels of competition, achieving fame and fortune along the way, and a few more earn a comfortable living, even if they do not quite achieve superstardom. If a man really is good enough at his chosen athletic pursuit, there is a decent chance that sports can be his job.

The fact that this represents a genuine, if remote, possibility for men is due to the financial resources that flood many men's sports. Fans buy team paraphernalia and tickets to games. They watch their teams play on television and pay for subscription streaming services, and because they do all these things, advertisers pay millions of dollars to show commercials during breaks in the action. For superstar athletes, endorsement dollars are also available. Be famous enough for what you do on the field, and a company will pay you significant money to wear their shoes or appear in an ad drinking their latest sports beverage. Without all the dollars that consumers inject into the proceedings, the financial rewards available to male athletes would not be nearly as substantial as they are.

The situation is much different for women. For the most part, girls do not grow up knowing that if they are among the best in the world at their sport, they may be able to earn a living playing the games that they love. They may aim for athletic scholarships to help ease the financial burdens of college. But the likelihood of comfortably supporting themselves with an athletic career—already small for males—is even smaller for girls.

Individual sports seem to hold out somewhat greater hope in this regard. Purses for women's tennis and golf, though not as large as the men's, allow for the top players in the world to earn reasonable sums of money. Indeed, the woman in 100th place on the WTA prize money list for 2018 made $367,524 while the 100th spot on the LPGA money list garnered $113,220.[16] While these numbers aren't enough to buy a private island in the Caribbean, they certainly constitute a decent living. Individual endorsement contracts for women's track and field, swimming, gymnastics, and a handful of winter sports are enough to keep careers afloat in those sports, and during some Olympic cycles, endorsements can help gold medal winners obtain a greater level of financial security. For all those who don't stand atop the podium, the chances of a significant endorsement contract are, unsurprisingly, less than stellar. Wheaties is not going to put a fifth-place middle distance runner with zero name recognition on the front of their cereal boxes.

For women competing in the most popular team sports, the disparities are even starker. In her excellent book profiling the lives of professional women soccer players, Gwendolyn Oxenham details the remarkable career of Marta Vieira da Silva—one that, by almost any measure, contains accomplishments rivaling the great Pele:

> Between 2006 and 2010, Marta wins FIFA World Player of the Year an unprecedented five times in a row. On the professional level, she has kept pace with Pele: he scored 650 goals in 694 appearances; as of March 2017, Marta has 358 goals in 321 games. For the national team, Pele scored 77 goals in 91 national appearances; Marta has scored 105 goals in 101 national games.[17]

Despite not winning a World Cup title, a feat Pele managed to accomplish an unprecedented three times, Marta clearly stands as one of the best female soccer players to ever set foot on a pitch.

Nevertheless, when her home club in Brazil—the storied Santos FC, where Pele also began his career—faced the prospect of losing a player on their men's team to one of the large European clubs, they cut the entire women's team in order to secure enough money to keep him.[18] In 2010, Santos began receiving transfer offers for Neymar, at the time a 19-year-old rising star of undeniable talent. In order to meet his salary demands, Santos discontinued a women's squad that, because of Marta's presence on the field, was one of the best in South America and had drawn a respectable 13,000 fans to the Copa Libertadores final. As Oxenham points out, the entire operating budget for the women's team was $826,000 in 2012. Neymar was making $558,000 a month.[19] At the end of 2011, he had scored 80 goals in 153 first team appearances for Santos and 8 goals in 15 appearances for Brazil's national team—impressive accomplishments, to be sure, but notably short of the goal scoring pace Marta had been setting for years.[20] Neymar had also not won a World Cup.

Neymar would go on to leave Santos for Barcelona in 2013 for a transfer fee of 57 million euros.[21] From there, he would move to Paris St. Germain in 2017 for a world record fee of 198 million pounds.[22] By contrast, Marta has had trouble finding consistent employment. "Of the eight professional teams she's played for in the past, seven have folded, unable to stay financially afloat."[23] As I write, she plays for the Orlando Pride in NWSL, a league where the maximum salary is $42,600.[24] According to some reports, Neymar is paid 700,000 Euros *a week* by PSG.[25]

The disparate challenges faced by male and female athletes can also be seen in basketball. For financial reasons, roughly two-thirds of players in the WNBA play for a European team once the WNBA season is over.[26] With average WNBA salaries currently around $75,000, players look to supplement their income by playing for European clubs who often pay better than teams in the United States.[27] Detailed salary information is not easy to find, but according to some reports,

> a player with no WNBA experience can earn between $6,000 and $7,000 a month while playing in the top leagues in countries like Spain and Italy. A player with WNBA experience can earn an average of $13,000 a month while playing in the same tier league.[28]

This practice is not confined to midlevel players either. Prior to the 2015 season, Diana Taurasi (already a three-time WNBA champion and a seven-time All-Star) announced that she would be taking a break from the WNBA to rest her body and focus instead on European competition.[29] While the current WNBA league maximum of $113,500 is obviously a good salary in a country where the median household income is a little over $60,000, it paled in comparison to the $1.5 million that Taurasi's Russian club was willing to pay her.[30] For athletes who often retire in their early or mid-30s, it is understandable why players would take the chance to maximize their earnings in whatever way they can during their playing careers.

Suffice it to say that the top male athletes in the world do not look for side jobs to supplement their income in the offseason. The idea of Lebron James spending his summers in Latvia so he can provide increased financial security for his family would likely strike readers as preposterous. And yet, even though James and Taurasi have won the same number of league titles in their respective careers, Taurasi has regularly looked for opportunities to earn extra money by playing basketball.

Another choice that top male athletes typically do not have to make is whether they want to market themselves in an explicitly sexualized manner. To be sure, some of them choose to do so. David Beckham and Cristiano Ronaldo come immediately to mind as examples of men who have chosen to make their sex appeal a central part of (at least some of) their product endorsements. But they have both been among the highest paid athletes in the world at one time or another and have made more than enough money solely from their athletic labor to last several lifetimes. If they decided that they didn't want to market their appearance in a particular way, they might be limiting their earning potential, but their place among the very rich would not be at all threatened. By contrast, many top female athletes rely much more heavily on endorsements to obtain a measure of financial security, and given the way that women are often used in advertising campaigns, they often face one of two options for how to present themselves. As Olympic gold medalist Mary Lou Retton puts it, you're "either wholesome American squeaky clean or sexy vixen. Why do women have to be like that and the men don't?"[31]

Importantly, when women choose to deliberately market their appearance, they are often criticized for their decision on the grounds that it demeans their status as topflight athletes. For example, American hurdler Lolo Jones was the target of a scathing editorial in the *New York Times* during the 2012 Olympics. Pointing out that Jones had posed nude for *ESPN the Magazine* and appeared on the cover of *Outside* in a "bathing suit made of nothing but strategically placed ribbon," Jere Longman argued that Jones's popularity at the time "was based not on achievement but on her exotic beauty and on a sad and cynical marketing campaign."[32] Longman wrote:

> Women have struggled for decades to be appreciated as athletes. For the first time at these Games, every competing nation has sent a female participant. But Jones is not assured enough with her hurdling or her compelling story of perseverance. So she has played into

100 Egalitarian Fandom

the persistent, demeaning notion that women are worthy as athletes only if they have sex appeal. And, too often, the news media have played right along with her.

Anne Griffin sums up the tension. "Appearance, sex appeal and charisma are among myriad factors that can turn an athlete—or any public entertainer—into a media star," she writes. But it is a difficult line to walk as some athletes end up portraying "themselves in a way that's good for their personal brand but potentially detrimental to their sport or other female athletes."[33]

This tension extends even to the way in which women's sports are marketed by various leagues and governing bodies. Charlene Weaving thus criticizes the rule that used to require women's beach volleyball players to wear bikinis:

> The message sent out via the uniform rule perpetuates the belief that women's beach volleyball only attracts viewers and a fan base by promoting the sexualization of the women athletes. It also promotes the notion that women's sport is not a good enough product to sell on its own, and that women athletes are not talented enough to attract viewership—that we need to market them as sexualized, "sexy" women rather than strong, powerful, athletic women. I see this as a step backward for women's participation and positioning in the Olympics, as well as their overall perception in society.[34]

On the one hand, it is not difficult to see how explicitly marketing the attractiveness of female volleyball players might draw more attention to the sport and thereby bolster the financial rewards available to the athletes. On the other hand, that very strategy has the potential to undermine an appreciation for the very same women *qua* athletes.

My intention here isn't at all to criticize the choice that any particular woman has made about how she wants to market herself. It is rather to highlight the fact that the conditions under which they have made those decisions are much different than those affecting the marketing strategies of high-profile male athletes. And while I certainly think that league policies *requiring* athletes to present themselves in a sexualized manner are inappropriate, I nevertheless think it is possible to see those policies as at least potentially motivated by a genuine desire to promote women's sports *as sports*. In our current cultural landscape, using the sex appeal of athletes might just be a distasteful means of getting people to pay attention, the hope being that over time, viewers will come to appreciate the athletic competition for its own sake. But even if this interpretation is plausible, it still illustrates the marginalized role that women generally occupy in the world of sports. After all, those in charge of men's leagues aren't contemplating similar marketing strategies.

Fan Preference and Standards of Excellence

I suspect that many people, sports fans included, will assess the challenges faced by female athletes by arguing that there is no inherent right to be able to make a decent living playing a game that you love, much less any right to achieve fame and fortune. Put even more strongly, one might argue that there is no inherent right to make a living at *any* particular thing you might want to do, and as a result, the plight of female athletes might be somewhat unfortunate, but it is not at all unjust. You might want to make a living writing experimental fiction about dope smoking sea turtles struggling with their sense of identity, but your inability to do so does not represent a wrong that needs to be righted, much less impose on me any obligation to spend money on your work. By the same token, the fact that Marta has a deep desire to be a professional soccer player does not entail that the disparities between her career and Neymar's represent any kind of injustice. If fans want to buy tickets to watch her play or tune into her games on television, they are obviously free to do so. But if they would rather devote that money to other things, that is fine too, and because fans have decided to spend more time and money watching men play soccer, men reap a larger share of the financial rewards on offer. That's just the way things play out given the preferences people happen to have.

To be sure, I don't think the basic thought underlying this objection is very controversial. There was a time in my life when I genuinely desired to be a professional golfer. Unfortunately, I wasn't nearly good enough to play at that level, and so nothing more than some very modest success as a player on my high school team ever materialized. Did my deep desire to play golf for a living somehow entitle me to that kind of career? Conditions in the world sometimes mean that our deepest desires go unfulfilled. Sometimes the reasons are that we simply aren't good enough to do what we want to do. Other times, the explanation is that people simply aren't interested in what we have to offer. I could devote the next year of my life to abstract painting in the hopes of bolstering my son's college fund. But if no one likes my pictures, they certainly don't have to buy them, no matter how much I might want the money. Justice doesn't require that we always get what we want in life.

Despite the general plausibility of this line of thought, I don't think it ultimately undermines the idea that disparities between men's and women's sports should legitimately concern those who claim to value gender equality. For while it is generally true that justice does not demand that we always get what we want in life, it does seem to demand that failures to get what we want in life should not result from our gender. This is importantly different from saying that biological limitations do not sometimes affect our ability to get what we want. No matter how much I might want to be pregnant, biological limitations prohibit that from happening (at least at this point in human history). Similarly for my desire to be an NBA power forward, a desire that is clearly contravened by my 5'10" height and insufficiently broad shoulders. If your athletic career is limited because you lack the physical characteristics necessary to excel in your sport of choice, you can shake your fist at the universe in frustration, but you don't really have a legitimate complaint.

Moreover, I think it is also reasonable to grant that the preferences of others can sometimes legitimately affect our ability to get what we want. If people just happen to prefer watching basketball to reading your experimental fiction, so be it. You might just be a bit before your time. And if there is not a significant market for field hockey, because the public doesn't have much interest in the sport, then you probably shouldn't complain about the injustice of failing to get a multimillion-dollar contract as a center forward.

But the limitations that are sometimes placed on athletes' careers because of their gender seem to be different in kind from these sorts of limitations. After all, there are plenty of people who clearly love sports, and millions around the world are perfectly happy to devote significant portions of their time and money to supporting athletes. And there are clearly plenty of women who can play their respective sports at a very high level. Marta is good enough at soccer to compete at the highest echelons of the game. At a certain point, it is difficult to conclude that the main reason she has struggled to make a living at the game she loves is that she is a woman. Imagine a female writer who loves writing experimental fiction about sea turtles, and suppose further that she is very skilled at writing such books (using whatever standards of excellence might be appropriate for this obscure genre). If she is unable to sell her books because no one really wants to read any books in this genre, she might be disappointed, but that disappointment would not constitute an ethical concern for the reading public. People just aren't interested in sea turtle fiction. However, if she is unable to sell her (excellent) books even as her male colleagues are funding lavish lifestyles with the sales of their (okay but not excellent) books about sea turtles, the reading public will have reason to be concerned. One's ability to sell their books shouldn't depend on their gender.

The basic idea here is, I think, similar to one pressed by Jane English in her seminal essay "Sex Equality in Sports." In that paper, English makes a distinction between the basic benefits of sports—goods like health, "the chance to improve one's skills," and "just plain fun"—and the scarce benefits of sports which she seems to limit to "fame and fortune."[35] According to English, while everyone has an equal right to the basic benefits of sports, regardless of their gender or any other characteristic they might possess, not everyone has an equal right to scarce benefits. For example, I don't have a right to the fame and fortune lavished on famous athletes, because I am not that great of an athlete.

However, English argues that the scarce benefits of sports should not accrue disproportionately to various social groups. In other words, every individual may not have a right to become a famous athlete or to make a living playing a game that they love. But in a society (such as ours) that accords some people those opportunities, it should not be the case that only white men (for example) have access to them. English frames the stakes here in terms of self-respect:

> When there are virtually no female athletic stars, or when women receive much less prize money than men do, this is damaging to the self-respect of all women. Members of disadvantaged groups identify strongly with each other's successes and failures. If women do not attain roughly equal fame and fortune in sports, it leads both men and women to think of women as naturally inferior. Thus, it is not a right of women tennis stars to the scarce benefits, but rather a right of all women to self-respect that justifies their demand for equal press coverage and prize money.[36]

Because there is clearly a market for spectator sports, failing to provide women access to the benefits of that market explicitly marginalizes them and sends the message that their talents and abilities are not as valuable. The effect of that marginalization can be a corresponding erosion of self-respect among members of the marginalized group.

Pamela Sailors has recently criticized English on this point. At least in the case of gender segregated sports, where men and women do not compete against each other, she argues that the self-respect of women may not be enhanced. Citing the work of Eileen McDonagh and Laura Pappano, she suggests that "imposing segregation reflects the notion that women are unable to be competitive with men and, thus, must be protected. The result is the drawing of an able/disabled binary, which only perpetuates the idea that women are lesser than men."[37] In other words, efforts to promote the self-esteem of women and girls by offering them the chance to compete against other girls may backfire by reinforcing an athletic hierarchy that consistently places men above women.

Sailors's assessment may draw support from a general suspicion of the athletic ability of female athletes. According to this sort of objection, the claim that women like Marta or Diana Taurasi are among the best athletes in the world is simply mistaken. They might very well be among the best *women* who play their particular sport. But if forced to compete against men, their performance would not be nearly as impressive. Could Marta so much as make the squad of a Major League Soccer team, to say nothing of one of the top flight teams in the Champions League? Could Taurasi get on the roster of a top Division I men's basketball team, much less earn a significant amount of playing time? The fact that women require separate divisions thus illustrates their inferiority, and any corresponding complaint they have about the difficulty of making a living at their chosen sport goes away. Consumer demand is for the highest levels of athletic competition, and women are unable to satisfy that demand, not because they are women, but simply because they are not good enough. If they can hold their own against the boys, then so be it. Otherwise, fans are simply recognizing that the product on the field that women are able to produce does not warrant the support garnered by men.

This sort of objection suffers from a number of problems—problems that also undermine Sailors's response to English. To begin with, I suspect that a lot of those who disparage the quality of women's sports—at least in such venues as social media and sports talk radio—often do so in a more sweeping fashion than my representation of their view might suggest. In other words, they often seem to be implying (though they rarely come right out and say it) that the overwhelming majority of men who are even moderately athletic are superior to the women who compete at the highest levels of their respective sports. In their minds, the 35-year-olds who play pickup basketball every Saturday morning would certainly compete with—and probably beat—the local college's women's team. Scan Twitter the next time a prominent women's sporting event is going on—the Women's World Cup or the NCAA Women's College Basketball tournament. It's not hard to find guys who will argue that their son's high school team would easily defeat the tournament champions.

However, the idea that nearly every moderately coordinated male is a superior athlete to nearly every female, is quite clearly false. I am moderately athletic and, for a man in his mid-40s, in decent physical condition. But any player on Wake Forest's women's basketball team would make me look patently ridiculous on the court. Why? Because they are all vastly superior to me at playing basketball. The co-ed adult soccer league I played in a couple of years ago has a rule that each team must have a woman on the field at all times, otherwise they have to play with six players instead of the standard seven. I understand the justification for this rule, and it is certainly well-intentioned, but I also found it a bit patronizing to the women in the league. Our team, in particular, had a woman who was probably the second or third best player on the squad. If I subbed in for her, the overall quality of the team would go down significantly. Why? Because she is a much better soccer player than I am.

Being better at sports than I am might be a fairly low bar for female athletes to clear. But I think skeptics about the quality of women's sports probably underestimate the quality of play at its highest levels in a fairly systematic way. For example, WNBA teams regularly put together practice squads of men in an effort to challenge themselves against players whose size and strength are difficult to find in women, and Natalie Weiner thus describes the experience of such men as follows:

> [T]he men anxiously trying to prove their worth on the hardwood are aware of how they look to so many of their peers, who use social media to share memes that make the same sexism women basketball players have always faced nearly inescapable. "Get back in the kitchen," "Who cares?" and, of course, "I could beat a WNBA player one-on-one" are all familiar refrains.
>
> "I just laugh," says 30-year-old Garvin McAlister, who is an assistant coach at Post University, a DII school in Waterbury. He's been on the Sun practice squad for years, and knows better than most just how implausible those online claims to on-the-court dominance really are. "I'm like, 'You will get killed, what are you talking about?'"[38]

The Phoenix Mercury probably would not be able to beat the Phoenix Suns, but they are still better than a sizeable number of men's squads who step on the court.

In a similar vein, Oxenham details professional soccer player Allie Long's foray into the male-dominated world New York City's futsal leagues. Trying to sharpen her own skills in the off-season (and earn some extra money), she is initially treated with skepticism and as something of an oddity. But when the men find out she can play—and play well—they are disappointed when she doesn't show up on a given week. "Where's my *gringa*?" they ask, knowing that Long will be able to help their competitive prospects.[39] The players that Long is playing with are good, and she notes her dismay that "they never made it" at the professional level.[40] I'm guessing that most of them are better than the kids on my son's high school team, and by implication, I suspect the odds of my son's high school team defeating the women's world champions (for whom Long has played as a member of the US Women's National Team) would be, well, really low.[41]

If this kind of (admittedly) anecdotal evidence about the athletic ability of women isn't convincing, Eileen McDonagh and Laura Pappano have pointed out that there are plenty of cases in which women are able to straightforwardly outperform men in athletic competition. Women, in particular, seem to do quite well in ultra-endurance sports. For example, Pamela Reed won the 2002 Badwater Ultra Marathon, beating all other male and female competitors by almost five hours, and of the four course records kept for the Catalina Swim—22 miles between Santa Catalina Island and the California coast—three are held by women.[42] Girls have won state wrestling championships competing directly against boys, and Lynn Hill was the first person—male or female—to free climb the nose of El Capitan in Yosemite National Park.[43] Perhaps these are niche sports that do not garner the kind of fan attention lavished on football or basketball, but these examples should be enough to show, at the very least, that not all men are better than all women at any given sport. Indeed, my strong suspicion is that most of the men talking about the clear inferiority of female athletes on social media would not be able to compete on anything like equal terms with many of the best women athletes in the world.[44]

Some fans may be inclined to dig in their heels and argue that they are happy to watch women who are, in fact, the best in the world at their given sports. Women who can beat men at ultra-distance running or swimming, for example, would be worthy of support. But because the best women soccer players in the world cannot compete with the best men in the world, fans cannot be expected to invest significant time and energy in following women's soccer. Similarly for basketball or ice hockey—team sports where the best men's teams in the world would beat the best women's teams in the world. And if the reason why they choose not to support women's teams has to do with the excellence of their play rather than the gender of the athletes who are competing, then they can't really be accused to failing to satisfy any particular ideal of fandom. They are just being consistent in their appreciation of excellence.

I suppose purist fans would be able to maintain this kind of position in certain cases. If, in fact, their appreciation of sport is tied to the quality of play on the field—measured in some quasi-objective manner—then perhaps they could insist that watching men play is always preferable to watching women, at least in sports where the best men are clearly better than the best women. However, for partisan fans, this sort of defense is untenable for one simple reason: such fans are not at all consistent in their commitment to only support teams composed of the best athletes in the world. As I've detailed, my passionate devotion to the Badgers doesn't have anything to do with their excellence. Indeed, in my childhood years, I knew that the Badger football and basketball teams were not made up of the best players in the Big Ten Conference, much less the world. Fans of lower-division soccer teams around the globe know they are not watching the best players in the world, and yet such knowledge has absolutely no effect on the tenacity of their commitment. In the United States, people can be committed to minor league teams that have deep ties to the local community even as they know that most of the players on those teams will never make it to the majors. Why, then, should the fact that a women's team could not defeat a men's team have any effect at all on one's support? The Wisconsin Badgers football team couldn't defeat the New England Patriots either. That doesn't mean I won't support them as enthusiastically as I can. If the North Carolina Courage cannot beat the Columbus Crew, so be it. If I like soccer, I may still have good reason to buy tickets to their games, watch them on television, and wear team paraphernalia, just as I do for the Crew.

As Emily Ryall has pointed out, our engagement with sports really only requires three things—"excellence of skill, uncertainty of outcome, and a crescendo of drama that isn't relinquished until the last second"—none of which are limited to men or, for that matter, only the best athletes in the world.[45] Ryall thus continues:

> A battle where players and fans are on edge, mettles are tested, and the game flows in favor of one opponent, then the other, then—depending on who you're cheering for—back to the other side's favor again. Those are the kinds of games we hunger to see and the ones that enter into the history books: Whether they're played by men or women is neither here nor there.[46]

If, as I have argued, we are drawn to sports by the excitement they are able to provide and the way they can challenge us to reflect on the nature of the good life, and if, as I have also argued, we often attach ourselves to teams because of factors other than their excellence on the field, then there is no reason to think that women's sports cannot provide fans everything that men's sports can provide. And if it is excitement and our love of teams that leads us to devote our financial resources to sports at all, then there is no reason to think that women should not have a sizable share of those resources.

Protesting Misogyny

Cynical readers may be forgiven for thinking that there are other, less principled explanations for a general failure to support women's sports teams—explanations that require us to acknowledge a basic misogyny at work in the world of sports. In her compelling book *Down Girl*, Kate Manne has argued that misogyny "should be understood as the 'law enforcement' branch of a patriarchal order, which has the overall function of *policing* and *enforcing* its governing ideology."[47] Thus, if patriarchy is a "social milieu" in which "all or most women are positioned as subordinate in relation to some man or men therein," misogyny is the tool that men (and perhaps even some women) use to ensure that patriarchy is not threatened.[48] In practice, "misogynistic social forces" will "target girls and women (in the relevant class) for actual, perceived, or representative challenges to or violations of applicable patriarchal norms and expectations."[49] Challenge the patriarchal structure, and the misogynistic police will step in to make sure things get back to the way they want them.

Importantly, Manne does not think that either patriarchy or misogyny require any overt hostility toward women. Misogynists may like women very much, provided they behave according to the expectations of the misogynist. Usually, this involves staying confined to fairly proscribed gender roles in which women provide things *for* men. Manne thus writes that women are often viewed as "givers" of particular kinds of goods: "love, sex, attention, affection, and admiration, as well as other forms of emotional social, reproductive and caregiving labor, in accordance with social norms that govern and structure the relevant roles and relations."[50] As long as women continue to give men what they want, men are likely to be quite happy with women; they may even love them. However, when women act contrary to these expectations, either by failing to provide what men want or, even worse, challenging men's dominant place in a particular sphere, the attitudes of the misogynist are likely to change, and women are likely to run headlong into the social structures that keep patriarchy the entrenched force that it is.

I think the application of this account to the realm of women's sports is troublingly straightforward. Perhaps the reason why people who are otherwise passionate sports fans are resistant to supporting women's teams in any robust way is that they have fallen prey to misogyny. Whether or not they are actively misogynist themselves, they have given in to a policing of the world of sports

106 Egalitarian Fandom

that enforces its patriarchal structure.[51] On this view, women's teams are not marginalized because they are inferior. They are instead marginalized primarily because they threaten the dominance of men.

This analysis would explain why male fans are happy to support female athletes in ways that confine them to roles traditionally played by women where they can provide what Manne calls "feminine-coded goods."[52] Men, in particular, are happy to express their admiration for female athletes whom they regard as physically attractive, even as they are not interested in taking those same women seriously *as athletes*. And women who compete in sports outside the hegemonic team sports that fill the world's stadiums are likewise regarded as unthreatening. Such fans might, therefore, happily display a poster of the USWNT's Alex Morgan posing alluringly in a bikini but never give any serious consideration to supporting the Orlando Pride. Viewed in this way, Morgan is able to provide men with goods that women are supposed to provide them—aesthetic and sexual pleasure—in a way that doesn't require her to be taken seriously as an athlete.

By the same token, women who play beach volleyball (in bikinis) or women gymnasts and figure skaters do not awaken the forces of misogyny because they are able to compete while simultaneously offering men a dose of the aesthetic pleasure they expect. The uniforms of beach volleyball players explicitly signal that the women on the court are not sacrificing any of their stereotypically feminine characteristics in the pursuit of their athletic goals. And sports like figure skating and gymnastics do not threaten patriarchal expectations not only because of the attire of the participants but also because the sports themselves are coded as feminine. Boys who want to be gymnasts or figure skaters will be fighting against cultural assumptions that regard these pursuits as "girly" or for "sissies." However, when women play basketball or soccer, they are participating in traditional strongholds of male dominance in uniforms that are essentially the same as those worn by their male counterparts. They aren't doing anything coded as feminine, and as a result, their only real contribution is negative: to detract attention from the men who feel entitled to it.

If this application of Manne's view is plausible, then it presents another reason for fans to support female athletes (and in particular women's teams in sports traditionally played by men), namely, that such support represents a direct challenge to patriarchy. By following women's games with the same passion and intensity as they devote to men's teams, fans are able to subvert the assumption that the realm of competitive athletics is the special province of men—one that they deign to open to women only as a grudging concession to the forces of political correctness. Moreover, as Erin Tarver has argued, such support has the potential to have a wider impact on the self-conception of women and girls as they contemplate the various paths they can take through the world. She thus writes:

> The identification with women athletes as agents and heroes is important not only because it rejects the dominant discourse of femininity as unimportant apart from women's appeal as sexual objects but also because it offers girls and women a means of cultivating a more robust sense of bodily agency.[53]

In other words, the more that women and girls plausibly conceive of themselves as athletes, the more they might be able to "imaginatively inhabit the world as a subject who says 'I can.'"[54]

Of course, the choices of individual fans are probably not enough to radically transform the landscape of sports all on their own. In the same way that combating large scale problems like climate change requires input from large-scale actors like governments, corporations, philanthropic initiatives, and non-governmental organizations, any significant change to the role that female athletes play in our broader sporting culture will almost certainly require those in positions of influence make it their explicit aim to promote women's sports. For example, Santos had a chance to make a notable statement by trying to keep their women's team alive, even if it meant losing Neymar. They instead chose to keep Neymar and thereby sacrifice their women's team. The NBA could choose to direct even more of its resources into promoting the WNBA and paying its players wages that don't require them to take a second job. And the US Soccer Federation could leave all questions about revenue generation to the side and simply choose to pay its four-time World Cup winning women's team equally to the US men.[55] Organizations make statements with the use of their resources and advocating for a greater appreciation of women's sports would be a worthy statement to make with their expenditures.

Even when the goals are purely financial, it is worth noting how willing investors are to lose money on men's sports in the short term in order to reap rewards down the line. As Lindsay Gibbs points out, Vince McMahon has publicly stated that he expects to lose $375 million in the first three years of the newly reconstituted XFL—a football league created to play in the NFL's offseason.[56] McMahon's hope is that the early losses will be recouped in a few years when the XFL is an established commodity with a regular presence on television. By contrast, the NBA supports the WNBA with a mere $12 million dollars annually—an amount less than the salaries of 117 NBA players. There isn't an immediate demand at present to justify McMahon's investment, but he believes that he can increase that demand over time by guiding the league through some growing pains.

Only time will tell whether McMahon's gamble will pay off. For my purposes, what is important is the following comment from Gibbs:

> Men's pro sports succeed because people with power and money have given them the investment and the time that is needed to succeed. They succeed because the people with power and money want them to. Yes, market forces are a part of it. But there's always someone pulling the strings of those forces, deciding when they're a challenge and when they're a dagger, picking and choosing which messages to take from them.[57]

What if a wealthy investor decided to drop $100 million to help promote the WNBA or NWSL? Might they find that they could help to make those leagues established commodities? As Gibbs concludes: "The XFL provides us yet another reminder that in men's sports, the rules are simply different."[58]

I am inclined to think that individuals willing to invest large sums of money in women's sports is probably the single best way to move the needle regarding their popularity. Improving the infrastructure surrounding women's teams—from the quality of training facilities and coaching to the experience in the stadiums—will almost certainly produce a better product on the field. And more prominent distribution of women's games on television can make it easier for fans watch games and develop attachments to particular players and teams.

Nevertheless, fans make statements with their behavior as well, and by directing their time and financial resources toward women's sports, they also have the opportunity to change the economic realities that female athletes face. Those who are disconcerted by the fact that Marta's career has followed such a circuitous route or who think it unfortunate that the best women basketball players in the world earn a little more than one-eighth of the NBA's league minimum can help to alter the market. They can inject more money into women's sports by buying game tickets and team apparel. They can draw advertising dollars by watching games on television and online subscription services. And they can shift cultural perceptions by devoting the same kind of time and emotional energy to the fortunes of women's teams as they do to the men's teams around which they organize their lives. Doing so can send a message to those around them that sports need not be—and, indeed, should not be—a male-dominated space, whether in the stands or on the field. In this way, being a fan of female athletes and women's teams can be a explicitly political act, one which puts yet another nail in the coffin of purely escapist fandom.

As readers might suspect, given the tone I've worked to strike in the preceding chapters, I don't think that focusing on a rigid set of rules to govern fan support of women's sports is likely to be particularly helpful, in part because I confess that I am not sure what a sufficiently egalitarian sporting landscape ultimately looks like. English seems to suggest that it is one where fully equal resources go to men's and women's sports and the overall pie of money and fame devoted to sports is, therefore, divided equally between men and women. Perhaps this vision is the right one. I certainly wouldn't object to it in principle.

However, there seem to be too many variables for me to be confident that this is the only acceptable goal toward which to strive. For example, the overwhelming popularity of football in the United States—a sport played only by men but popular among fans of all genders—may skew the numbers in ways that make it difficult to know what sorts of outcomes are desirable. As another illustration, the soccer club where I coach regularly fields more boys teams than girls teams at almost every level of competition, even though they work hard to promote an egalitarian ethos in all of their programs. It just happens that more boys than girls tend to want to play soccer in our area of North Carolina.

By the same token, it isn't clear to me that those who genuinely want to promote equality for women in sports can only do so by devoting the same amount of time and energy to women's sports as they do to the men. If you are a serious football fan, does that mean that you have to devote an equal amount of time to a sport that women play? What if you don't really like soccer or basketball, whether it is played by men or women? Does that make you insufficiently committed to the equality of women as athletes, given that women don't play football?

What I think is preferable is that rather than agonizing over the specific allocation of the time and money they spend on men's and women's sports, fans should simply look for ways to increase resources and promote opportunities for female athletes through their fandom. This may strike some die-hards as unsatisfying, but I think analogies with other large-scale problems like climate change end up being fairly instructive here. As I've noted, I think that successfully addressing climate change is not something that can be done entirely at the level of individual choice. Any meaningful progress requires significant changes in all sorts of national and international policies as well as the investment of huge sums of money in various technological innovation, and those of us who want to mitigate the effects of global warming should vigorously advocate for those policies.

At the same time, anyone who claims to be concerned about the environment should probably have that concern reflected somewhere in their behavior. There should probably be *something* that they do—or something that they refrain from doing—because they care about the effect of such actions on the environment. These actions may be small, like recycling or refraining from burning leaves in one's yard, or large, like installing solar panels on one's house and driving electric cars. But either way, such choices have tangible effects on the environment, make a statement about one's commitments to the cause, and perhaps spark interest in making further progress, both in oneself and others. These things are, it seems to me, part and parcel of what it means to be committed to improving the environment, and while such a commitment might not require that one do absolutely everything one can for the cause, someone who did none of them would rightfully have their commitment questioned.

In the same way, fans should look for tangible ways to support women's sports even as they advocate for the kinds of policies and financial investments that will be required to more fully level the playing field in the long run. This support may take a variety of forms. One might opt to become a full-blown fan of a women's team and devote similar amounts of time and financial resources to that endeavor as they devote to the men's teams they follow. Or they might resolve to attend the local college's women's soccer or basketball game with their kids, even if those aren't sports they would typically set aside time to watch. Doing so would not only provide some level of financial support for those teams; it would also introduce the next generation to the enjoyment that all sports can provide, no matter who is playing them.

Again, the point isn't to lay out a specific formula for how to go about this process. Nor is it to deny that individuals can always do more. As in the case of climate change, I have no doubt that most fans can do more to support the equality of women in the athletic realm. Nevertheless, I think that acknowledging the problem and setting out some tangible ways to proceed is a good start. Indeed, if the majority of fans take even these small steps, my suspicion is that there would start to be a notable shift in the material conditions of female athletes and that the enjoyment fans would derive from the experience would spur even further change.

And Yes, You Can Adopt a New Team

I want to conclude this chapter by responding to one final objection—a response that fills out the comparison I drew in Chapter 3 between loving teams and loving our family members. On the view I defended there, most fans don't really choose the teams they support but instead simply find themselves attached. I no more chose to become a fan of the Milwaukee Brewers than I chose to love my parents or my sister. But if this analysis is right, then one might worry that it poses a significant problem for my contention that sports fans should support women's teams much more robustly than they currently do. After all, if we can't choose which teams we end up loving, then we can't decide to become emotionally invested in the prospects of a women's team just because we think we should. I can no more choose to become a fan of the Atlanta Dream than I can resolve to be a fan of the Charlotte Hornets. Genuine fandom develops organically—a fact that will stubbornly resist whatever commitments we have about women's equality. Acknowledging the value of supporting women's sports does not, therefore, bring about a corresponding obligation to actively support any women's teams.

While I am obviously sympathetic with the basic ideas underlying this objection, I think they nevertheless fail to undermine the main points I make in this chapter. To begin with, it isn't clear that this particular line of thought cuts against a more purist approach to engaging with women's sports. Thus, one might think that a useful way to bolster the profile of female athletes is simply to watch more games on television or even attend events in which one has no particular rooting interest. Even this kind of dispassionate fandom would increase TV ratings and team revenue, and it would also seem to send a social message about the significance of women's athletics. If one thinks that it is important to achieve these kinds of goals, then one has a number of concrete ways to help bring them about that do not require the love of particular teams.

However, for those who (like me) prefer to engage with sports as a partisan, I think the model of adoptive parenting that I introduced in Chapter 3 provides a useful template for thinking about the relationships we might develop with new teams. The experiences of people who decide to adopt children are, no doubt, as varied as the experiences of those who have their own biological children, and I do not intend anything I say here to imply that there is any universal experience of parenting, much less adoptive parenting. That said, it is worth noting that at least some people who make the decision to adopt children do so out of a sense of obligation. That is, they do so because they think it is something they should do. They see that there are children who do not have families of their own, believe they have the resources and ability to provide a good home for those children, and thereby resolve to help at least one child through adoptive parenting. It is, therefore, not a grudging sense of obligation that leads them to pursue this course of action—something they endure through gritted teeth—but rather a sense of responsibility and a desire to make the world a slightly better place in whatever small way they can.

Moreover, as I've argued, the children that adoptive parents end up parenting are very rarely selected on the basis of any criteria of excellence. Many times, the particular children they parent are assigned to them or selected (if that is even the correct term) only because they are available to be adopted. There is no previous relationship to explain why one child is adopted rather than another, nor may the parents really know anything about the child's appearance or personality traits. And even in cases where prospective parents do know these sorts of facts about a child, such knowledge does not serve as any kind of basis for the adoption. Many adoptive parents I know (and I happen to know quite few) are happy simply to have the opportunity to adopt any child, no matter what that child happens to be like.

If the decision to adopt a child is sometimes motivated by a sense of responsibility, and if the children who end up being adopted are not chosen on the basis of any particular characteristics, the emotional attachments that result are, ultimately, no different than the emotional attachments that people develop with their biological children. Parents love and care for their adoptive children in ways that are largely indistinguishable from the ways that nearly all parents love and care for their children, even though their decision to become parents may have been motivated by a sense of responsibility. They grieve their adopted children's pain and rejoice in their happiness. They pursue their adopted children's interests to the best of their ability. And they cannot imagine exchanging their adopted children for any other, even if those others might, in various ways, be superior to their own kids. If they happen to also have biological children of their own, the idea of imposing some hierarchy of value on their kids probably strikes them as anathema. Their children are their children, no matter how the parenting relationship may have originated.

I think these features of adoptive parenting are important for thinking about the idea that we might have an obligation to support women's sports teams. On the one hand, they show that it is possible to decide to enter into an emotionally significant relationship because you think you should do so. If some adoptive parents can be motivated by this sense of responsibility, there is no obvious reason why sports fans could not be similarly motivated. On the other hand, the analogy with adoptive parenting suggests that the emotional attachments that result from such a decision can be as strong and meaningful as attachments whose history is somewhat different. My attachment to the Milwaukee Brewers might have come about simply because my dad is a Brewers fan. But that doesn't mean that a decision to support the OL Reign would not ultimately produce a similar kind of affection.

To be sure, I think it would be unreasonable to expect such affection to arise immediately. My entire life as a sports fan has involved the Milwaukee Brewers. I have suffered through many of their losing seasons and enjoyed their (comparatively few) triumphs. I have watched them play in person numerous times and know their current roster well enough to have opinions about the performance of various players. Their seasons have structured non-trivial portions of my life, and expecting to immediately respond to the successes and failures of a newly adopted team in precisely the same way would not be realistic.

However, the fact that affection for a team may not be instantaneous is not a reason to think that any resulting affection would not be genuine or, eventually, just as strong as the love that one has for the other teams one supports. When the Columbus Blue Jackets came into existence as an NHL expansion team in 2000, fans in the city did not immediately love them in the same way that they loved the Ohio State Buckeyes football team. They may have been excited about having a top-flight professional sports team in their town and looked forward to the prospect of attending games, but it would have been unreasonable to expect them to immediately have the same level of affection for the Jackets as the Buckeyes. Nevertheless, after over 20 years, there are now plenty of fans who care just as passionately about the Jackets as they do any other team they support, including the Buckeyes. If fans can adopt a brand-new team just because of its presence in their city, there is no reason why they cannot similarly adopt a women's team because of their commitment to gender equality.

Egalitarian Fandom **111**

A slightly different objection to my proposal is that the presence of existing loyalties leaves little space to develop new ones. Given limited time and emotional resources, it is not reasonable to expect fans to add to their list of sporting commitments. This sort of argument is framed (though not advocated) by Markovits and Albertson as the "sports space" argument—the idea "that consumers simply do not have 'room' left to care about and closely follow women's team sports, considering the space that is taken up by the hegemonic sports."[59] If you already follow the exploits of a college and professional football team, a college basketball team, a professional baseball team, and two professional soccer teams (as I do), then you might not be able to find the time, much less the enthusiasm, to devote to any other teams. As much as we don't like to admit it, our time is limited, and there are not enough hours in the day to do all the things that are worth doing. If we are going to avoid devoting every waking second of our lives to following sports, there have to be limits. Simply adding an item to an already long list of fan commitments is not a recipe for a well-rounded existence.

However, I do not think that the "sports space" argument ultimately provides convincing reasons to refrain from supporting women's teams. To begin with, while our time may be limited, it is not at all obvious that our affections are limited in similar ways. The love I have for my son does not at all limit the amount of love I have for my daughter, and while there may be good reasons for people to limit the number of children they have, the fact that they only have a finite amount of love is probably not one of them. Similarly, my love for the Green Bay Packers doesn't affect how much I love the Columbus Crew, and my fairly recent attachment to Tottenham has done nothing to inhibit my affection for the Wisconsin Badgers football team. Neither would adopting a women's team exhaust my supply of sports related love.

Moreover, there is a way in which the addition of new sporting loyalties might help fans to keep existing commitments in perspective. Because our time is indeed limited, it is true that following the exploits of one team will sometimes mean that we cannot follow the exploits of another. And if we want to devote ourselves to anything other than sports, sometimes we will have to forego watching games entirely. Round the clock sports watching on multiple screens is, perhaps, one way to live, but it is probably not a good way to live. Adding new loyalties may, therefore, force us to make decisions about which games we are going to watch in ways that are healthy. Allowing ourselves to miss some of the games of our favorite teams can reinforce the idea that we are not ultimately responsible for their fortunes. Whether they win or lose is not up to us, and our lives will continue no matter the outcome of the game. This is no less true if we are missing one of our team's games because we are watching another game than it is if we miss a game for some pursuit that has nothing to do with sports. Missing games is okay, and doing so doesn't make anyone less of a real fan.

So, follow women's sports. Adopt a women's team. Challenge patriarchy. Your other teams won't mind, and your relationships to them may even be better for it.

Notes

1. Alia Wong, "Where Girls Are Missing Out on High-School Sports," *The Atlantic*, June 26, 2015, www.theatlantic.com/education/archive/2015/06/girls-high-school-sports-inequality/396782.
2. Wong, "Where Girls Are Missing Out."
3. "NCAA Sports Sponsorship and Participation Rates Database," *NCAA.org*, October 2018, www.ncaa.org/about/resources/research/ncaa-sports-sponsorship-and-participation-rates-database.
4. "High School Sports Participation Increases for 29th Consecutive Year," September 11, 2018, www.nfhs.org/articles/high-school-sports-participation-increases-for-29th-consecutive-year.
5. "Title IX and the Rise of Female Athletes in America," *Women's Sports Foundation*, September 2, 2016, www.womenssportsfoundation.org/education/title-ix-and-the-rise-of-female-athletes-in-america.
6. "Youth Sports Facts: Participation Rates," *The Aspen Institute Project Play*, Accessed June 11. 2021, www.aspenprojectplay.org/youth-sports-facts/participation-rates.

112 Egalitarian Fandom

7. Jon Lewis, "Ratings: WNBA, NFL Pregames, NFL OOH, CFB," *Sports Media Watch*, September 2018, www.sportsmediawatch.com/2018/09/wnba-finals-ratings-nfl-pregame-ooh-cfb.
8. Jon Lewis, "NBA Finals Ratings Hit Low, But Not Bad for Sweep," *Sports Media Watch*, June 2018, www.sportsmediawatch.com/2018/06/nba-finals-ratings-least-watched-four-years.
9. Joe Otterson. "NCAA Championship Game Viewership Drops 28% from 2017," *Variety*, April 3, 2018, https://variety.com/2018/tv/news/2018-ncaa-championship-game-ratings-1202742895.
10. "2018 Women's Final Four Makes History in Columbus," *NCAA.com*, April 13, 2018, www.ncaa.com/news/basketball-women/article/2018-04-13/2018-womens-final-four-makes-history-columbus.
11. Richard Deitsch, "USA's Women's World Cup Win Is the Most-Watched Soccer Game in U.S. History," *Si.com*, July 6, 2015, Accessed April 28, 2020, www.si.com/soccer/2015/07/06/usa-japan-womens-world-cup-tv-ratings-record.
12. Joe Otterson, "World Cup Final U.S. Ratings Fall from 2014," *Variety*, July 17, 2018, https://variety.com/2018/tv/news/world-cup-final-us-ratings-1202875655.
13. "2018 NWSL Attendance," *Soccer Stadium Digest*, Accessed April 28, 2020, https://soccerstadiumdigest.com/2018-nwsl-attendance.
14. "International League Attendance," *International League*, Accessed April 28, 2020, www.milb.com/milb/stats/stats.jsp?y=2018&t=l_att&lid=117&sid=l117.
15. The Ashes are a series of cricket matches played between England and Australia.
16. This information is available at the official websites of the Women's Tennis Association and the Ladies Professional Golf Association.
17. Gwendolyn Oxenham, *Under the Lights and in the Dark: Untold Stories of Women's Soccer* (London: Icon Books, 2018), 167.
18. Santos r-established its women's team in 2015.
19. Oxenham, *Under the Lights*, 168–169.
20. "Brazil—Neymar—Profile with News, Career Statistics and History—Soccerway," Accessed April 30, 2020, https://us.soccerway.com/players/neymar-da-silva-santos-junior/102697.
21. Oxenham, *Under the Lights*, 171.
22. "Most Expensive Transfers of All-Time," *ESPN.com*, July 10, 2018, www.espn.com/soccer/blog/soccer-transfers/3/post/2915603/most-expensive-transfers-of-all-time-neymar-mbappe-pogba-ronaldo-and-more.
23. Oxenham, *Under the Lights*, 171.
24. Frank Pingue, "Soccer: U.S. Women's League Increases Roster Size, Player Pay," *Reuters*, January 10, 2019, www.reuters.com/article/us-soccer-women-nwsl-idUSKCN1P42MA.
25. Oli Platt, "What Is Neymar's Net Worth and How Much Does the PSG Star Earn?" *Goal.com*, Accessed November 25, 2020, www.goal.com/en-us/news/neymar-net-worth-salary-contract-psg/1kvfsexg0npxf15gn60ol0zknl.
26. Lyndsey D'Arcangelo, "'There's No Break': Overseas Double Duty Is an Offer Many WNBA Stars Can't Refuse," *The Guardian*, May 19, 2018, www.theguardian.com/sport/2018/may/19/theres-no-break-overseas-double-duty-is-an-offer-many-wnba-stars-cant-refuse.
27. Nancy Lough, "The Case for Boosting WNBA Player Salaries," *The Conversation*, August 9, 2018, http://theconversation.com/the-case-for-boosting-wnba-player-salaries-100805.
28. Jonathan Lister, "The Average Salary of a Women's Professional Basketball Player," *Career Trend*, August 5, 2019, https://careertrend.com/the-average-salary-of-a-womens-professional-basketball-player-13657126.html.
29. Kate Fagan, "Taurasi Opts for Rest, to Skip WNBA Season," *ESPN.com*, February 3, 2015. www.espn.com/wnba/story/_/id/12272047/diana-taurasi-opts-sit-2015-wnba-season.
30. Fagan, "Taurasi Opts for Rest."
31. My source for this quote and the examples in this section is the 2013 ESPN documentary *Branded*, directed by Heidi Ewing and Rachel Grady.
32. Jeré Longman, "For Lolo Jones, Everything Is Image," *The New York Times*, August 4, 2012, www.nytimes.com/2012/08/05/sports/olympics/olympian-lolo-jones-draws-attention-to-beauty-not-achievement.html.
33. Anna Griffin, "Marketing Women Athletes Often Walks Careful Line between Savvy and Sexist," *Oregon Live*, Accessed January 10, 2019, www.oregonlive.com/business/2013/04/marketing_women_athletes_can_w.html.
34. Charlene Weaving, "Buns of Gold, Silver, and Bronze: The State of Olympic Women's Beach Volleyball," in *The Olympics and Philosophy*, ed. Heather Lynne Reid and Michael W. Austin (Lexington: University Press of Kentucky, 2012), 235.
35. Jane English, "Sex Equality in Sports," *Philosophy and Public Affairs* 7, no. 3 (Spring 1978): 271–272.

36. English, "Sex Equality in Sports," 273.
37. Pamela R. Sailors, "Mixed Competition and Mixed Messages," *Journal of the Philosophy of Sport* 41, no. 1 (January 2014): 68.
38. Natalie Weiner, "The WNBA's Male Practice Squads Lose to Women All the Time—and Enjoy It," *SBNation.com*, May 23, 2019, www.sbnation.com/wnba/2019/5/23/18636639/wnba-male-practice-squads.
39. Oxenham, *Under the Lights*, 9.
40. Oxenham, *Under the Lights*, 24.
41. While I suspect that speculations on whether boys could be the world champion women are generally ill-informed, it is worth noting that stories about the USWNT competing against boys do periodically surface. See, for example, Roger Gonzalez, "FC Dallas Under-15 Boys Squad Beat the U.S. Women's National Team in a Scrimmage," *CBSSports.com*, April 4, 2017, www.cbssports.com/soccer/news/a-dallas-fc-under-15-boys-squad-beat-the-u-s-womens-national-team-in-a-scrimmage.
42. Eileen L. McDonagh and Laura Pappano, *Playing with the Boys: Why Separate Is Not Equal in Sports* (New York: Oxford University Press, 2008), 58–59. There are two one-way records for the Catalina Swim, one each depending on the starting location, and two two-way records distinguished in the same manner. McDonagh and Pappno's book was published in 2009, but their claim is still accurate as of this writing. See Catalina Channel Swimming Federation, "Individuals Records," Accessed April 30, 2020, https://swimcatalina.org/individuals-records.
43. McDonagh and Pappano, *Playing with the Boys*, 62–63.
44. On this point, see Törbjörn Tännsjö, "Against Sexual Discrimination in Sport," in *Ethics in Sport*, ed. William John Morgan, 2nd ed. (Champaign, IL: Human Kinetics, 2007), 347–358.
45. Emily Ryall, "Sex, the World Cup and Breaking Up the Boys' Club," *The New York Times*, June 11, 2019, www.nytimes.com/2019/06/11/opinion/womens-world-cup-us-gender-pay.html.
46. Ryall, "Sex, the World Cup and Breaking Up the Boys' Club."
47. Kate Manne, *Down Girl: The Logic of Misogyny* (New York: Oxford University Press, 2018), 63.
48. Manne, *Down Girl*, 45.
49. Manne, *Down Girl*, 63.
50. Manne, *Down Girl*, 301.
51. It is a prominent feature of Manne's account that misogyny can exist without misogynists. See *Down Girl*, Chapter 2.
52. Manne, *Down Girl*, 110.
53. Erin C. Tarver, *The I in Team: Sports Fandom and the Reproduction of Identity* (Chicago: The University of Chicago Press, 2017), 197.
54. Tarver, *The I in Team*, 197.
55. Thomas Barrabi, "Women's World Cup: USWNT's Fight for Equal Pay Looms Over Tournament," *FOXBusiness.com*, June 6, 2019, www.foxbusiness.com/features/womens-world-cup-uswnt-pay-lawsuit.
56. All the information in this paragraph is from Lindsay Gibbs, "Losing $375 Million in the Name of Men's Sports," *Power Plays*, February 10, 2020, www.powerplays.news/p/losing-375-million-in-the-name-of.
57. Gibbs, "Losing $375 Million."
58. Gibbs, "Losing $375 Million."
59. Andrei S. Markovits and Emily K. Albertson, *Sportista: Female Fandom in the United States Politics, History and Social Change* (Philadelphia: Temple University Press, 2012), 103.

7

COSMOPOLITAN FANDOM

On November 11, 2016, the US Men's National Team played Mexico in a qualification match for the 2018 World Cup in Russia. Three days earlier, Donald Trump had defeated Hilary Clinton in the presidential election. Because Trump had made immigration policy a centerpiece of his campaign—in particular, insinuating that the majority of Mexican immigrants are rapists and drug dealers—the atmosphere surrounding the game was politically charged in a way that is unusual for soccer games in the United States. A team representing the country that had just elected Trump was taking on the team representing the country Trump had spent months disparaging, and the elephant in the room was large enough that players felt the need to address it with a pre-game photo demonstrating their lack of animosity toward one another.[1]

The early part of the Americans' qualifying schedule was difficult, and a home result against Mexico would go a long way toward securing a trip to Russia. Nevertheless, for one of the only times I can remember, I felt ambivalent about rooting for the United States. I was troubled by the election results and deeply opposed to Trump's anti-immigrant sloganeering and the policies his rhetoric foreshadowed. A win for the Americans in these circumstances felt too much like a win for Trump and all those who vowed, inchoately, to make America great again. When the United States lost the game 2–1, I was officially disappointed. Unofficially, I found it difficult to muster any of the angst that would normally accompany a loss in such circumstances.

One of the only other times I remember being ambivalent about the performance of a US national team actually occurred 35 years after the game in question took place. On February 22, 1980, the United States played the Soviet Union in the Olympic ice hockey tournament. The USSR, a team of de facto professionals supported full-time by the Soviet government who played together year-round, had won gold medals at the previous 4 Olympics and 13 of the previous 16 World Championships. The United States, on the other hand, was an ad hoc team of college players put together for international tournaments. In exhibition play leading up to the Olympics, the Soviets went 5–3–1 against teams from the National Hockey league, ostensibly the best hockey teams in the world. They also beat the United States 10–3 in an utter rout at Madison Square Garden.

When the Americans subsequently won their Olympic matchup 4–3, it was dubbed the "Miracle on Ice" (at least in the United States), and known ever after as one of the great upsets in sports history. At the height of the Cold War, it was also touted as a victory for capitalism and freedom over the evil totalitarianism of Soviet-style communism. I was only 3 at the time, so I have no

DOI: 10.4324/9781003223696-8

memories of watching the game and was obviously unaware of the drama surrounding it. But as I was growing up in the 1980s and 1990s, the remarkable facts of the American victory took on the status of myth—a process completed in 2004 with the release of the Walt Disney Studios film *Miracle*. Plot summary: a ragtag group of college kids fighting for the Stars and Stripes take down the soulless enemies of freedom. It was the perfect recipe for making Americans feel good about being Americans.

I suspect that most of my fellow citizens who think at all about the Miracle on Ice do so in roughly these terms. I certainly did, at least until 2015, when ESPN aired the remarkable documentary *Of Miracles and Men*. If *Miracle* offers a Disneyfied version of the 1980 Olympics from the perspective of the Americans, *Of Miracles and Men* looks at events from the perspective of the Soviets and in so doing, reveals players who are far from robotic sycophants to communist ideology. Indeed, highlighting the truly artistic nature of their hockey is one of the great achievements of the film, surpassed only by the way in which it fully humanizes the players. The Soviets, at that time, were laboring under a tyrannical coach. They faced enormous pressure from their government. They had families they rarely saw. They loved the sport they played and were devastated by the loss. In some cases, they longed to move to the United States and eventually used their status as world-class athletes to escape the communist regime. By the end of the film, American viewers can be forgiven for wishing the Soviets had won.

This kind of ambivalence challenges the way that fans generally take the support of their country's national teams for granted. Most of us simply assume that Americans should root for those who represent the United States in international competition just as Germans should support Germans, South Africans should support South Africans, and the Balinese should support Bali. Perhaps some dispensation can be given to immigrants. American citizens who grew up in Rome are allowed to support Italy in the World Cup. And if you have deep family ties to another country, it might be okay to follow that country in a secondary capacity. If your grandparents are Dutch, you can root for the United States *and* the Netherlands (though you should probably support the Americans if they play each other). Nevertheless, the presumption that fans should support the teams that represent their country of citizenship is one that has to be overridden. It is the rule rather than the exception.

I suspect that the reasoning behind this assumption (if there is any such reasoning) is that the players on a national team represent a country's citizens in a particular way—that there is a connection between the players on the field and their fan base that is more robust than it is in other sporting contexts. As a result, international competition offers an opportunity to identify with the fortunes of athletes more deeply than in club sports. The achievements of the team become the achievements of the nation, and fans can indulge their desire to use "we" because it reflects an uncomplicated patriotism. In the same way that "we" won the Second World War or put a man on the moon, American sports fans might glory in "our" victory over the Soviets in the Miracle on Ice.

As readers who have made it this far will no doubt surmise, I think this view of the relationship between a nation and the players on its national teams runs afoul of my argument in Chapter 1 concerning fans' use of the first-person plural. Thus, it is no more true that fans win games (or are part of the team) when those games are played by one's countrymen in international competition than it is when they are played by professional football or basketball players in the NFL or NBA. To invoke the comparison I introduced in Chapter 1, I think fans saying otherwise are more like civilians talking about how they won the battle among a group of combat veterans than they are like citizens talking about the collective political actions of their country. "We" didn't win the Miracle on Ice in 1980 or lose to the Mexican national team in November of 2016. The US hockey team won just as the USMNT lost.

116 Cosmopolitan Fandom

However, I think that identifying our national teams too closely with the nations they ostensibly represent is also problematic in ways that are unique to the international context. On the one hand, this approach can encourage stringent tests for determining who can properly represent a nation (and thereby encourage nationalistic insularity more broadly). On the other hand, it can lead us to view sporting events as proxies for ideological and political disputes that have nothing to do with sports (and that certainly cannot be settled on the field of play). My aim in this final chapter is thus to explore the ways in which these problems emerge and to outline an alternative way of thinking about the exploits of national teams that might avoid them.

I begin by looking at some controversies involving dual nationals—athletes who are eligible to represent more than one country—which often involve the search for a national essence that I argue is both futile and corrosive: futile, because there is no such thing as a national essence; corrosive, because it leads to insularity and a hostility to cultural diversity and immigrants. I then introduce an approach to fandom that I label cosmopolitan according to which fans recognize that their own national identities are contingent features of history and that the imperative to support one's own national teams is not nearly as strong as ardent nationalists might think. If this view is plausible, I think it helps to de-politicize much of the action on the field without gutting international competitions of some of their distinctive joys. I therefore conclude by suggesting some of the ways that the cosmopolitan fan might think about such issues.

The "Problem" of Dual Nationals and the Futile Search for National Essence

The idea that there is some special connection between players on a national team and the nation those players represent is perhaps best illustrated in controversies surrounding the composition of various national teams. For example, questions swirled around France's 2018 World Cup winning soccer team concerning whether the 12 players of African descent on the roster were sufficiently French. Despite the remarkable success of the squad, some members of the team felt that the legitimacy of their claim to represent France had come under fire, especially when the team was not performing well. Fans of Les Bleus may be happy to claim players like Paul Pogba (born in France to Guinean parents) and Kylian Mbappe (born in France to a Cameroonian father and mother of Algerian descent) when they were securing results on the field and winning world championships. But when those results were less than ideal, those very same players were often dismissed as foreigners.[2]

Similar comments have been directed at the US Men's National Team in recent years, a team that has explicitly courted dual-nationals, particularly during the managerial tenure of Jurgen Klinsmann. No less a figure than Abby Wambach—all-time leading goal scorer for the women's national team—has questioned whether foreign-born players "have that killer instinct" when they play for the national team. Wambach thus noted that it

> feels a little bit odd to me that you have some guys that have never lived in the United States that play for the United States because they were able to secure a passport. To me, that just feels like they weren't able to make it for their country and earn a living, so they're coming here.[3]

And in the wake of the team's failure to qualify for the 2018 World Cup, former USMNT goalkeeper Tim Howard raised similar concerns, arguing that "having American roots doesn't mean you are passionate about playing for that country."[4]

These sorts of thoughts are far from new. Michael O'Hara and Connell Vaughan thus point out that similar controversies arose during the tenure of the Jack Charlton—a former England international—as manager of the Republic of Ireland's national soccer team. They write:

> With no players from the domestic league the team were labelled "England B" and "Plastic Paddies." Only six of the 22 players that travelled to Italy in 1990 were born in the Republic. At USA '94 only seven of the players were born in the Republic. The rest were born in England (13) and Scotland (2). Furthermore, none of these players were playing for League of Ireland teams. The sense of *ersatz* Irishness was reinforced by the fact that these players were second- and third-generation emigrants.[5]

In this minds of some, a team couldn't truly be Irish if it was made up of a bunch of Scots and Englishmen.

The idea lying in the background of all of these cases thus seems to be that there is some national essence that players on a national team should exemplify. In order to represent France on the international stage, athletes must be sufficiently French. Similarly for the United States, Ireland, or indeed any other country that participates in international athletics. By the same token, when players are not regarded as sufficiently French (or American or Irish)—whether because of their dual citizenship, the nationality of their parents, or the amount of time they have spent in the country they represent—they can be dismissed as foreigners. Such foreignness can then be employed as an explanation for the team's failures—"They aren't really committed to representing their country"—or it can be used by critics of all stripes to paint the team's achievements as counterfeit. How truly American is an American victory when it is secured by a bunch of Germans?

Unfortunately (at least for advocates of this sort of sports-related nationalism), it is not at all clear what should be invoked as necessary and sufficient conditions for adequately exemplifying any country's national essence. What qualities, at the end of the day, make one sufficiently French such that they are entitled to represent France on the world's athletic stage? What is the essence of being an American that needs to be exemplified by all members of the US national teams? And how, exactly, is the Irishness of players to be measured so that fans who support the Republic of Ireland's national soccer team can be sure that all the players on the pitch are sufficiently Irish?

One might, of course, point to a shared language or culture that is supposed to constitute the essence of any particular nation. On this view, those concerned about the purity of a national team would want members of the team to be robustly committed to certain linguistic and cultural practices as definitive of the nation's unique character. However, as Kwame Anthony Appiah has recently argued, the problem with such a position is that "the reality of linguistic and cultural variation within a community" is regularly "in tension with the romantic nationalist version of a community united by language and culture."[6] "Indeed," writes Appiah, "this tension is the rule, rather than the exception," so if you are looking for language and culture to provide a distinct national essence, you might find yourself looking for something that simply doesn't exist.[7]

As an illustration of this phenomenon, Appiah points to Scotland—a place that might, at first blush, seem to have a clear national identity, at least when viewed from afar. However, Appiah writes:

> For hundreds of years, it has been a country of more than one language (Gaelic, Lallans or Broad Scots, and English) of more than one religion (the Church of Scotland, Anglicanism, Catholicism) with regional differences between the cultures of the Highlands and the Lowlands, the Islands and the mainland, country and city, even Edinburgh and Glasgow. What the Scots mostly have in common is more than a millennium of institutional connection to

the crown of Scotland. . . . Many of the things that are identified with Scots culture aren't widely shared. Fewer than 60,000 Scots speak Gaelic today; it hasn't been the mother tongue of the majority of the people of Scotland in five hundred years. People speak of Scotland as the land of the Protestant Kirk (the Church of Scotland), but Catholics outnumber adherents of the kirk in Glasgow, Scotland's largest city. And, like most of Europe, Scotland has a long-established Jewish presence and a growing Muslim population.[8]

Given this variety, what essential Scottishness might fans hope for members of Scotland's national soccer team to exemplify? A particular religious commitment? A knowledge of Gaelic? It isn't at all obvious what characteristic might play the role.

The de facto criteria for determining who can represent Scotland, at least in international soccer competitions, is that someone must simply have born in Scotland or have a parent or grandparent who was born in Scotland. One doesn't need to demonstrate that they understand Scotland's cultural heritage, much less prove to fans that they embrace that heritage in any robust way. They simply have to meet the conventionally defined standards that the governing body of international soccer has set for being allowed to play for the country in question.

In practice, as astute readers will have discerned, the criteria for representing Scotland are somewhat more complicated than the criteria for representing, say, the United States. After all, Scotland is not, strictly speaking, an independent country; it exists as part of the United Kingdom—a country that has four territories, each with its own soccer governing body: England, Scotland, Wales, and Northern Ireland. As a result, there has been a series of agreements about how to determine which "home nation" a player who would otherwise play for the UK is eligible to represent. Thus, players who hold UK citizenship but do not have ties to any of the four territories may represent the association of their choice. Talented soccer players born in the British Virgin Islands could, should they so choose, elect to represent Northern Ireland, provided neither their parents nor their grandparents have ties to any of the other British football associations. Moreover, after a 2009 agreement, players who received five years of education in the UK prior to their 18th birthday are likewise eligible to represent the territory in which their schooling took place. A Syrian refugee who sought asylum in Wales as a 10-year-old could, therefore, represent Wales on the soccer field.[9]

The UK is not unique in this regard. Players born in Northern Ireland are eligible to play for both Northern Ireland and the Republic of Ireland (though individuals born in the Republic cannot play for Northern Ireland).[10] Similarly, Puerto Ricans can represent Puerto Rico—a territory with its own soccer association—and as US citizens, they can also represent the United States, after they have lived in one of the 50 states continuously for at least two years.

These sorts of criteria may be unsatisfying for those of a strongly nationalistic bent, but no matter how fervently some partisans may want their country's national team to reflect a deep and singular national essence, the composition of most national teams is likely to be as messy as the composition of most every nation. Supporters of France's national teams may want players who embody some kind of essential Frenchness. However, in the absence of any clear sense of what that Frenchness might be, we have nothing to fall back on except the sorts of rules imposed by FIFA. Were you born here? Sure, you can play for us. Were your parents or grandparents born here? Sure, you can play for us too. By these sorts of criteria, all members of the French national team who won the 2018 World Cup had as much right to represent France as any other French citizen. And same for the German-American dual nationals on the USMNT and all of the Plastic Paddies fielded by Jack Charlton.

If this minimalist criterion does not require that players exemplify some mythical national essence, I don't think it guts an athlete's decision to play for a national team of all significance, particularly when they have more than one option for which nation to represent. The Englishmen who played for Charlton's Irish squad might not have known a word of Irish (or even had any fondness for the language). Nor might they have known the finer details of Irish history. Nevertheless, in choosing to represent Ireland, they were identifying themselves with the complex and messy inheritance of the Irish nation and thereby choosing to play *as Irishmen*. That sort of identification may mean different things to different people, athletes no less than anyone else. It may have been deeply meaningful for some of them, whereas others might have simply viewed it as a means to play a sport they love on the international stage. But regardless of the particular motivations, that identification is not entirely meaningless, even on the minimalist criteria for inclusion on national teams that I am advocating here.

Perhaps more importantly, for my purposes, I think this kind of minimalist approach encourages the idea that "every member of a nation is as much a member as any other."[11] As Bernard Yack has put it, this feature of national membership is significant in that "it links people directly and equally rather than by means of hierarchical subcommunities."[12] According to Yack, then, there are no second-class members of national communities (of the sort that might be entailed by more robust appeals to national essence) and I would regard this commitment as an important means of resisting some problematic social attitudes. Objecting to Pogba and Mbappe on the grounds that they aren't sufficiently French isn't bad because it is wrong to invoke any and all criteria for representing France. It is bad because it invokes a multi-tiered sense of being a part of the French nation—one according to which some people are truly French and others are merely permitted to call themselves French for certain purposes.

There are clearly numerous philosophical and political issues that intersect with my discussion at this point: the relationship between nations and states, the rights of citizenship, and how we should understand the ideal of national self-determination, to name but a few.[13] That caveat in place, I want to suggest that the invocation of any extensive criteria for national membership is often a way to divide various communities and exclude those we want to exclude on other grounds, rather than unite people around a shared sense of identity. Not being "one of us" in terms of language, skin color, religion, or any other marker of national essence can easily become a pretext for denying others full standing in the moral community constituted by the nation in question. In this vein, concerns about the degree to which members of the USMNT are really American may simply reflect a more general desire to marginalize non-white people who do not speak English. The trait to be preserved is not a unifying American identity but rather whiteness and a sense of one's own cultural superiority. Insofar as it serves to combat such attitudes, a much less stringent sense of who counts as "one of us" is, no doubt, to be preferred. Far better, it seems to me, to be inclusive when identifying who is a genuine member of the nation than to be rigorously exclusive.

If people want to identify as French (or American or Irish), why not celebrate that desire? There may, of course, be logistical challenges to that process, particularly where membership in a nation is connected to citizenship in a state. But considered in its own right, I think we should be happy when people want to join us. And if they want to represent France (or the United States or Ireland) as part of a national team, why not treat that decision as an opportunity—and a compliment to our national heritage—rather than a reason to question their motives or their commitment to the flag and the nation it represents?

The Landscape of Cosmopolitan Fandom

The general approach to international sports that emerges from this picture is, then, one that I would label cosmopolitan. In politics, the cosmopolitan is one who, as Appiah puts it, regards oneself first and foremost as a citizen of the world.[14] While acknowledging that "living in political communities narrower than the species is better for us than would be our engulfment in a single

120 Cosmopolitan Fandom

world-state," the cosmopolitan nevertheless believes that the whole of humanity comprises an important moral community and that this fact should shape our loyalties and obligations.[15] Wherever we happen to be born, and wherever we choose to live, we should work to leave the world "better than we found it" and to help all humans to fulfill their "highest destiny."[16] And no matter how much one loves one's country, county, city, town, or village, that love does not permit one to pursue the interests of those close to home at the expense of those on the other side of the world. As much as possible, the cosmopolitan will work for the flourishing of all peoples.

In the context of sports, the cosmopolitan will thus recognize that all of our national identifications are, to a large extent, accidents of a history that could have unfolded differently. There are nations within states and states within nations; states and nations go in and out of existence over time; and people now move all around the world with a freedom we have never seen before. In light of such realities, it is unreasonable to expect our sporting loyalties to reflect the world that ardent nationalists would have us pursue. If the entities our national teams represent are more fragile than the nationalist wants to acknowledge, the mobility of both fans and athletes makes it likely that our sporting loyalties will likewise evolve in a variety of different ways. Americans who move to the Netherlands may very well develop an affection for the Dutch national team (and the country it represents) even if they never pursue citizenship. And just as fans often inherit other sporting commitments from their parents or grandparents, their rooting interests on the international stage might also reflect their particular family history. If your grandfather is from Germany, and you grow up following the exploits of Germany's national soccer team as a result, you might very well carry that attachment into adulthood just as a parent who roots for the Green Bay Packers may bequeath that love to his children.

Because of this recognition, the cosmopolitan fan can also take pleasure in the various differences that obtain in sporting cultures and traditions around the world. Nationalist critics sometimes allege that cosmopolitanism leaves individuals rootless and that it will, over time, drive out cultural variation—that a commitment to being a citizen of the world threatens to make us all the same. But this criticism clearly misses the mark. What cosmopolitans want more people to do is to *appreciate* the differences among cultures and communities, not work to make them conform to a bland ideal. As Appiah puts it, cosmopolitans

> value the variety of human forms of social and cultural life; we do not want everybody to become part of a homogeneous global culture; and we know that this means that there will be local differences (both within and between states) in moral climate as well. As long as these differences meet certain general ethical constraints—as long, in particular, as political institutions respect basic human rights—we are happy to let them be.[17]

In this way, the cosmopolitan fan will enjoy the fact that different national teams (along with their fan bases) have different histories, traditions, and playing styles: the Dutch legacy of total football contrasted with the historically defensive approach of Italy's national soccer teams; the haka of New Zealand's All Blacks rugby team; the physicality of American basketball players against the more finesse oriented game played by Europeans; the varied fan chants, songs, and dances practiced in stadiums around the world.

Moreover, even as cosmopolitans grant that individuals might support national teams that represent countries other than their own, they needn't worry that such a concession will undermine the enthusiasm with which individuals root for their home country's national teams. In the same way that fans often simply root for their hometown teams because they are the hometown team, it seems to me that fans are overwhelmingly likely to support their home country's national team simply because it is their home country's team. To be sure, there are fans who root for teams that are not based in the place where they reside. Though I live in North Carolina, I support the Packers rather than the Carolina Panthers, and I am a Tottenham fan despite having only visited London twice. However, the existence of fans like me does nothing to undermine the support that the Panthers and Tottenham get from their local fan bases. I might not support my hometown team in certain sports, but millions of people around the world certainly do.

If the existence of fans who are less attached to their hometown teams in other sports does not threaten the enthusiasm of local fans, I see little reason to think that it will do so in international sports. There may be some Americans who root for Germany in international soccer tournaments, but most Americans who care about such events will nevertheless support the United States simply because it is the team of their home country. In this way, cosmopolitan fans can appreciate the different experiences that people bring to international fandom without feeling insecure about the legitimacy of their own local attachments. They can, in other words, revel in the variety of sporting cultures throughout the world while still rooting for their home country to win.

For fans who consciously embrace cosmopolitanism in the realm of sports, then, criticisms of players for being insufficiently patriotic should probably be off the table. It is, of course, perfectly legitimate for observers to note when a player is not performing well. While everyone involved with sports should avoid objectifying athletes—and therefore remember that they are not simply bodies but are individual persons with a variety of beliefs, projects, relationships, commitments, and emotions—it doesn't follow that they are immune from criticism. It is even sometimes appropriate to point out when players seem disinterested or when they are not putting forth maximum effort on the field. As I argued in Chapter 4, preparation and effort seem to be part of what athletes owe to fans, and if they are not satisfying these demands of the job, it is legitimate to point out this fact. Philosophy professors who are simply going through the motions in their classes are not doing their jobs sufficiently well and neither are footballers or professional basketball players.

What is out of bounds is for fans to view an athlete's poor performance or lack of effort as a sign that they are not sufficiently committed to the country they are representing. For example, if part of the assessment of the failure of the USMNT to qualify for the 2018 World Cup is that the players on the field did not exhibit sufficient effort—that they were, at various points in the qualifying campaign, too lackadaisical or just going through the motions—that may very well be a fair criticism. But if the lack of effort is attributed disproportionately to the German dual nationals on the squad on the grounds that they did not take enough pride in representing their country, it would seem that an inappropriately nationalistic metric is being employed. The cosmopolitan response will be to point out that the players on the field are eligible to represent the United States, that they have chosen to do so, and that an athlete's performance should be judged by the standards appropriate to sports rather than invoked as a litmus test for how much they love their country or embody the mythical essence of the nation.

This conclusion may seem to rob international sports of their distinctiveness by making the support of one's national team too much like support for any other team and, as a result, robbing fans of the pride that comes from a sporting triumph on the world stage. After all, international sports generally operate under the guise that there is a deeper connection between the players on the field and the fans who support them. Reducing the significance of what it means to be "one of us" thereby threatens to rob fans of the distinctive joy they might experience when their national teams succeed. Simply having an American passport does not feel like the kind of bond between players and fans that can support deep nationalistic pride.

But it is not clear why fans cannot take the same sort of pleasure in the exploits of their national teams as they derive from the professional and collegiate teams that represent their cities and states. Fans of the Green Bay Packers may be happy when their team wins the Super Bowl, and residents of Green Bay or the state of Wisconsin may feel a corresponding sense of pride in their city or

122 Cosmopolitan Fandom

state. However, such fans know that they are rooting for players whose only real connection to their community is that they are being paid to play football by an organization that is based there. Very few, if any, members of the team were born or grew up in Wisconsin, much less Green Bay, and most of them have played for other teams or will do so in the future, so their status as Packers is only temporary. Nevertheless, 80,000 spectators fill Lambeau Field for every home game, often in winter weather that is ill-suited for the preservation of human life. They do so in order to support their team—one that is embraced enthusiastically as a representative of the community—and millions of fans around the world similarly support their hometown teams even though they know that the players on the field are not from the cities they now represent.

To be sure, natives will occasionally end up with professional careers close to home, and those players may very well have a special place in fans' hearts. As a player who grew up near Tottenham's stadium, Harry Kane may evoke a particular affection from Spurs fans (at least those based in London), but they are also more than happy to embrace anyone who will play hard for the team they love. The cheers in the stadium aren't any louder for goals scored by Kane than they are for the South Korean Son Heung Min. Indeed, I would even argue that there is a certain cosmopolitan beauty on display when players represent communities to which they have no previous connection. There was a time when two of the most popular athletes in Columbus, OH, were the Russian goaltender Sergei Bobrovsky (who was playing for the Blue Jackets) and the Argentinian midfielder Federico Higuain (who was playing for the Crew), and I think the relationship they developed with the city was an encouraging illustration of the ways that we can all benefit from openness to other places, people, and cultures.

Cynics might argue that such affection is only the expression of a mercenary desire for victory—that fans will be happy to have anyone on their team who will help them win—and I have no doubt that the popularity of Bobrovsky and Higuain owed in large part to the fact that they were very good players who helped secure results on the field. But that is true of pretty much all athletes who are embraced by the communities they represent, whether they are native to those communities or not. Bad players on bad teams don't become beloved just because they are locals, and it is fine for us to acknowledge that the beauty of integrating individuals into a team that can connect emotionally with the community it represents is tied up with results on the field. That fact doesn't undermine the distinct kind of beauty involved in kids who have never left Ohio cheering for Argentinians and Russians as representatives of their community.

If fans in general lavish this kind of affection on teams composed of players who are not from the locales they represent, then there is little reason to worry that support for national teams will be muted because some of the players on the field were born in a different country or are eligible to represent more than one nation. This is not to suggest that it is entirely clear what it means for the Green Bay Packers to represent the city of Green Bay when players on the team were born in California and now spend the off-season in Texas. I confess that I find that relationship somewhat vexing. My point is simply that because fans are untroubled by this phenomenon when they root for their favorite club teams, they should be equally untroubled by it when they root for their national team. Thousands of Mancunians cheer on Manchester United even though few, if any, players on the field hail from Manchester, and supporters of England's national teams should likewise feel free to be equally enthusiastic about supporting anyone on the field who is eligible to represent their nation.

Politics and Sports (or Why the Miracle on Ice Was Just a Hockey Game)

There is a further implication of a cosmopolitan approach to fandom—one that connects back to the examples with which I began this chapter. For many people, if the United States plays Iran in a soccer match, it becomes more than a soccer match. It becomes a chance to make a statement about the competing ideologies that the two countries are thought to represent. In the same way that Hitler saw the 1936 Olympics in Berlin as an opportunity to demonstrate the promise of National Socialism to the world via success in athletic competition (and non-Germans equally viewed the games as a way to challenge that very same ideal), observers of international competitions today might invest the outcome of various games with political significance. Neutrals might, therefore, approach such contests by rooting for the "good guys" and hoping that the "bad guys" take the loss. These days, teams representing North Korea are unlikely to get much support outside the country's borders, because viewers might think that a North Korean victory is too much like a victory for the North Korean regime, and rooting for the United States during the Trump administration might feel rather different for many Americans than it did during the Cold War.

Fans view sports through this kind of political lens all the time. Argentinians clearly viewed their 1986 World Cup contest with England as a way to gain revenge for the Falklands War.[18] Germany and the Netherlands are still rivals on the soccer pitch, in part because of the Dutch's crushing loss to Germany in the 1974 World Cup final (at a time when the Dutch had a legitimate claim to being the best team in the world and, indeed, one of the best teams of all time). But that game was also infused with a spirit of revenge for the evils of the Second World War, and while these tensions may have cooled in recent years, as late as 1989 a game between the two teams in Rotterdam featured a Dutch banner comparing Lothar Matthaus to Adolf Hitler. And a German loss to Denmark in the final of Euro 1992 produced almost as much celebration in the Netherlands as in Denmark.[19]

Indeed, these sentiments don't require contests between national teams in order to gain a footing. The rivalry between Real Madrid and Barcelona is often characterized in ideological terms. Because Francisco Franco had supported Madrid, the club is often contrasted with the democratic commitments of Barcelona, whose motto "More Than a Club" is a rallying cry for those in favor of Catalan independence.[20] And Old Firm matches between Celtic and Rangers are similarly infused with sectarian conflict between Catholics and Protestants—conflict that, in Scotland, has as much to do with political questions about Northern Ireland as the authority of the Pope in matters of theology.[21]

In contrast to such politicized views of action on the field, the cosmopolitan fan will insist that sporting contests are just that: contests of athletic talent, strategy, and preparation. As such, their outcome is decided by how well athletes perform against their competitors, not by political or philosophical means. Thus, whether capitalism is a superior economic system to communism had no bearing on the outcome of the 1980 Olympic hockey tournament that was, at the end of the day, just a hockey tournament. The broader political context in which the events took place certainly added to the drama for fans (and likely for participants as well). It also made for storylines that were more intriguing to Hollywood producers. Absent such a politically charged backdrop, one doubts whether a movie like *Miracle* would have been made.

Nevertheless, it is an irreducible feature of sports that—at least when they are played on fair competitive terms—they are contests of athletic skill and performance. Nothing more, though certainly nothing less. The United States performed the Miracle on Ice because, on that particular day, they scored more goals than the Soviets.[22] An American victory no more proved the superiority of capitalism over communism than did the Houston Rockets' victory over the Utah Jazz that same day (which a quick Google search reveals happened by a score of 94–82). Such an assessment might come across as deflating, something of a philosophical downer. But I don't intend it as anything of the sort. If the central argument of this book is at all compelling, then it follows that sports have sufficient value taken solely on their own terms. We don't have to transform them into something else in order to enjoy them or to justify the effort we invest in playing and watching

124 Cosmopolitan Fandom

them. A hockey game can be thoroughly compelling even when it is simply viewed as a hockey game. It doesn't have to be a contest between political ideologies in order to captivate us.

To advance this view is not at all to deny that sports and geopolitical events can sometimes be related in complex ways. In 1969, the so-called Soccer War broke out between El Salvador and Honduras. Though the conflict was pretty clearly the result of economic tensions caused by Salvadorian migration into Honduras (and a history of ineffective efforts by military juntas in both countries to stabilize relations), the proximate cause of hostilities in the popular imagination was a series of World Cup qualifying matches that produced violence between fan bases.[23] Neither country had ever previously qualified for the World Cup, and the chance to project a positive image to the world increased the perceived stakes involved. When El Salvador won a tightly contested match to earn a trip to the 1970 World Cup, diplomatic relations between the two countries were severed—a prelude to a military conflict that, despite spanning only five days, killed nearly 6,000 people and wounded approximately 12,000.[24] The fighting had no real connection to soccer; Hondurans and Salvadorians were not killing each other because of results on the pitch. Rather, the sporting conflict served to heighten the preexisting political tension and give each side a reason to settle quite different scores.[25]

Acts of terrorism can also draw the world of sports and politics together in unsettling ways, as terrorists use the communal significance of sports to draw greater attention to their causes. One thinks here of the murder of 11 Israeli athletes by Palestinian militants at the 1972 Olympics in Munich, a suicide bombing ahead of a cricket match between New Zealand and Pakistan in 2002 that killed 14, or the Boston Marathon bombing in 2013. In all such cases, a sporting event is made the occasion for ostensibly political violence even though that connection is contingent. Other communal events that could provide similar opportunities would do just as well.

If the Soccer War and various acts of terrorism illustrate the dark side of intermingling politics and sports, it is also worth noting that sports can provide a venue for constructive political speech. In Chapter 3, I discussed the problems with attempts to silence athletes who wish to speak out on controversial political issues. Athletes who choose to use the celebrity at their disposal for such purposes should certainly be free to do so. To be sure, it does not seem that that their status as athletes gives their speech any particular moral weight. When Colin Kaepernick protests racial injustice, the fact that he is an NFL quarterback does not mean that we should accord his words greater significance than anyone else who speaks out on racial injustice any more than George Clooney's status as a famous movie star means that we should pay particular attention to his thoughts about human rights. Nevertheless, the fact that many athletes have a larger platform than most people means that they may choose to use that platform to draw attention to worthy causes.

Finally, sports have the potential to unite and inspire communities that are going through difficult times. Nelson Mandela famously used the 1995 Rugby World Cup to unite a South Africa trying to recover from the evils of apartheid—a saga portrayed in the Hollywood film *Invictus*, starring Matt Damon and Morgan Freeman. The Iraqi men's soccer team's run to the Asian Games title in 2007 provided a much-needed sense of national pride to a country that had been ravaged, in succession, by the totalitarian rule of Saddam Hussein and the invasion of American military forces. James Dorsey highlights the significance of the victory as follows:

> The multi-ethnic and multi-sect character of the team gave its winning of the Asian Cup added significance. The decisive goal was scored by a Sunni Muslim after taking a pass from a Kurdish team mate. The team's Shiite goalkeeper contributed his part by ensuring that his Saudi opponents remained goalless. Their teamwork constituted a rare ray of hope for Iraqis. It offered a glimpse of life beyond conflict in a war-ravaged country devoid of prospects and inclusive institutions.[26]

Cosmopolitan Fandom **125**

For one month, at least, "the beautiful game was the one institution in which Kurds, Sunnis, and Shias focused on a common goal."[27]

But if sports can be intertwined with, and surrounded by, events of political significance, I want to insist that the games themselves are not proxies for political or ideological disputes. If one wants to root for Barcelona because of the club's support of Catalan self-determination or likes what Gregg Popovich has to say about racial injustice in the United States and therefore decides to become a fan of the San Antonio Spurs, that's fine. Such reasons are as good as any other for supporting teams (and probably better than many). The mistake is simply in thinking that those commitments have any special connection to the outcome of games or that sporting events are contests in political ideology. You can root for Barcelona because you support Catalan independence, but such a cause is neither vindicated nor defeated by the results of games against Real Madrid any more than the fight against racial injustice depends on whether San Antonio beats the Lakers.

Moreover, I think we should be wary of placing too much weight on sports as engines of lasting social and political change. South Africa did not transform itself into a racially just society simply because they won the Rugby World Cup. Problems in Iraq were not resolved with a gold medal in the Asian Games. Those results might have provided a temporary moment of uplift in places that were in desperate need of emotional encouragement, but the ongoing transformation of South Africa probably would have happened anyway, and as history has shown, the respite in Iraq was only temporary.

In a similar way, sports were able to provide some positive emotional energy in the United States after the attacks of 9/11. As Howard Bryant puts it, "From the moment the games resumed across all sports after the attacks, sports sold the idea of healing, of everyone coming together at the ballpark in a combined show of force."[28] However, Bryant argues, I think convincingly, that sports in this period "also sold another product: conformity and obedience cloaked in an ostensibly benign patriotism."[29] In particular, Bryant thinks that the subsequent marriage between sports and American militarism undermined a robust commitment to social activism on the part of athletes, and specifically athletes of color, thus reinforcing the "stick to sports" posture I discussed in Chapter 4. The impulse that created a communal experience in stadiums across America in the fall of 2001 thus laid the groundwork for Colin Kaepernick's troubles in 2016.

As one final illustration of this idea, consider England's run to the semifinals of the 2018 World Cup. For a region unsettled by the controversies of Brexit and grappling with its identity as a multiethnic society, such a performance afforded a rare glimpse of unity. As Ceylan Yeginsu wrote in the *The New York Times* during the tournament:

> [I]n a week when the government of Prime Minister Theresa May has been plunged into new chaos—with ministers resigning and the fate of the country's effort to exit the European Union more uncertain than ever—much of the nation seems determined to take a timeout from the acrimonious politics and bask in something recently in short supply: Unity, not to mention blind hope.[30]

England manager Gareth Southgate explicitly appealed to this sentiment in his media appearances that summer, noting: "We're a team with our diversity and our youth that represent modern England."[31] For a nation that has anxiously viewed the fortunes of its football team as a symbol of its broader cultural and political decline, success on the international stage presented an opportunity to change the narrative.[32]

England lost in the semifinals to Croatia 2–1 when a goal from Mario Mandžukić in the 109th minute dashed England's hopes for a world championship, and subsequent events in Great Britain

126 Cosmopolitan Fandom

have shown that the unity created by success on the pitch was ephemeral. As I write, debates are still raging about how to handle Brexit: whether to maintain some connection between the UK and the European Union, sever ties completely, or even hold another national referendum on the question. Boris Johnson, now Prime Minister, has made controversial remarks about Muslims.[33] Jeremy Corbyn, former leader of the Labor Party, somehow managed to respond by drawing charges of anti-Semitism.[34] Less than a year after the blind hope offered by the Three Lions, multiple voices would be writing about Britain's political crisis.[35] If we want lasting societal change, victories by our national teams aren't going to be able to provide it.

Rooting for the United States in Complicated Times

What, then, is the appropriate cosmopolitan response to my ambivalence about rooting for the US Men's National Team against Mexico back in 2016? As a provisional answer to this question, it seems that I was wrong to invest the game with any real political significance. It was, at the end of the day, just a soccer game, and as a fan of the USMNT, I shouldn't have felt any reticence about wanting them to win. Put differently, rooting for the United States did not signal any particular support for Donald Trump or animosity toward either the people of Mexico or Mexican immigrants in the United States. It merely expressed my desire that a soccer team I support would win the game it had to play.

At the same time, a genuinely cosmopolitan appreciation for the world's sporting cultures would not render the event entirely meaningless from a political point of view. After all, an appreciation for the diversity of sporting cultures and traditions around the world should have its roots in an appreciation for the individuals who embody those cultures and practices those traditions: their value as human beings and the beautiful and varied forms that human life can take. A robustly cosmopolitan fandom depends on a more general commitment to the idea that we are all, first and foremost, citizens of the world. Thus, while fans needn't feel any compunction about rooting for their national teams to win games, we should expect an appreciation for the teams and fans of other nations to fuel reflection on more general political questions about what kinds of societies we want to live in and how we want the world to be.

Viewed in this way, a cosmopolitan might say that my ambivalence surrounding the US–Mexico game was not really about events on the field as much as it was about the state of the world that those events brought into sharp relief. I opened this book by suggesting that we reject any hard and fast distinction between sports and "real life." International sporting contests can be a useful reminder of why such a rejection is justified. All of the Mexicans participating in that game—whether as fans, players, or coaches—were individuals with their own lives to live. Appreciating their investment in the proceedings, even as I hoped for a US victory, could serve as a challenge to the way in which various public policies and political rhetoric either paid those individuals sufficient respect or marginalized them in troubling ways. Sports, in this case, shed important light on troubles at home.

A similar assessment might be directed at the Miracle on Ice. If the US triumph was a compelling underdog victory, it was also a game that involved human beings on the other side—human beings who were not, in any meaningful sense, the enemies of anyone involved. Indeed, they were very much victims of the Soviet regime, manipulated to serve the state's ends rather than enabled by the state to pursue their own. If this fact did not require Americans to root for the Soviets (or to mute their enthusiasm at an American victory), perhaps it could have played a more prominent role in the subsequent rhetoric surrounding the game than it did. Had it done so, the lesson of the Miracle on Ice would not have been about American superiority. Rather, it would have been that a mere hockey game can serve as an important reminder of our common humanity.

Notes

1. Des Bieler, "US and Mexico Players Make Statement of Unity Before World Cup Qualifier," *The Washington Post*, November 12, 2016, www.washingtonpost.com/news/early-lead/wp/2016/11/12/u-s-and-mexico-players-make-statement-of-unity-before-world-cup-qualifier/?noredirect=on&utm_term=.287292411ecb.
2. Rokhaya Diallo, "On Football, Identity and 'Frenchness'," *AlJazeera.com*, August 2, 2018, www.aljazeera.com/indepth/opinion/football-identity-frenchness-180801080257299.html.
3. Gianni Verschueren, "Abby Wambach Criticises USMNT's Use of Players with Dual Citizenship," *Bleacher Report*, October 11, 2016, https://bleacherreport.com/articles/2668948-abby-wambach-criticises-usmnts-use-of-players-with-dual-citizenship.
4. Andrew Joseph, "Ex-USMNT Player Blames Foreign-born Players," *USA Today*, May 31, 2018, www.usatoday.com/story/sports/ftw/2018/05/31/exusmnt-player-blames-foreignborn-players-lack-of-fight-for-world-cup-failure/111170244.
5. Michael O'Hara and Connell Vaughan, "Caveman Stuff: Ireland's Soccer Struggle with Identity, Style, and Success," in *The Aesthetics, Poetics, and Rhetoric of Soccer*, ed. Ridvan Askin, Catherine Diederich, and Aline Bieri (London: Routledge, 2018), 173.
6. Kwame Anthony Appiah, *The Lies That Bind: Rethinking Identity* (New York: Liveright Publishing Co., 2018), 86.
7. Appiah, *Lies that Bind*, 86.
8. Appiah, *Lies that Bind*, 86–87.
9. Peter Jardine, "Exclusive: Smith's Blueprint Will Open Door to Non-Scots Playing for National Team," *The Daily Mail*, February 26, 2009, www.dailymail.co.uk/sport/football/article-1156743/Exclusive-Smiths-blueprint-open-door-non-Scots-playing-national-team.html.
10. The guidelines are different in other sports. For example, anyone born in Northern Ireland or the Republic of Ireland can play for Ireland's national team in rugby union.
11. Bernard Yack, *Nationalism and the Moral Psychology of Community* (Chicago, IL: The University of Chicago Press, 2012), 70.
12. Yack, *Nationalism*, 70
13. Yack outlines one way to put these pieces together in *Nationalism*.
14. Kwame Anthony Appiah, "Cosmopolitan Patriots," *Critical Inquiry* 23, no. 3 (April 1997): 618.
15. Appiah, "Cosmopolitan Patriots," 624.
16. Appiah, "Cosmopolitan Patriots," 618.
17. Appiah, "Cosmopolitan Patriots," 621.
18. David Randall, "Maradona Admits 'Hand of God' Goal Was Revenge for Falklands," *Independent*, October 10, 2011, www.independent.co.uk/sport/football/news/maradona-admits-hand-of-god-goal-was-revenge-for-falklands-550743.html.
19. See David Winner, *Brilliant Orange: The Neurotic Genius of Dutch Soccer* (New York: The Overlook Press, 2008), Chapter 18.
20. The complexities in this rivalry are explored in Sid Lowe, *Fear and Loathing in La Liga: Barcelona, Real Madrid, and the World's Greatest Sports Rivalry* (New York: Nation Books, 2014).
21. For an intriguing discussion of the Old Firm Rivalry, see Franklin Foer, *How Soccer Explains the World: An Unlikely Theory of Globalization* (New York: Harper Perennial, 2005).
22. I'm not even sure the United States was the better team on the day of the Miracle. Two of the goals scored by the Americans were, I think it's fair to say, exceedingly lucky. And as *Of Miracles and Men* highlights, some of the decisions made by the Soviet coach, Viktor Tikhonov, were highly questionable. This is not at all to suggest that the United States didn't earn the victory, fair and square. In hockey, much like soccer, there are often victories earned by teams that do not necessarily play better than their opponents. And, to be fair, the American goaltender, Jim Craig, had a tremendous game, as even the Soviet players acknowledged.
23. Tamir Bar-On, *Beyond Soccer: International Relations and Politics as Seen Through the Beautiful Game* (New York: Roman and Littlefield, 2017), 43ff.
24. Tamir Bar-On, *Beyond Soccer*, 43.
25. I think this is the pervasive logic of hooligan violence. Violence between fan bases of different clubs is not about what is happening on the field. Sporting rivalries are merely serving as pretext for indulging other violent impulses. See, for example, Bill Buford, *Among the Thugs* (New York: Vintage, 1993) and Foer, *How Soccer Explains the World*, Chapter 4.
26. James Dorsey, *The Turbulent World of Middle East Soccer* (Oxford: Oxford University Press, 2016), 192–193.
27. Dorsey, *The Turbulent World*, 193–194.

28. Howard Bryant, *The Heritage: Black Athletes, a Divided America, and the Politics of Patriotism* (Boston, MA: Beacon Press, 2018), 107.
29. Bryant, *The Heritage*, 107.
30. Ceylan Yeginsu, "World Cup Brings England Together at a Time of Division," *The New York Times*, July 10, 2018, www.nytimes.com/2018/07/10/world/europe/uk-world-cup-england.html. It is worth highlighting, as the Times article does, that the positive sentiment about England's fortunes did not extend to Scotland and Wales. As in many other facets of British society, "English" and "British" can be two very different things.
31. Jamie Grierson, "England Celebrates Gareth Southgate as Hero of World Cup," *The Guardian*, July 8, 2018, www.theguardian.com/football/2018/jul/08/england-celebrates-gareth-southgate-as-hero-of-world-cup-waistcoast.
32. On the anxiety of the English soccer fan, see David Winner, *Those Feet: A Sensual History of English Football* (London: Bloomsbury Publishing, 2005), particularly Chapters 4 and 6.
33. Jessica Elgot, "Boris Johnson Accused of 'Dog-whistle' Islamophobia Over Burqa Comments," *The Guardian*, August 7, 2018, www.theguardian.com/politics/2018/aug/06/boris-johnsons-burqa-remarks-fan-flames-of-islamophobia-says-mp.
34. Isobel Thompson, "Jermey Corbyn's Anti-Semitism Scandal Is Spiraling Out of Control," *Vanity Fair*, August 15, 2018, www.vanityfair.com/news/2018/08/jeremy-corbyn-anti-semitism-scandal-spiraling-out-of-control.
35. Vernon Bogdanor, "Britain's Crisis Isn't Constitutional. It's Political," *Foreign Policy*, April 1, 2019, https://foreignpolicy.com/2019/04/01/britains-crisis-isnt-constitutional-its-political-brexit-tories-theresa-may-corbyn-customs-union-eu. Jane Merrick, "Securing a Brexit Deal Will Not End the UK's Political Crisis," *CNN.com*, March 28, 2019, www.cnn.com/2019/03/28/uk/brexit-turmoil-ongoing-intl-gbr/index.html. Jon Worth, "Britain's Political System is at the Breaking Point," *AlJazeera.com*, March 13, 2019, www.aljazeera.com/indepth/opinion/britain-political-system-breaking-point-190313131636062.html.

CONCLUSION

A Few Guidelines for Being a Good Fan

Sports began to return throughout 2020 and into 2021. The process came in fits and starts, and sometimes in unprecedented circumstances. Games were played in empty stadiums. Prerecorded crowd noise was added to television broadcasts in an effort to improve the viewing experience of fans at home. Numerous events were canceled because of positive COVID tests among players. League and playoff schedules were altered significantly in order to make up for lost time. The 2020 NBA Playoffs were played entirely on the grounds of Walt Disney World in Orlando, Florida, in an effort to create a "COVID bubble" and prevent the spread of the virus. The College Football Championship featured a team that had only played 7 games against a team that had played 12.

At a much different level, my son's high school and club soccer teams had their seasons compressed into remarkably tight scheduling windows, first playing in masks and then not. My girls youth soccer team had their fall and spring seasons as well: they began playing without masks, then had to wear them, and finished their last few games maskless. Nothing felt altogether normal; rather, there was a constant sense that everyone at every level of sport was just making up plans on the fly (as they probably were). But sports did steadily return, as I more or less assumed they would at the start of the pandemic.[1]

What also returned were the myriad controversies that always seem to surround the action on the field. If fans wanted sports to provide a complete escape from the draining stress of pandemic life, the world of sports was, as usual, unable to oblige. A list of such examples could probably fill another 10,000 word chapter, but here are just a few that stood out to me as I was completing work on the book:

- Naomi Osaka, the second-ranked women's tennis player in the world, withdrew from the French Open after refusing to hold press conferences during the tournament. Citing the mental health consequences of continually dealing with a media she regarded as intrusive and insensitive, Osaka's refusal officially put her in violation of tournament rules that require players to make themselves available to reporters. Rather than be disqualified, Osaka preemptively withdrew from the competition.[2]
- Reports surfaced during the NFL draft that Green Bay Packers quarterback Aaron Rodgers no longer wanted to play for the team and wished to be traded. The saga has provided plenty of fodder for the 24-hour "take machine" that is sports media, and as I write, has yet to be resolved.[3]

DOI: 10.4324/9781003223696-9

130 Conclusion

- Closer to home, donors to the Wake Forest women's basketball team threatened to end their financial support of the team if players continued to kneel for the national anthem—a practice they had begun (along with many other teams around the country) to protest racial injustice as well as the January 6 insurrection at the United States capital building. The threats came on the back of donor complaints that the Wake Forest football team had been wearing "Black Lives Matter" stickers on their helmets throughout the season. The basketball team resumed standing for the national anthem prior to the Atlantic Coast Conference tournament.[4]

To these off-field issue can be added one particularly harrowing incident on the field when Danish midfielder Christian Eriksen suffered cardiac arrest and collapsed during Denmark's European Championship soccer game against Finland. As Eriksen received CPR and defibrillation on the field, his teammates formed a circle around him in an effort to shield the events from television producers who aired the incident live while repeatedly cutting to shots of his distraught girlfriend on the sidelines. Miraculously, Eriksen survived, and by the evening, was asking about his teammates while in stable condition in a Copenhagen hospital. The Danish team doctor summed up events by saying, "He was gone, and we did cardiac resuscitation. It was a cardiac arrest. How close were we [to losing Eriksen]? I don't know."[5]

The particular issues that are highlighted by these examples are obviously varied, and each one probably warrants their own extended treatment. I could have easily devoted stand-alone chapters to the relationship between athletes and the media, how fans should view workplace issues in professional sports, and any number of thorny problems that beset college athletics (at least in the United States). Drilling down on the specifics of these topics is, no doubt, a good agenda for future work. But what I want to do here instead is step back from those specifics and consider a few of the ways in which my discussion in the foregoing pages might provide a framework for thinking about issues such as these in the future.

By way of conclusion, then, I offer a few schematic guidelines that I think can aid us all in our efforts to be better fans. My hope is that they can serve as some memorable slogans to help us think through the never-ending stream of controversies that the world of sports seems to provide and to continue to appreciate the talents and sacrifices of the athletes who make sports worth watching in the first place.

1. Always Remember That Athletes Are People Too

If there is one overarching thesis that I hope readers take away from the preceding pages, it is this one. The fact that it is a platitude doesn't prevent all fans from forgetting it at various times, and because most of us are fairly removed from the athletes we watch compete, we all periodically lose track of a few important facts. Athletes do not cease to be human when they step on the field; nor do they lose their individuality as they make more money or reach higher and higher echelons of competition. They have thoughts, feelings, plans, and goals of their own. They have friends and families and interests that don't have anything to do with sports. Their prodigious talents do not render them undeserving of the same kind of sympathy and compassion that is due every other human being.

Of course, as I have noted at points throughout the book, the fact that athletes are people does not entirely exempt them from criticism. They certainly make mistakes, both on the field and off, and I think the nature of sports as a public activity certainly makes it appropriate to analyze their performance in competition; when they do things in the public eye that are particularly noteworthy, those actions probably also warrant comment. However, we should be wary of applying standards to athletes that we would not apply to regular private citizens or that we could not begin to live up to ourselves. How would we act if we had to do our jobs in front of thousands of people? What would our lives look like if they were exposed to the harsh lights of the media on a regular basis? How would we spend our money if we had significantly more of it than we do? And what sort of scrutiny would we want when grappling with our anxieties or, God forbid, staring death in the face? The point here isn't necessarily that answers to these questions are obvious or that we would all answer them the same way. It is rather that they are the sorts of questions we should be asking as we think about how to respect athletes as individuals.

If the idea that athletes are people has implications for our general sporting culture, I think it also has implications for the ways in which partisan fans think about players on the teams they support (as well as those they don't). I noted in Chapter 4 that I think fan hatred of players on rival teams is more or less harmless, but if such an attitude is to *remain* harmless, we must hold it at a certain ironic distance. That is, we must remember that our reactions to rival players are often based on their persona on the field—the part of themselves that is presented to the world in the heat of competition—and therefore colored by the fact that we want them to lose. By the same token, the love we have for players on the teams we support is easily tinged with our hopes for victory. All players, no matter the teams on which they play, are people—with strengths and weaknesses who make mistakes and also do good things. If the teams we support probably aren't really better at "doing things the right way" than other teams (just as our kids probably aren't better than other people's kids), then it is worth thinking about whether the players we love are really better people than those we "hate." Perhaps, in some cases, they really are. Far more often, I suspect, they are not.

2. Think Carefully About What Athletes Owe You as a Fan

This guideline is, I think fairly clearly, connected to the first. However, I include it as a separate point because I think there is a tendency for fans to invoke their status as fans to justify a corresponding sense of entitlement over the athletes they support. Thus, one might not think that athletes owe anything in particular to the public, beyond the rudiments of human decency, but also think that athletes have more specific obligations *to the fans*. The same people who think that Osaka does not owe the general public her daily thoughts during a tournament, might think she owes those thoughts to the fans. People in general might have a right to work wherever they can find employment, but players owe a greater measure of loyalty to the fan bases that support them. And it is one thing to engage in political speech that displeases the public as a whole and something different to engage in that same speech when it displeases the fans, particularly the fans of one's own team.

The idea that the fan/athlete relationship might carry with it a unique set of obligations and entitlements strikes me as plausible. In the same way that professors might have obligations to their students (and vice versa) that result from the specific constraints of the professor/student relationship, athletes might have obligations to fans that they do not have to non-fans. And if athletes have such obligations, then fans may be justified in having certain expectations of athletes that they do not have of other people.

However, it isn't at all clear what sorts of rights fans have *as fans* beyond an expectation that athletes will work hard to prepare themselves for competition and will put forth significant effort to win the games they play. If athletes are not really trying—and certainly if they are engaged in any sort of match-fixing or systematic violation of the rules—then I think fans have every right to be upset. The fundamental terms of the tacit agreement between fans and spectators have been violated. But once we move much beyond the bounds of the stadium, matters become a fair bit murkier. Fans certainly can't claim any sort of ownership of athletes' lives off the field, and so they

132 Conclusion

don't have any right to expect that athletes will behave in exactly the ways they want when matters have nothing to do with sports.

To be sure, individual fans may have a right as private citizens to do all sorts of things: criticize a player's performance as well as their political beliefs; use their money in more or less any way they see fit; give up following sports altogether because athletes aren't behaving in the ways they would prefer. But it is one thing for fans to justify these choices by appealing to their rights as citizens in a free society and something else to justify them by appealing to the distinctive norms of the fan/athlete relationship. Thus, in expressing political opinions with which they disagree, athletes are not violating any specific obligation they have to their fans because fans are not entitled to root for teams who only express political opinions with which they agree. Indeed, being a good fan may require that one refrain from using one's fandom to manipulate the political speech of athletes, because (as I've argued) athletes are people too. The point here might be a subtle one, but I think it is nevertheless worth keeping in mind. It means that there may be a conflict between what we are entitled to do as citizens in a free society and what we are entitled to do as fans. And what we *should* do, all things considered, may be a matter of figuring out how best to navigate these competing norms.

One final point to keep in mind on this score. Fans who are inclined to spend a lot of time thinking about what athletes owe them as fans should also think about the corresponding obligations that fans might have *as fans*. One who thinks only about what they are entitled to receive from their friends without ever giving a moment's thought to what they owe their friends is, to put it mildly, not a very good friend. Similarly, fans who only think about what athletes owe them without ever thinking about what they owe to athletes has failed to take the fan/athlete relationship all that seriously. As in nearly every other area of human life, whatever special rights fans may possess are limited by a corresponding set of obligations, and fans who never think about how they can be better fans even as they confidently opine about what athletes owe them are hardly fulfilling their end of the bargain.

3. Be Exceedingly Wary of Online Spaces (and Always Avoid the Comments)

My original version of this guideline was: "Avoid fan Twitter. It's a cesspool." I still more or less endorse that formulation, but in the interest of nuance, I'm officially willing to soften my stance.

I have generally been resistant to the idea that social media is the source of great societal ills, instead choosing to view it (like a great many other things in the world) as a tool that does some good but also some harm. Social media platforms may allow people to hurl insults that they would never utter in person at people they have never met, but they also enable forms of human connection that wouldn't happen otherwise. Provided we can keep their costs at a minimum, the benefits we receive may justify paying them.

The pandemic has placed considerable pressure on this view. Perhaps it is just a function of spending more time online while being cooped up at home, or perhaps we are simply experiencing some uniquely fraught tensions in our culture at this historical moment, but the dark side of the internet has begun to strike me as a deeply insidious problem that may very well threaten the fabric of our society. Rampant disinformation—both deliberate and unwitting—coupled with anonymity and copious amounts of grandstanding send innumerable online interactions off the rails before they even start. If there is good to be salvaged in these spaces, we are going to have to work exceptionally hard to preserve it.

If it seems that the comparative unimportance of sports makes online interactions about sporting-related matters less fraught with animus, my experience has generally been the opposite. To be clear, I'm on Twitter (though I rarely tweet) and I follow a lot of sports journalists there because I find it a good way to get news about the teams I support. I'm often curious to hear their thoughts on games (sometimes while the action is still ongoing), and they regularly link to informative articles that enhance my understanding of what's happening in the world of sports, both on and off the field.

However, I consistently try to stay away from the replies to sports-related Twitter posts because in my view, they tend to reflect the most reactionary tendencies of sports fans. On fan Twitter (to say nothing of the various fan-related message boards out there), every coach should be fired, every player is trash, and no one knows what they are doing (except, of course, the fan disparaging every player and coach). Anyone who departs from such views gets labelled as an "apologist" who is happy with the status quo and doesn't really care about important things like winning championships.

I understand perfectly well that coaches should sometimes be fired and that players do not always perform to the best of their ability. (I even understand that some players are better than others!) What I object to is the knee-jerk quality of the thinking that is so frequently expressed in these forums. Everyone is in the grip of the moment, and rarely is there any effort to step back from recent developments and see the bigger picture. Even after victories, fans who are active online often focus on the negative: a particular player's performance, a poor coaching decision, the inferior quality of the opponent, or how the team just got lucky. It is a remarkably discouraging and toxic environment—one that can lead to serious doubts about the intelligence and goodness of humanity.

Then there are the ways in which fans interact directly with athletes. I have no doubt that these interactions are sometimes positive—fans who simply want to praise a player's effort or get a "shout out" from someone they admire. But far too often, fans use online venues to attack not only an athlete's performance, but also their character or various aspects of their life off the field. Explicitly racist abuse is startingly common,[6] as fans use the cover of anonymity to say things to athletes they would never say to their faces, and a startling number of athletes receive death threats (keeping in mind that I consider one such threat startling).[7] In light of these sorts of incidents, it's hard not to think of Justin Reid's comment (noted in Chapter 4) about people tweeting at athletes like they are animals. (If you find yourself treating athletes like animals, see guideline #1.)

I don't know whether, at the end of the day, the benefits of social media interaction outweigh its costs, but I do think that anyone who wants to be a good fan should approach online spaces with exceptional caution. We should think about why we are there, what we want to get out of the interactions, and whether there are more productive ways to spend our time. Perhaps, rather than dive into Twitter spats with other fans right after a game, it's better to simply turn off the television and get on with our day. Maybe, rather than trying to have engaging conversations with people who have no interest in dialogue, we should find the information we want and leave it at that. And if we feel inclined to interact with athletes, we could do far worse than follow the motherly admonition that if we can't say something nice, we probably shouldn't say anything at all.

4. Try to Appreciate Other Fans, Especially New Ones

Rivalries are part of the fun of sports. They furnish a broader historical context for the games we watch and heighten the drama that unfolds on the field. Games against rival teams may not matter more than other games in any plausibly objective way (as it were, from the point of view of the universe). But if they matter more to the fans and players involved, then the stage is set perfectly for the storylines that captivate us.

If rivalries add to the fun of sports, they can also distance us from other fans in corrosive ways. Someone's support of a rival team can be a reason to dislike that person, or at least dislike that fact about them. Sporting loyalties become moralized such that they are an important facet of someone's character, and the overall character of fan bases is essentialized such that we paint all fans of certain teams (particularly rival teams) with a remarkably broad brush. ("Ugh. Vikings fans are all

134 Conclusion

[fill in the blank with negative attribute].") This is a feature of the world of sports that non-fans rightly find baffling but which, I suspect, longtime partisans will recognize instantly.

There is also a puzzling hostility that fans seem to have toward newcomers, even when those fans support the teams we like. My guess is that we think the long histories we have with our teams make us uniquely entitled to suffer with their misfortunes and rejoice in their triumphs. For example, when someone who has only lived in North Carolina for a couple of years (and has no previous attachment to the Panthers) reacts negatively to Carolina's loss in the Super Bowl, lifelong fans may be inclined to brush off their disappointment as counterfeit. "You can't really know what this feels like. We've suffered for years!"

Finally, I think there is a dismissal of fans who are new to various sports that might be even more common than the skepticism directed at fans who are new to various teams. Long time soccer fans are notoriously skeptical of those who are new to the game, often mocking them for their lack of knowledge about the sport's nuances and history.[8] And while the posture that many men adopt toward women who are newly interested in sports may simply exemplify a misogyny that is all too common in other areas of society, it is also an expression of a broader phenomenon: Sports fans love their sports, but they can be wary of—even downright unwelcoming to—those who have not long been a member of the club.

Whatever the exact form of such insularity, it seems to be exactly the opposite of what those who love sports should be striving to cultivate. If there is something about sports that is worth loving (and I have argued throughout this book that there is), then we should be happy when others discover that love for themselves, not bitter that they are trampling on something that only we—the true fans—can really appreciate. And we should be patient as newcomers gradually find their way with the games and teams to which we have devoted years. After all, we were all new fans at one time. Why not welcome everyone to the joys and pains that life as a fan has to offer?

Notes

1. I'm going to leave aside a consideration of whether sports *should* have returned when they did or whether any particular decision or policy regarding playing conditions was justified. My unexciting opinion on this question is that the issues were complex (as they were throughout the pandemic, well beyond the realm of sports) and that the people tasked with making choices about what to do were largely doing the best they could while serving a wide variety of constituencies with a wide variety of interests in the midst of tremendous uncertainty. Some of them got it right; some got it wrong; some were motivated by greed; and some of them genuinely wanted to serve the athletes, fans, and communities that give life to sports. I have thoughts about some specific cases but, as elsewhere, am resistant to sweeping generalizations.
2. Katherine Acquavella, "Naomi Osaka Withdraws from Tournament after Being Fined for Skipping Media Obligations," *CBSSports.com*, May 31, 2021, www.cbssports.com/tennis/news/french-open-2021-naomi-osaka-withdraws-from-tournament-after-being-fined-for-skipping-media-obligations.
3. Jake Curtis, "Aaron Rodgers' Mind Reportedly Is Made Up—He Wants Out," *Si.com*, May 3, 2021, www.si.com/college/cal/news/aaron-rodgers-wants-out-of-green-bay.
4. Essex Thayer, "Threats from Donors Paused Women's Basketball's Protest," *Old Gold and Black*, April 8, 2021, https://wfuogb.com/12590/sports/protests-lead-to-threats-from-boosters.
5. Connor O'Halloran, "Denmark's Christian Eriksen Suffered Cardiac Arrest, Was 'Gone' before Resuscitation," *ESPN.com*, June 13, 2021, www.espn.com/soccer/denmark-den/story/4407267/denmarks-christian-eriksen-gone-before-cardiac-resuscitation-team-doctor.
6. Ryan Conway (and more), "In Their Own Words: The Damage Social Media Abuse Causes in Football and the Frustrations in Tackling It," *The Athletic*, April 30, 2021, https://theathletic.com/2549195/2021/04/30/in-their-own-words-the-damage-social-media-abuse-causes-in-football.
7. Billy Heyen, "Packers' Marquez Valdes—Scantling Tweets He Received Death Threats after Fumble vs. Colts," *The Sporting News*, November 23, 2021, www.sportingnews.com/us/nfl/news/packers-marquez-valdes-scantling-death-threats-fumble-colts/pdw3zuk1djlo144ofs7xuqqpx.
8. Erin Tarver has a very compelling discussion of the role that knowledge acquisition plays in distinguishing fans from non-fans. See *The I in Team* (Chicago: The University of Chicago Press, 2017), 30ff.

WORKS CITED

Acquavella, Katherine. "Naomi Osaka Withdraws from Tournament after Being Fined for Skipping Media Obligations." *CBSSports.com*, May 31, 2021. www.cbssports.com/tennis/news/french-open-2021-naomi-osaka-withdraws-from-tournament-after-being-fined-for-skipping-media-obligations.

American Academy of Pediatrics' Committee on Bioethics. "Informed Consent in Decision-Making in Pediatric Practice." *Pediatrics* 138, no. 2 (August 2016): 1–7. https://doi.org/10.1542/peds.2016-1484.

Appiah, Kwame Anthony. "Cosmopolitan Patriots." *Critical Inquiry* 23, no. 3 (April 1997): 617–639. https://doi.org/10.1086/448846.

Appiah, Kwame Anthony. *Lies That Bind: Rethinking Identity*. New York: Liveright Publishing Co., 2018.

Aspen Institute Project Play. "Youth Sports Facts: Participation Rates." Accessed June 11, 2021. www.aspen-projectplay.org/youth-sports-facts/participation-rates.

Badhwar, Neera, and E. M. Dadlez. "Love and Friendship: Achieving Happiness in Jane Austen's Emma." In *Jane Austen's Emma: Philosophical Perspectives*, edited by E. M. Dadlez, 25–54. Oxford: Oxford University Press, 2018.

Barash, David P. "The Roar of the Crowd." *The Chronicle Review*, March 20, 2009. www.chronicle.com/article/The-Roar-of-the-Crowd/32744.

Bar-On, Tamir. *Beyond Soccer: International Relations and Politics as Seen through the Beautiful Game*. Lanham, MD: Rowman & Littlefield, 2017.

Barrabi, Thomas. "Women's World Cup: USWNT's Fight for Equal Pay Looms Over Tournament." *FOXBusiness.com*, June 6, 2019. www.foxbusiness.com/features/womens-world-cup-uswnt-pay-lawsuit.

Bieler, Des. "U.S. and Mexico Players Make Statement of Unity before World Cup Qualifier." *The Washington Post*, November 12, 2016. www.washingtonpost.com/news/early-lead/wp/2016/11/12/u-s-and-mexico-players-make-statement-of-unity-before-world-cup-qualifier.

Bishop, Greg. "A Family's Search for Why after QB's Suicide." *Si.com*, June 26, 2018. www.si.com/college/2018/06/26/tyler-hilinski-suicide-washington-state-qb-cte.

Bogdanor, Vernon. "Britain's Crisis Isn't Constitutional. It's Political." *Foreign Policy*, April 1, 2019. https://foreignpolicy.com/2019/04/01/britains-crisis-isnt-constitutional-its-political-brexit-tories-theresa-may-corbyn-customs-union-eu/.

Bonagura, Kyle. "Police: WSU QB Hilinski Dies in Apparent Suicide." *ESPN.com*, January 17, 2018. www.espn.com/college-football/story/_/id/22125232/washington-state-qb-tyler-hilinski-found-dead-apparent-suicide-police-say.

Boston University CTE Research Center. "Frequently Asked Questions about CTE." Accessed May 31, 2019. www.bu.edu/cte/about/frequently-asked-questions.

Bryant, Howard. *The Heritage: Black Athletes, a Divided America, and the Politics of Patriotism*. Boston: Beacon Press, 2018.

Buford, Bill. *Among the Thugs*. New York: Vintage Departures, 1993.

136 Works Cited

Carson, Harry. *Captain for Life*. New York: St. Martin's Press, 2011.

Catalina Channel Swimming Federation. "Individuals Records." Accessed April 30, 2020. https://swimcatalina.org/individuals-records/.

Centers for Disease Control and Prevention. "CDC, Washington State Report First COVID-19 Death." *CDC Online Newsroom*, February 29, 2020. www.cdc.gov/media/releases/2020/s0229-COVID-19-first-death.html.

Chin, Jimmy, and Elizabeth Chai Vasarhelyi. *Meru* (Little Monster Films, 2015).

Conway, Ryan (and more). "In Their Own Words: The Damage Social Media Abuse Causes in Football and the Frustrations in Tackling It." *The Athletic*, April 30, 2021. https://theathletic.com/2549195/2021/04/30/in-their-own-words-the-damage-social-media-abuse-causes-in-football.

Curtis, Jake. "Aaron Rodgers' Mind Reportedly Is Made Up—He Wants Out." *Si.com*, May 3, 2021. www.si.com/college/cal/news/aaron-rodgers-wants-out-of-green-bay.

D'Arcangelo, Lyndsey. "'There's No Break': Overseas Double Duty Is an Offer Many WNBA Stars Can't Refuse." *The Guardian*, May 19, 2018. www.theguardian.com/sport/2018/may/19/theres-no-break-overseas-double-duty-is-an-offer-many-wnba-stars-cant-refuse.

Dayen, David. "How Teddy Roosevelt Saved Football." *Politico*, September 20, 2104. www.politico.com/magazine/story/2014/09/teddy-roosevelt-saved-football-111146.html.

Deadspin Staff. "We Asked 14 Retired NFL Players: Would You Do It Again?" *Deadspin*, March 17, 2015. https://deadspin.com/we-asked-14-retired-nfl-players-would-you-do-it-again-1691919600.

Deitsch, Richard. "USA's Women's World Cup Win Is the Most-Watched Soccer Game in U.S. History." *Si.com*, July 6, 2015. www.si.com/soccer/2015/07/06/usa-japan-womens-world-cup-tv-ratings-record.

Diallo, Rokhaya. "On Football, Identity and 'Frenchness'." *AlJazeera.com*, August 2, 2018. www.aljazeera.com/indepth/opinion/football-identity-frenchness-180801080257299.html.

Dixon, Nicholas. "Boxing, Paternalism, and Legal Moralism." *Social Theory and Practice* 27, no. 2 (April 2001): 323–344. https://doi.org/10.5840/soctheorpract200127215.

Dixon, Nicholas. "The Ethics of Supporting Sports Teams." *Journal of Applied Philosophy* 18, no. 2 (January 2001): 149–158. https://doi.org/10.1111/1468-5930.00182.

Dixon, Nicholas. "In Praise of Partisanship." *Journal of the Philosophy of Sport* 43, no. 2 (May 2016): 233–249. https://doi.org/10.1080/00948705.2015.1112234.

Dorsey, James M. *The Turbulent World of Middle East Soccer*. Oxford; New York: Oxford University Press, 2016.

Dreyfus, Hubert L., and Sean Kelly. *All Things Shining: Reading the Western Classics to Find Meaning in a Secular Age*. New York: Free Press, 2011.

Elgot, Jessica. "Boris Johnson Accused of 'Dog-Whistle' Islamophobia over Burqa Comments." *The Guardian*, August 7, 2018. www.theguardian.com/politics/2018/aug/06/boris-johnsons-burqa-remarks-fan-flames-of-islamophobia-says-mp.

Elias, Norbert, and Eric Dunning. *Quest for Excitement: Sport and Leisure in the Civilizing Process*. London: Blackwell, 1986.

English, Jane. "Sex Equality in Sports." *Philosophy and Public Affairs* 7, no. 3 (Spring 1978): 269–277.

ESPN. "Most Expensive Transfers of All-Time." *ESPN.com*, July 10, 2018. www.espn.com/soccer/blog/soccer-transfers/3/post/2915603/most-expensive-transfers-of-all-time-neymar-mbappe-pogba-ronaldo-and-more.

Ewing, Heidi, and Rachel Grady. *Branded* (ESPN, 2013).

Fagan, Kate. "Taurasi Opts for Rest, to Skip WNBA Season." *ESPN.com*, February 3, 2015. www.espn.com/wnba/story/_/id/12272047/diana-taurasi-opts-sit-2015-wnba-season.

Fainaru, Steve, and Mark Fainaru-Wada. "Why Chris Borland Is the Most Dangerous Man in Football." *ESPN.com*, August 20, 2015. www.espn.com/nfl/story/_/id/13463272/how-former-san-francisco-49ers-chris-borland-retirement-change-nfl-forever.

Feezell, Randolph M. *Sport, Philosophy, and Good Lives*. Lincoln: University of Nebraska Press, 2013.

Findler, Patrick. "Should Kids Play (American) Football?" *Journal of the Philosophy of Sport* 42, no. 3 (September 2015): 443–462. https://doi.org/10.1080/00948705.2015.1079132.

Flanigan, Jessica. *Pharmaceutical Freedom*. New York: Oxford University Press, 2017.

Foer, Franklin. *How Soccer Explains the World: An Unlikely Theory of Globalization*. New York, NY: Harper Perennial, 2005.

Works Cited 137

Fort, Rodney, and John Fizel. *International Sports Economics Comparisons*. Santa Barbara: ABC-CLIO, 2004. http://qut.eblib.com.au/patron/FullRecord.aspx?p=554186.

Foxworth, Domonique. "Domonique Foxworth: Why I Love Football." *The Undefeated*, August 12, 2016. https://theundefeated.com/features/domonique-foxworth-why-i-love-football.

Frankfurt, Harry G. *The Reasons of Love*. Princeton, NJ: Princeton University Press, 2004.

Gibbs, Lindsay. "2 More NFL Players Retire Early as Evidence Linking Football and CTE Mounts." *Think Progress*, April 8, 2016. https://archive.thinkprogress.org/2-more-nfl-players-retire-early-as-evidence-linking-football-and-cte-mounts-f170cbe5f4f1.

Gibbs, Lindsay. "Losing $375 Million in the Name of Men's Sports." *Power Plays*, February 10, 2020. www.powerplays.news/p/losing-375-million-in-the-name-of.

Golliver, Ben. "NBA Suspends Season after Jazz's Rudy Gobert Tests Positive for Coronavirus." *The Washington Post*, March 12, 2020. www.washingtonpost.com/sports/2020/03/11/nba-suspends-play-player-test-coronavirus.

Gonzalez, Roger. "FC Dallas under-15 Boys Squad Beat the U.S. Women's National Team in a Scrimmage." *CBSSports.com*, April 4, 2017. www.cbssports.com/soccer/news/a-dallas-fc-under-15-boys-squad-beat-the-u-s-womens-national-team-in-a-scrimmage.

Goodman, Rob. "Cognitive Enhancement, Cheating, and Accomplishment." *Kennedy Institute of Ethics Journal* 20, no. 2 (June 2010): 145–160. https://doi.org/10.1353/ken.0.0309.

Gottschall, Jonathan. *The Professor in the Cage: Why Men Fight and Why We like to Watch*. New York: Penguin Press, 2015.

Greenblatt, Stephen. "General Introduction." In *The Norton Shakespeare*, edited by Walter Cohen, Jean E. Howard, Katharine Eisaman Maus, and Stephen Greenblatt, 1–58. New York: W.W. Norton and Co., 2000.

Grierson, Jamie. "England Celebrates Gareth Southgate as Hero of World Cup." *The Guardian*, July 8, 2018. www.theguardian.com/football/2018/jul/08/england-celebrates-gareth-southgate-as-hero-of-world-cup-waistcoat.

Griffin, Anna. "Marketing Women Athletes Often Walks Careful Line between Savvy and Sexist." *Oregon Live*. Accessed January 10, 2019. www.oregonlive.com/business/2013/04/marketing_women_athletes_can_w.html.

Gubar, Justine. *Fanaticus: Mischief and Madness in the Modern Sports Fan*. Lanham: Rowman & Littlefield, 2015.

Gumbrecht, Hans Ulrich. *In Praise of Athletic Beauty*. Cambridge, MA: Harvard University Press, 2006.

Haner, Jim. *Soccerhead: An Accidental Journey into the Heart of the American Game*. New York: North Point Press, 2006.

Helm, Bennett W. *Love, Friendship, and the Self: Intimacy, Identity, and the Social Nature of Persons*. Oxford: Oxford University Press, 2010.

Hornby, Nick. *Fever Pitch*. New York: Riverhead Books, 1998.

"Individuals Records—Catalina Channel Swimming Federation." Accessed April 30, 2020. https://swim-catalina.org/individuals-records/.

International League. "International League Attendance." Accessed April 28, 2020. www.milb.com/milb/stats/stats.jsp?y=2018&t=l_att&lid=117&sid=l117.

Jamieson, Jeremy P. "The Home Field Advantage in Athletics: A Meta-Analysis." *Journal of Applied Social Psychology* 40, no. 7 (July 2010): 1819–1848. https://doi.org/10.1111/j.1559-1816.2010.00641.x.

Jardine, Peter. "Exclusive: Smith's Blueprint Will Open Door to Non-Scots Playing for National Team." *The Daily Mail*, February 26, 2009. www.dailymail.co.uk/sport/football/article-1156743/Exclusive-Smiths-blueprint-open-door-non-Scots-playing-national-team.html.

Jones, Chris. "What Do You Mean, 'We?'." *Grantland*, October 25, 2011. https://grantland.com/features/what-do-mean-we.

Joseph, Andrew. "Ex-USMNT Player Blames Foreign-Born Players." *USA Today*, May 31, 2018. www.usatoday.com/story/sports/ftw/2018/05/31/exusmnt-player-blames-foreignborn-players-lack-of-fight-for-world-cup-failure/111170244.

Kadlac, Adam. "Irreplaceability and Identity." *Social Theory and Practice* 38, no. 1 (January 2012): 33–54. https://doi.org/10.5840/soctheorpract20123812.

Klein, Binnie. *Blows to the Head: How Boxing Changed My Mind*. Albany, NY: Excelsior Editions/State University of New York Press, 2010.

138 Works Cited

Klein, Gary. "NFL Myths: Some Players May Be '$10-Million Guys,' But Not All of Them Are Rich." *Los Angeles Times*, January 26, 2018. www.latimes.com/sports/nfl/la-sp-nfl-myths-20180126-story.html.

Klosterman, Chuck. *But What If We're Wrong? Thinking about the Present as If It Were the Past*. New York: Blue Rider Press, 2016.

Koestler, Arthur. *The Ghost in the Machine*. London: Arkana, 1989.

Kuper, Simon. "How Books about Sport Got Serious." *The Financial Times*, November 22, 2013. www.ft.com/content/d1d75a48-513c-11e3-9651-00144feabdc0.

Langton, Rae. *Sexual Solipsism: Philosophical Essays on Pornography and Objectification*. Oxford; New York: Oxford University Press, 2009.

Laskas, Jeanne Marie. "The People V. Football." *GQ*, February 21, 2011. www.gq.com/story/jeanne-marie-laskas-nfl-concussions-fred-mcneill.

Layden, Tim. "Coronavirus KO'd Spring Sports; Now We're Living without Them." *NBC Sports.com*, March 13, 2020. https://sports.nbcsports.com/2020/03/13/sports-crystallized-coronavirus-for-america-now-we-adjust-to-life-without-them.

Leitch, Will. "How Will Sports Recover from This Hiatus?" *The New York Times*, March 15, 2020. www.nytimes.com/2020/03/15/opinion/sports-coronavirus.html.

Levy, Neil. "Autonomy and Addiction." *Canadian Journal of Philosophy* 36, no. 3 (September 2006): 427–447. https://doi.org/10.1353/cjp.2006.0018.

Lewis, Jon. "NBA Finals Ratings Hit Low, But Not Bad for Sweep." *Sports Media Watch*, June 2018. www.sportsmediawatch.com/2018/06/nba-finals-ratings-least-watched-four-years.

Lewis, Jon. "Ratings: WNBA, NFL Pregames, NFL OOH, CFB." *Sports Media Watch*, September 2018. www.sportsmediawatch.com/2018/09/wnba-finals-ratings-nfl-pregame-ooh-cfb/.

Lewis, Lisa A., ed. *The Adoring Audience: Fan Culture and Popular Media*. London: New York: Routledge, 1992.

Lewis, Ori. "Fans of Jerusalem Club Fed up with Racism Form New Outfit." *Reuters*, February 22, 2018. www.reuters.com/article/uk-soccer-israel-nordia-idUKKCN1G61RJ.

Lisa, Andrew. "The Money Behind the March Madness NCAA Basketball Tournament." *Yahoo.com*, March 19, 2020. https://finance.yahoo.com/news/money-behind-march-madness-ncaa-194402803.html.

Lister, Jonathan. "The Average Salary of a Women's Professional Basketball Player." *Career Trend*, August 5, 2019. https://careertrend.com/the-average-salary-of-a-womens-professional-basketball-player-13657126.html.

Longman, Jeré. "For Lolo Jones, Everything Is Image." *The New York Times*, August 4, 2012. www.nytimes.com/2012/08/05/sports/olympics/olympian-lolo-jones-draws-attention-to-beauty-not-achievement.html.

Lough, Nancy. "The Case for Boosting WNBA Player Salaries." *The Conversation*, August 9, 2018. http://theconversation.com/the-case-for-boosting-wnba-player-salaries-100805.

Lowe, Sid. *Fear and Loathing in La Liga: Barcelona vs Real Madrid*. New York, NY: Nation Books, 2014.

Manne, Kate. *Down Girl: The Logic of Misogyny*. New York: Oxford University Press, 2018.

Markovits, Andrei S., and Emily K. Albertson. *Sportista: Female Fandom in the United States*. Philadelphia: Temple University Press, 2012.

Markovits, Andrei S., and Lars Rensmann. *Gaming the World: How Sports Are Reshaping Global Politics and Culture*. Princeton: Princeton University Press, 2010.

Marsden, Sam. "Messi to Pay Tax Fine, Avoid Prison Sentence." *ESPN.com*, June 23, 2017. www.espn.com/soccer/barcelona/story/3147554/barcelonas-lionel-messi-to-pay-fine-to-avoid-21-month-prison-sentence-for-tax-fraud.

McCabe, Robert W. "The Rise of American Sport and the Decline of American Culture." In *Sports in School: The Future of an Institution*, edited by John Gerdy, 138–150. New York: Teachers College Press, 2000.

McCaffery, Larry. "An Interview with David Foster Wallace." *Review of Contemporary Fiction* 13, no. 2 (Summer 1993): 127–150.

McDonagh, Eileen L., and Laura Pappano. *Playing with the Boys: Why Separate Is Not Equal in Sports*. New York: Oxford University Press, 2008.

McGinn, Colin. *Ethics, Evil, and Fiction*. Oxford: Clarendon Press, 1997.

McLeod, Carolyn. "Mere and Partial Means: The Full Range of the Objectification of Women." *Canadian Journal of Philosophy Supplementary Volume* 28 (2002): 219–244. https://doi.org/10.1080/00455091.2002.10717588.

Meggyesy, Dave. *Out of Their League*. Berkeley, CA: Ramparts Press, 1970.

Merrick, Jane. "Securing a Brexit Deal Will Not End the UK's Political Crisis." *CNN.com*, March 28, 2019. www.cnn.com/2019/03/28/uk/brexit-turmoil-ongoing-intl-gbr/index.html.

Mez, Jesse, Daniel H. Daneshvar, Patrick T. Kiernan, Bobak Abdolmohammadi, Victor E. Alvarez, Bertrand R. Huber, Michael L. Alosco, et al. "Clinicopathological Evaluation of Chronic Traumatic Encephalopathy in Players of American Football." *JAMA* 318, no. 4 (July 2017): 360–370. https://doi.org/10.1001/jama.2017.8334.

Mill, John Stuart. *On Liberty*. Indianapolis, IN: Hackett Publishing, 1978.

Mill, John Stuart. *Utilitarianism*. London: Longman's, Green, and Co, 1879.

Mohr, Richard D. *Gay Ideas: Outing and Other Controversies*. Boston: Beacon Press, 1992.

Morris, S. P. "The Limit of Spectator Interaction." *Sport, Ethics and Philosophy* 6, no. 1 (February 2012): 46–60. https://doi.org/10.1080/17511321.2011.598465.

Mullin, Amy. "Children, Autonomy, and Care." *Journal of Social Philosophy* 38, no. 4 (December 2007): 536–553. https://doi.org/10.1111/j.1467-9833.2007.00397.x.

Mullin, Amy. "Children, Paternalism and the Development of Autonomy." *Ethical Theory and Moral Practice* 17, no. 3 (June 2014): 413–426. https://doi.org/10.1007/s10677-013-9453-0.

Mumford, Stephen. "Allegiance and Identity." *Journal of the Philosophy of Sport* 31, no. 2 (2004): 184–195. https://doi.org/10.1080/00948705.2004.9714659.

Mumford, Stephen. *Watching Sport: Aesthetics, Ethics and Emotion*. New York: Routledge, 2012.

National Collegiate Athletic Association. "NCAA Recruiting Facts." *NCAA.org*, March 2018. www.ncaa.org/sites/default/files/Recruiting%20Fact%20Sheet%20WEB.pdf.

National Collegiate Athletic Association. "2018 Women's Final Four Makes History in Columbus." *NCAA.com*, April 13, 2018. www.ncaa.com/news/basketball-women/article/2018-04-13/2018-womens-final-four-makes-history-columbus.

National Collegiate Athletic Association. "NCAA Sports Sponsorship and Participation Rates Database." *NCAA.org*, October 2018. www.ncaa.org/about/resources/research/ncaa-sports-sponsorship-and-participation-rates-database.

National Federation of State High School Associations. "High School Sports Participation Increases for 29th Consecutive Year." September 11, 2018. www.nfhs.org/articles/high-school-sports-participation-increases-for-29th-consecutive-year.

Nevill, Alan M., Sue M. Newell, and Sally Gale. "Factors Associated with Home Advantage in English and Scottish Soccer Matches." *Journal of Sports Sciences* 14, no. 2 (April 1996): 181–186. https://doi.org/10.1080/02640419608727700.

Nozick, Robert. *The Examined Life: Philosophical Meditations*. New York: Simon and Schuster, 1989.

Nussbaum, Martha C. "Objectification." *Philosophy and Public Affairs* 24, no. 4 (Autumn 1995): 249–291.

O'Halloran, Connor. "Denmark's Christian Eriksen Suffered Cardiac Arrest, Was 'Gone' Before Resuscitation." *ESPN.com*, June 13, 2021. www.espn.com/soccer/denmark-den/story/4407267/denmarks-christian-eriksen-gone-before-cardiac-resuscitation-team-doctor.

O'Hara, Michael, and Connell Vaughan. "Caveman Stuff: Ireland's Soccer Struggle with Identity, Style, and Success." In *The Aesthetics, Poetics, and Rhetoric of Soccer*, edited by Ridvan Askin, Catherine Diederich, and Aline Bieri, 163–181. London: Routledge, 2018.

Orentlicher, David, and William David. "Concussion and Football: Failures to Respond by the NFL and the Medical Profession." *FIU Law Review* 8, no. 1 (September 2012). https://doi.org/10.25148/lawrev.8.1.6.

Otterson, Joe. "NCAA Championship Game Viewership Drops 28% From 2017." *Variety*, April 3, 2018. https://variety.com/2018/tv/news/2018-ncaa-championship-game-ratings-1202742895.

Otterson, Joe. "World Cup Final U.S. Ratings Fall from 2014." *Variety*, July 2018. https://variety.com/2018/tv/news/world-cup-final-us-ratings-1202875655.

Oxenham, Gwendolyn. *Under the Lights and in the Dark: Untold Stories of Women's Soccer*. London: Icon Books, 2018.

Papadaki, Lina. "What Is Objectification?" *Journal of Moral Philosophy* 7, no. 1 (January 2010): 16–36. https://doi.org/10.1163/174046809X12544019606067.

Pingue, Frank. "Soccer: U.S. Women's League Increases Roster Size, Player Pay." *Reuters*, January 10, 2019. www.reuters.com/article/us-soccer-women-nwsl-idUSKCN1P42MA.

Platt, Oli. "What Is Neymar's Net Worth and How Much Does the PSG Star Earn?" *Goal.com*, Accessed November 25, 2020. www.goal.com/en-us/news/neymar-net-worth-salary-contract-psg/1kvfsexg0npx fl5gn60ol0zknl.

Plenderleith, Ian. *The Quiet Fan*. London: Unbound, 2018.

Pollard, R., and G. Pollard. "Long-Term Trends in Home Advantage in Professional Team Sports in North America and England (1876–2003)." *Journal of Sports Sciences* 23, no. 4 (April 2005): 337–350. https://doi.org/10.1080/02640410400021559.

Randall, David. "Maradona Admits 'Hand of God' Goal Was Revenge for Falklands." *Independent*, October 10, 2011. www.independent.co.uk/sport/football/news/maradona-admits-hand-of-god-goal-was-revenge-for-falklands-550743.html.

Rob, Goodman. "Cognitive Enhancement, Cheating, and Accomplishment." *Kennedy Institute of Ethics Journal* 20, no. 2 (June 2010): 145–160. https://doi.org/10.1353/ken.0.0309.

Rowe, David. "Sports and Culture." In *The Blackwell Encyclopedia of Sociology*, edited by George Rizer, J. Michael Ryan, and Betsy Thorn, 4676–4685. London: Blackwell, 2007.

Rubin, Gayle. "Thinking Sex." In *The Lesbian and Gay Studies Reader*, edited by Henry Abelove, Michèle Aina Barale, and David M. Halperin, 3–44. New York: Routledge, 1993.

Russell, J. S. "The Ideal Fan or Good Fans?" *Sport, Ethics and Philosophy* 6, no. 1 (February 2012): 16–30. https://doi.org/10.1080/17511321.2011.579570.

Ryall, Emily. *Philosophy of Sport: Key Questions*. London: Bloomsbury, 2016.

Ryall, Emily. "Sex, the World Cup and Breaking Up the Boys' Club." *The New York Times*, June 11, 2019. www.nytimes.com/2019/06/11/opinion/womens-world-cup-us-gender-pay.html.

Sailors, Pamela R. "Mixed Competition and Mixed Messages." *Journal of the Philosophy of Sport* 41, no. 1 (January 2014): 65–77. https://doi.org/10.1080/00948705.2013.858398.

Sailors, Pamela R. "Personal Foul: An Evaluation of the Moral Status of Football." *Journal of the Philosophy of Sport* 42, no. 2 (May 2015): 269–286. https://doi.org/10.1080/00948705.2014.1000338.

Sanchez, Mark W. "ESPN's Mike Ditka to Colin Kaepernick: 'Get the Hell Out'." *New York Post*, September 24, 2016. https://nypost.com/2016/09/24/espns-mike-ditka-to-colin-kaepernick-get-the-hell-out/.

Sandel, Michael J. "The Case Against Perfection." *The Atlantic*, April 2004. www.theatlantic.com/magazine/archive/2004/04/the-case-against-perfection/302927.

Satz, Debra. *Why Some Things Should Not Be for Sale: The Moral Limits of Markets*. New York: Oxford University Press, 2010.

Simmons, Bill. "Rules for Being a True Fan." *ESPN.com*, 2002. www.espn.com/espn/page2/story?page=simmons/020227.

Simmons, R., and D. Forrest. "Buying Success: Team Performance and Wage Bills in U.S. and European Sports Leagues." In *International Sports Economics Comparisons*, edited by R. Fort and J. Fizel. Westport, CT: Praeger Publishers, 2004.

Slotnik, Daniel E. "Bill Buckner, All-Star Shadowed by World Series Error, Dies at 69." *The New York Times*, May 27, 2019. www.nytimes.com/2019/05/27/obituaries/bill-buckner-all-star-shadowed-by-world-series-error-dies-at-69.html.

Snow, Aurora. "This Is What It's Really Like to Work in Porn." *Fortune*, February 5, 2016. https://fortune.com/2016/02/05/this-is-what-its-really-like-to-work-in-porn.

Soccer Stadium Digest. "2018 NWSL Attendance." Accessed April 28, 2020. https://soccerstadiumdigest.com/2018-nwsl-attendance.

Soccerway. "Brazil—Neymar—Profile with News, Career Statistics and History—Soccerway." Accessed April 30, 2020. https://us.soccerway.com/players/neymar-da-silva-santos-junior/102697.

Solomon, Andrew. *Far from the Tree: Parents, Children, and the Search for Identity*. New York: Scribner, 2012.

St. John, Warren. *Rammer Jammer Yellow Hammer: A Road Trip into the Heart of Fan Mania*. New York: Three Rivers Press, 2005.

Stocker, Michael. "The Schizophrenia of Modern Ethical Theories." *Journal of Philosophy* 73, no. 14 (August 1976): 453–466. https://doi.org/10.2307/2025782.

Tännsjö, Törbjörn. "Is Our Admiration for Sports Heroes Fascistoid?" *Journal of the Philosophy of Sport* 25, no. 1 (May 1998): 23–34. https://doi.org/10.1080/00948705.1998.9714566.

Tännsjö, Törbjörn. "Against Sexual Discrimination in Sport." In *Ethics in Sport*, edited by William John Morgan, 2nd ed., 347–358. Champaign, IL: Human Kinetics, 2007.

Works Cited

Tarver, Erin C. *The I in Team: Sports Fandom and the Reproduction of Identity*. Chicago: The University of Chicago Press, 2017.

Taylor, Craig. "Literature and Moral Thought." *The British Journal of Aesthetics* 54, no. 3 (July 2014): 285–298. https://doi.org/10.1093/aesthj/ayu036.

Thayer, Essex. "Threats from Donors Paused Women's Basketball's Protest." *Old Gold and Black*, April 8, 2021. https://wfuogb.com/12590/sports/protests-lead-to-threats-from-boosters.

Thompson, Isobel. "Jeremy Corbyn's Anti-Semitism Scandal Is Spiraling Out of Control." *Vanity Fair*, August 15, 2018. www.vanityfair.com/news/2018/08/jeremy-corbyn-anti-semitism-scandal-spiraling-out-of-control.

Tosi, Justin, and Brandon Warmke. "Moral Grandstanding." *Philosophy & Public Affairs* 44, no. 3 (June 2016): 197–217. https://doi.org/10.1111/papa.12075.

Travis, Clay. "Colin Kaepernick Is an Idiot." *Outkick the Coverage*, August 27, 2016. www.outkickthecoverage.com/colin-kaepernick-is-an-idiot-082716/.

Vanhoutte, Kristof. "The Importance of Trivial Oppositions in Football Fandom." In *The Aesthetics, Poetics, and Rhetoric of Soccer*, edited by Ridvan Askin, Catherine Diederich, and Bieri Aline, 126–140. London: Routledge, 2018.

Velleman, J. David. "A Right to Self-Termination?" *Ethics* 109, no. 3 (April 1999): 606–628.

Verschueren, Gianni. "Abby Wambach Criticises USMNT's Use of Players with Dual Citizenship." *Bleacher Report*, October 11, 2016. https://bleacherreport.com/articles/2668948-abby-wambach-criticises-usmnts-use-of-players-with-dual-citizenship.

Wallace, David Foster. "Roger Federer as Religious Experience." *The New York Times Magazine*, August 20, 2006. www.nytimes.com/2006/08/20/sports/playmagazine/20federer.html.

Weaving, Charlene. "Buns of Gold, Silver, and Bronze: The State of Olympic Women's Beach Volleyball." In *The Olympics and Philosophy*, edited by Heather Lynne Reid and Michael W. Austin, 228–241. Lexington: University Press of Kentucky, 2012.

Weiner, Natalie. "The WNBA's Male Practice Squads Lose to Women All the Time—and Enjoy It." *SBNation.com*, May 23, 2019. www.sbnation.com/wnba/2019/5/23/18636639/wnba-male-practice-squads.

Wellman, Christopher. "Do Celebrated Athletes Have Special Responsibilities to Be Good Role Models?" In *Sports Ethics: An Anthology*, edited by Jan Boxill, 333–336. London: Blackwell, 2003.

Winner, David. *Those Feet: A Sensual History of English Football*. London: Bloomsbury, 2005.

Winner, David. *Brilliant Orange: The Neurotic Genius of Dutch Soccer*. Woodstock, NY: Overlook Press, 2008.

Witz, Billy. "This Time, Colin Kaepernick Takes a Stand by Kneeling." *The New York Times*, September 1, 2016. www.nytimes.com/2016/09/02/sports/football/colin-kaepernick-kneels-national-anthem-protest.html.

Wojtowicz, Jake. "Fans, Identity, and Punishment." *Sport, Ethics, and Philosophy* 15, no. 1 (2021): 59–73. https://doi.org/10.1080/17511321.2019.1703032.

Women's Sports Foundation. "Title IX and the Rise of Female Athletes in America." September 2, 2016. www.womenssportsfoundation.org/education/title-ix-and-the-rise-of-female-athletes-in-america.

Wong, Alia. "Where Girls Are Missing Out on High-School Sports." *The Atlantic*, June 26, 2015. www.theatlantic.com/education/archive/2015/06/girls-high-school-sports-inequality/396782.

Worth, Jon. "Britain's Political System Is at the Breaking Point." *AlJazeera.com*, March 13, 2019. www.aljazeera.com/indepth/opinion/britain-political-system-breaking-point-190313131636062.html.

Yack, Bernard. *Nationalism and the Moral Psychology of Community*. Chicago, IL: The University of Chicago Press, 2012.

Yeginsu, Ceylan. "World Cup Brings England Together at a Time of Division." *The New York Times*, July 10, 2018. www.nytimes.com/2018/07/10/world/europe/uk-world-cup-england.html.

INDEX

addiction 82
agency: weak 90–91; of women athletes 106; *see also* autonomy
Albertson, Emily 111
Ali, Laila 83
Ali, Muhammad 92
Anker, Conrad 85
Appiah, Kwame Anthony 117, 119, 120
athletes: children as 70–71; as commodities 72; criteria for playing on national teams 116–119; demands on 16–17; endorsement opportunities for 97–99; exceptional performances by 37–38; exploitation of 86–88; fans' affection for 22, 29n21, 38–39; fans' hatred of 63–64; foreign-born 116; human struggles of 61–62, 129–130; kneeling for the national anthem 68, 130; as mascots 73; media intrusions on 129–130; movement from team to team 26, 129; objectification of 10, 12, 41, 67–75; obligation to fans 74–75, 131–132; players of color 72–73; political views of 68–69, 124–125, 132; as resources to be plundered 39–42; respect for as individuals 130–131; as role models 39–42, 45n31; sacrificing for money and fame 77, 82, 86–88, 92; on team rosters 20–23; women as 10, 95–111
athletic trainers 20
Augustine of Hippo (saint) 34
autonomy: of children 88–91, 94n33; in football 80–83, 85–86, 88, 89, 94n15, 94n17, 94n33; and objectification 62, 64–67, 69, 76n26; *see also* agency

Badwater Ultra Marathon 104
Baltimore Ravens 18
Barash, David 30, 31, 35, 42
basketball: gender disparities in 99; March Madness 1; NBA 1, 96, 107, 115, 129; WNBA 96, 99, 103, 107

beach volleyball 67, 100, 106
Beckham, David 99
Bennett, Martellus 71
Bobrovsky, Sergei 122
Borland, Chris 78
Boston Marathon bombing 124
boxing 77, 79, 83, 84, 92
Bryant, Howard 125
Buchanan, Shamari 73
Buckner, Bill 63, 76n8

Carson, Harry 86
Catalina Swim 104, 113n42
Charlton, Jack 117, 118–119
children: autonomy of 88–91, 94n33; love for 51–54, 58, 60n31, 109–110; medical decisions involving 89; objectification of 70–71; playing football 10, 78–79, 81, 88–91
Chin, Jimmy 85
chronic traumatic encephalopathy (CTE) 61, 77–78, 86
Cleveland Browns 18
climate change 108
Collymore, Stan 68
COVID-19, effect on sporting events 1–2, 129
culture, high *vs.* low 30

Dayen, David 80
dementia pugilistica 77; *see also* chronic traumatic encephalopathy (CTE)
Diego Maradona (documentary) 39
Dixon, Nicholas 47, 48–50, 80
Dorsey, James 124
Down Girl (Manne) 105
Dreyfus, Hubert 36, 42–43
Duerson, Dave 61, 77
Dunning, Eric 32, 34

Elias, Norbert 32, 34
endurance sports 104
English, Jane 102, 108
Eriksen, Christian 130
escapism 2–6, 35–36
excitement: human need for 33–35; mimetic 35
exploitation 86–87

fandom: analogy with personal relationships 48–53;
   claims that team do it the "right way" 57, 60n30,
   131; as communal activity 42–43; cosmopolitan
   119–126; cultural value of 33–35; as escapism
   2–6, 35–36; and family history of team support
   51–52; guidelines for being a good fan 129–134;
   nationalist 115; political implications of 114–116;
   potential value of 32; purist/partisan debate
   46–59, 104, 109; as reflection on embodiment
   37–38; rituals associated with 4; rooting for the
   U.S. 126; "sports space" argument 111; value of
   8–10; as waste of time 30; and women's sports
   teams 96–111
fans: anger and grief over pandemic cancellations
   1–2; challenges experienced by 10; comments
   on social media 132–133; critique of 30, 58;
   damaging behavior of 5, 15; development
   of attachment to sports 6–8; dual national
   116–119; emotional investment of 25–28; group
   identification of 31–33, 42–43, 46, 58; and the
   home field advantage 24; of hometown teams
   51, 120–122; identification with sports teams 9,
   14–16, 32; identities of 22; influence of sports in
   lives of 6–8, 12n8; loss of individuality among
   42; mysogynist 106–109, 134; and the need
   for excitement 33–35; of new teams 110–111;
   obligation of athletes to 74–75, 131–132; online
   interaction with athletes 61–62, 133; positive
   impact on teams' performance 24–25; primitive
   impulses of 30–31; purchase of tickets and
   team paraphernalia by 24; racist chants by 11,
   19; respect for rival fans 133–134; response to
   teams' losses 27–28, 29n28, 47; trash talking by
   21; violence threatened/enacted by 11, 35; of
   women's sports 10, 95–97, 106, 107–109; see also
   objectification
fantasy sports 10, 71
Federer, Roger 21, 37
Feezell, Randolph 47, 48
feminism/feminist thought 10, 12, 62, 64, 66–67, 70
Ferguson, D'Brickashaw 78
Fever Pitch (Hornby) 25, 47, 56
figure skating 106
Findler, Patrick 80–81
Fitzgerald, Larry 92
Flanigan, Jessica 81
football: Baltimore Ravens 18; challenges
   confronting fans of 10; children's participation
   in 10, 78–79, 81, 88–91; Cleveland Browns 18;
   dangerous aspects as attraction 83–86; defense of
   watching 10, 79–93; demands on players 16–17;
   ethics of playing 10; Green Bay Packers 6, 23, 58,

111, 120, 121–122, 129; measure to limit violence
   in 93, 93n9; and mimetic excitement 35; NFL
   18, 115, 124, 129; risks to players 10, 61; as threat
   to autonomy 80–83; in the U.S. 97; value and
   dangers of watching 91–93; violent history of
   80; as voluntary slavery 80–82; XFL 107; see also
   chronic traumatic encephalopathy (CTE)
Foreman, George 92
Foxworth, Dominique 83
Frankfurt, Harry 52, 53–54
Free Solo (film) 83
free solo rock climbing 80, 84–85; see also rock
   climbing

gambling 71–72
gender equality 10, 96–97, 101, 108, 109, 110
geopolitical conflicts 11
Gibbs, Lindsay 107
Gobert, Rudy 1
Gotschall, Jonathan 83
Green Bay Packers 6, 23, 58, 111, 120, 121–122, 129
Greenblatt, Stephen 35
Griffin, Anne 100
group identification 31–33, 42–43, 46, 58
gymnastics 106

Higuain, Federico 122
Hilinski, Tyler 61–62
hockey see ice hockey
home field advantage 24
Hornby, Nick 25, 27–28, 47, 51, 56
Howard, Tim 116

ice hockey 1, 11, 114–115; 1980 Winter Olympics
   11, 114–115, 123–124, 126, 127n22
International Olympic Committee 1; see also
   Olympic Games
Invictus (film) 124

James, Lebron 99
Jones, Chris 14, 16, 21
Jones, Lolo 99
Jordan, Michael 73

Kaepernick, Colin 68, 74, 124, 125
Kane, Harry 122
Kelly, Sean 36, 42–43
Klein, Binnie 84
Klinsmann, Jurgen 116
Klosterman, Chuck 79, 92–93
Koestler, Arthur 31
Kournikova, Anna 67
Krakauer, Jon 83–84, 85
Kuper, Simon 30

Langton, Rae 66–67
language use 14–16; athletes' objections to fans' use
   of "we" 28n5; defense of using "we" 24–26;
   non-sports use of "we" 23–24; racist 11, 19,
   73–74; trash talk 21; use of "we" by fans 14–23

144 Index

Layden, Tim 1
Leitch, Will 1–2, 3
Long, Allie 103–104
Longman, Jere 99
love: for children 51–54, 58, 60n31, 109–110; for
    romantic partners 48–50; for sports teams 51–53,
    55–59, 109; value and lessons of 53–57

Mandela, Nelson 124
Mandžukić, Mario 125
Manne, Kate 105–106
Maradona, Diego 39
Markovits, Andrei 35, 111
Marta 98, 100, 101, 102, 107
Mbappe, Kylian 116, 119
McAlister, Garvin 103
McCabe, Robert 30
McDonagh, Eileen 102, 104
McLeod, Carolyn 66
McMahon, Vince 107
medical decision-making 89
Meggyesy, Dave 86
Meru (documentary) 83
Mill, John Stuart 40
Milwaukee Brewers 6, 7, 109–110
Min, Son Heung 122
Miracle (film) 115
Miracle on Ice 11, 114–115, 123–124, 126, 127n22
misogyny 105–109, 134
MMA 79, 84
Modell, Art 18
Mohr, Richard 64
Morgan, Alex 106
Morris, S.P. 21
Moss, Randy 63
mountain climbing *see* rock climbing
Mumford, Stephen 18, 19, 37, 46–47, 48, 55

nationalism 10–11, 115, 117–119
NBA *see* basketball
NCAA 1, 87, 96, 103
Neiner, Natalie 103
Neymar 98, 100, 107
North American Soccer League 7; *see also* soccer
Nozick, Robert 50
Nussbaum, Martha 62, 64–67

objectification 10, 12, 41; of athletes 67–70; benign
    vs. negative 64–65; of children 70–71; defined
    64–67; downstream effects of 70–71; less obvious
    forms of 71–74; manifestations of 62; pitfalls of
    61–75; and sex 63, 64; significance of 62–64; of
    women 64–67; of women athletes 99–100
Of Miracles and Men (documentary) 115
O'Hara, Michael 117
Olympic Games: 1936 Berlin Games 123; 1972
    Munich Games 124; 1980 U.S.-Russia hockey
    game 11, 114–115, 123–124, 126, 127n22;
    Summer 2020 postponement 1

On Liberty (Mill) 40
Osaka, Naomi 129, 131
Out of Their League (Meggyesy) 86
Oxenham, Gwendolyn 98, 103
Ozturk, Renan 85

Papadaki, Lina 64–67
Pappano, Laura 102, 104
paternalism, preemptive 80–81
patriarchy 105–106, 111
Pele 98
Plenderleith, Ian 33
Pogba, Paul 116, 119
politics and sports 122–126
Popovich, Gregg 125
pornography 12, 62–63, 64, 70, 75–76n7, 76n26

racial injustice 72–73, 124–125
racist language 11, 19, 73–74
Rammer, Jammer, Yellow Hammer (St. John) 51, 73
Reed, Pamela 104
Reid, Justin 61–62, 133
Rensmann, Lars 35
Retton, Mary Lou 99
rock climbing 80, 83–84, 85, 104
Rodgers, Aaron 74, 88, 92, 129
Ronaldo, Cristiano 99
Rowe, David 30
Rubin, Gayle 64
Rugby World Cup (1995) 124–125
Russell, J.S. 35, 48–49
Ryall, Emily 105

Sailors, Pamela 80, 102–103
Sandel, Michael 55–56
Satz, Deborah 90
Seau, Junior 61, 77
Shakespearean theater 34–37
Shrewsbury & Atcham Conservative Association 68
Simmons, Bill 14
soccer: on American television 7, 53, 57, 96, 104;
    Asian Games (2007) 124–125; demands on players
    17; El Salvador *vs.* Honduras 124; international
    leagues 7–8, 20, 25–28, 46–47, 97, 98, 114,
    117–119, 123, 124–126; National Women's
    Soccer League (NWSL) 96; Republic of Ireland
    team 117; Scotland's national team 117–118; U.S.
    Men's National Team 114, 116, 119, 121, 126;
    U.S.-Mexico qualifying match (2016) 114, 126;
    U.S. Soccer Federation 107; U.S. teams 8; women
    players 98, 103; Women's World Cup 96; World
    Cup 7–8, 54–55, 96–97, 103, 114, 115–116, 121,
    124, 125; youth leagues 2, 7, 95, 129
Soccer War 124
social media 21, 132–133
Southgate, Gareth 125
sports: aesthetic value of 44n24; benefits of 102;
    college teams 2; dangerous (attractions of)
    83–86; effect of the pandemic on 1–2, 129;

gambling on 71–72; hometown 51, 120–122; and the human condition 37; integrity of 21; investment in 107; as low culture 30; news stories related to 5; and the participant/observer distinction 21–22; and politics 122–126; and sex 8; value of watching 91–93; violent 82–83, 84, 86–87, 92; youth leagues 2, 70–71, 95, 129; *see also* football; soccer

sports teams: cancellation of games by 1, 129; changing identity of 17–20, 25–26; doing things the "right way" 57, 60n30, 131; employees of 20–21; ethical identity of 18–19, 29n17; national 10–11, 115; new teams 110–111; post-pandemic return to play 129, 134n1; social media pages of 21; team rosters 20–23; *see also* women's sports teams

St. John, Warren 51, 73

suicide 5, 61, 75n3, 77

Tarpley, A. J. 78

Tarver, Erin 22, 38, 73, 106

Taurasi, Diana 99, 102

team paraphernalia 24, 97, 104

tennis, Australian Open 21

terrorism 124

ticket purchases 24

Title IX legislation 95–96

trash talk 21

traumatic brain injury (TBI) 78; *see also* chronic traumatic encephalopathy (CTE)

Trump, Donald 114, 126

Twitter *see* social media

ultra-endurance sports 104

US Soccer Federation 107; *see also* soccer

Vaughan, Connell 117

Vieira da Silva, Marta *see* Marta

violence, from fans 11, 35; *see also* sports, violent

Wallace, David Foster 36, 37

Wambach, Abby 116

Weaving, Charlene 100

Weber, Jim 2

Winter Olympics *see* Olympic Games

Wisconsin Badgers 6, 7, 8, 47, 50–51, 53, 104, 111

Wojtowicz, Jake 18–19

women: as athletes 10, 67, 95–111; objectification of 64–67, 99–100

Women's College Basketball 103

women's sports teams 10; compared to men's teams 102–104, 113n41; and fan preference 100–105; fan support for 10, 95–97, 106, 107–109; investment in 107; and professional sports 97–100; protesting misogyny 105–109; reduced earnings in 98; separate from men's sports teams 102–103; soccer 98; standards of excellence for 100–105; and title IX legislation 95–96; WNBA 96, 99, 103, 107; *see also* sports teams

Woods, Tiger 22

XFL 107

Yack, Bernard 119

Yeginsu, Ceylan 125

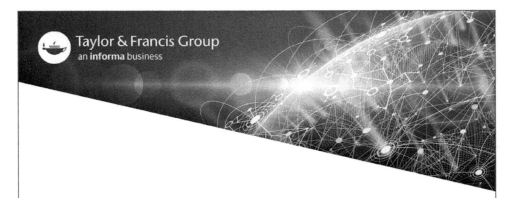

Ingram Content Group UK Ltd.
Milton Keynes UK
UKHW052242100523
421267UK00031B/130